Posthuman Research Practices in Education

Posthuman Research Practices in Education

Edited by

Carol A. Taylor
Sheffield Hallam University, UK

Christina Hughes
University of Warwick, UK

POSTHUMAN RESEARCH PRACTICES IN EDUCATION
Selection, introduction and editorial matter © Carol A. Taylor and Christina Hughes, 2016
Individual chapters © Respective authors, 2016

Softcover reprint of the hardcover 1st edition 2016 978-1-137-45307-5

All rights reserved. No reproduction, copy or transmission of this publication may be made without written permission. No portion of this publication may be reproduced, copied or transmitted save with written permission. In accordance with the provisions of the Copyright, Designs and Patents Act 1988, or under the terms of any licence permitting limited copying issued by the Copyright Licensing Agency, Saffron House, 6–10 Kirby Street, London EC1N 8TS.

Any person who does any unauthorized act in relation to this publication may be liable to criminal prosecution and civil claims for damages.

First published 2016 by
PALGRAVE MACMILLAN

The authors have asserted their rights to be identified as the authors of this work in accordance with the Copyright, Designs and Patents Act 1988.

Palgrave Macmillan in the UK is an imprint of Macmillan Publishers Limited, registered in England, company number 785998, of Houndmills, Basingstoke, Hampshire RG21 6XS.

Palgrave Macmillan in the US is a division of Nature America, Inc., One New York Plaza, Suite 4500, New York, NY 10004-1562.

Palgrave Macmillan is the global academic imprint of the above companies and has companies and representatives throughout the world.

ISBN: 978-1-349-68687-2
E-PDF ISBN: 978–1–137–45308–2
DOI: 10.1057/9781137453082

Distribution in the UK, Europe and the rest of the world is by Palgrave Macmillan®, a division of Macmillan Publishers Limited, registered in England, company number 785998, of Houndmills, Basingstoke, Hampshire RG21 6XS.

Library of Congress Cataloging-in-Publication Data
Names: Taylor, Carol Ann, editor. | Hughes, Christina, 1952– editor.
Title: Posthuman research practices in education / edited by Carol
   A. Taylor, Sheffield Hallam University, UK ; Christina Hughes, University of Warwick, UK.
Description: New York, NY : Palgrave Macmillan, 2016. | Includes index.
Identifiers: LCCN 2015039325

Subjects: LCSH: Education—Philosophy. | Education—Research. | Social sciences–Philosophy. | Social sciences—Research. | BISAC: EDUCATION / Experimental Methods. | EDUCATION / Non-Formal Education. | EDUCATION / Research.
Classification: LCC LB1025.3 .P6828 2016 | DDC 370.1—dc23
LC record available at http://lccn.loc.gov/2015039325

A catalogue record for the book is available from the British Library.

Contents

List of Figures vii

Acknowledgements viii

Notes on Contributors ix

Introduction 1
Carol A. Taylor and Christina Hughes

1 Edu-crafting a Cacophonous Ecology: Posthumanist Research Practices for Education 5
   Carol A. Taylor

2 Rethinking the Empirical in the Posthuman 25
   Elizabeth Adams St. Pierre

3 Deleuzo-Guattarian Rhizomatics: Mapping the Desiring Forces and Connections between Educational Practices and the Neurosciences 37
   Hillevi Lenz Taguchi

4 Thinking like a Brick: Posthumanism and Building Materials 58
   Luke Bennett

5 A Mark on Paper: The Matter of Indigenous–Settler History 75
   Alison Jones and Te Kawehau Hoskins

6 Thinking with an Agentic Assemblage in Posthuman Inquiry 93
   Alecia Youngblood Jackson and Lisa A. Mazzei

7 Flickering, Spilling and Diffusing Body/Knowledge in the Posthuman Early Years 108
   Rachel Holmes and Liz Jones

8 'Local Girl Befriends Vicious Bear': Unleashing Educational Aspiration through a Pedagogy of Material-Semiotic Entanglement 128
   Susanne Gannon

9   Decentring the Human in Multispecies Ethnographies   149
    Veronica Pacini-Ketchabaw, Affrica Taylor and Mindy Blaise

10 Girls, Camera, (Intra)Action: Mapping Posthuman
    Possibilities in a Diffractive Analysis of Camera-Girl
    Assemblages in Research on Gender, Corporeality and
    Place   168
    Gabrielle Ivinson and Emma Renold

11 Decolonizing School Science: Pedagogically Enacting
    Agential Literacy and Ecologies of Relationships   186
    Marc Higgins

12 Student Community Engagement through a Posthuman
    Lens: The Trans-corporeality of Student and Sea   206
    Jocey Quinn

13 Cows, Cabins and Tweets: Posthuman Intra-active Affect
    and Feminist Fire in Secondary School   220
    Jessica Ringrose and Emma Renold

14 Theorizing *as* Practice: Engaging the Posthuman as
    Method of Inquiry and Pedagogic Practice within
    Contemporary Higher Education   242
    Ken Gale

15 A Femifesta for Posthuman Art Education: Visions and
    Becomings   258
    Anna Hickey-Moody

Index   267

Figures

3.1	Santiago Ramón y Cajal. Line drawing of the retina	43
3.2	Fernando de Castro Rodríguez, 1896–1967. Cell morphologies within a typical sympathetic ganglia	44
5.1	Hongi Hika's tā moko drawn on paper by him in 1819	76
5.2	The Kerikeri land deed of 1819	87
7.1	Francesca Woodman, untitled	109
7.2	Caterina Silenza, untitled	119
7.3	Kira O'Reilly, stair falling	124
8.1	Slide 1, Zoologist	137
8.2	Slide 2, *The Daily Star:* 'Local girl befriends vicious bear'	137
10.1	'Still Running'	179
13.1	Feminism is for everybody	234
13.2	I need feminism because…	236
13.3	Who needs feminism?	237

Acknowledgements

We would like to give heartfelt thanks to our contributors for their engaging and engaged involvement in the becoming of this book. With generosity of time and critique they have been with us, side-by-side, as co-collaborators in shaping and progressing the originality and innovation in this significant field. It has been a truly generative entanglement.

Carol and Christina want to say thank you to our editors at Palgrave Macmillan: Andrew for the getting going and Eleanor for seeing it through with us. Thanks to our families, friends and furry ones for their love and support during this process. Thanks also to each other: it was a breeze.

Carol Taylor
Sheffield Hallam University

Christina Hughes
University of Warwick

September 2015

Contributors

Luke Bennett is a senior lecturer in the Department of the Natural and Built Environment, Sheffield Hallam University (SHU), UK. After over 15 years in legal practice as an environmental law specialist, he started teaching at SHU in 2007. His research work explores the intersection of ideas and materialities in the built environment via a series of empirical investigations of land managers' 'anxious' human–thing relations (e.g., with tombstones, elderly trees, derelict land and abandoned quarry workings) and in a recreational trespasser's enthusiastic meaning-making within the ruins of abandoned military bunkers. His work has been published in geography, law and management journals, and formed the basis of his PhD thesis entitled 'Interpretive Communities at Work and Play in the Built Environment' (2015). His human–thing ruminations continue in his voluminous blog, http://lukebennett13.wordpress.com.

Mindy Blaise is a professor in the College of Education at Victoria University, Melbourne, Australia. She publishes across both early childhood education and gender studies. Her book *Playing It Straight! Uncovering Gender Discourses in an Early Childhood Classroom* brings together feminism, queer theory and early childhood to rethink childhood, teaching and learning. Her most recent book, *The SAGE Handbook of Play and Learning*, was co-edited with Liz Brooker and Susan Edwards and showcases how postdevelopmentalism is being taken up in early childhood.

Ken Gale works in the Institute of Education at Plymouth University and has published widely and presented at a number of international conferences on the philosophy of education and anti-positivist approaches to education research and pedagogy. His co-authored books include *Between the Two: A Nomadic Inquiry into Collaborative Writing and Subjectivity, Deleuze and Collaborative Writing: An Immanent Plane of Composition, How Writing Touches: An Intimate Scholarly Collaboration* and *Philosophy and Education: An Introduction to Key Questions and Themes.* He has recently co-edited journal special editions on collaborative writing for the *International Review of Qualitative Research* and on collaborative writing as a method of inquiry for *Cultural Studies<=>Critical Methodologies*. He is an associate member of the Higher Education Academy, and a member of the International Association of Qualitative Inquiry and the Narrative Inquiry Centre at the University of Bristol, where he is also a visiting fellow.

Susanne Gannon is an associate professor and equity theme leader in the Centre for Educational Research at Western Sydney University, Australia. Her expertise includes diverse qualitative methodologies for investigating racialized and gendered subjectivities and place; media, popular culture and policy; aspirational trajectories of young people from diverse backgrounds; and creativity and writing. She draws on theories of place, bodies, affects and new materialities in order to better understand how particular ways of being are enabled or closed down for young people. She is interested in all sorts of materialities and representations, including and exceeding the 'real' accounts of lived experience that are privileged in much empirical research.

Anna Hickey-Moody is Senior Lecturer in Educational Studies and Head of the Centre for the Arts and Learning at Goldsmiths University, and her work focuses on disability, arts practice, gender and cultural geography. She is interested in generating new stories about disadvantaged and disabled youth in ways that do not re-inscribe marginalization. Her work is philosophically informed and can broadly be described as a cultural studies approach to youth arts as a subcultural form of humanities education. Her recent publications include (edited with Page) *Practice, Pedagogy, Resistance: A New Materialism* (2015); *Youth, Arts and Education* (2012); (edited with Vicki Crowley) *Disability Matters: Pedagogy, Media and Affect* (2011); and *Unimaginable Bodies* (2010).

Marc Higgins is Social Sciences and Humanities Research Council of Canada Doctoral Fellow and a doctoral candidate in Cross-Faculty Inquiry in Education at the University of British Columbia. Drawing from longstanding involvement in Indigenous education, science education and media-technology education, he continues to explore pedagogical possibilities in and across these fields. His interdisciplinary work explores the spaces between Indigenous, decolonizing, postcolonial, poststructural and posthumanist theories in order to think and practice education in ways that make space for Indigenous ways-of-knowing (i.e., epistemology) and ways-of-being (i.e., ontology). He has recently been involved in the design, development, delivery, as well as assessment of one of the first required Indigenous education courses for pre-service teachers in Canada at the University of British Columbia. He also continues to support Faculty of Education/school district collaborations by facilitating professional development for teachers on the topic of Indigenous and decolonizing science education in the Metro Vancouver area.

Rachel Holmes has been a teacher for 19 years, working across the fields of early years, Key Stage 1, further and more latterly higher education. She works in the Educational and Social Research Institute at Manchester Metropolitan University as a professor, leading the Children and Young People Research Group. Her research moves across the interstices of applied educational research, social science research and arts-based research within cultures of childhood. Her interests are located around notions of 'childhood territories' such as ways childhood becomes imag(in)ed through fictional, documentary and ethnographic film; children's child(self)hood, identities and objects and ways to (left)field childhood via opening up off-centre research methodologies.

Te Kawehau Hoskins is a Maori writer, scholar and activist from the tribal groups Ngāti Hau and Ngāpuhi. She is a senior lecturer in Te Puna Wānanga, School of Maori Education, University of Auckland, New Zealand. Her main academic interests are in governance, environment and settler–Indigenous relationships. Her community activism is focused on school governance as partnership, and her most recent writing brings 'face to face' the philosophical work of Levinas with Maori political thought.

Christina Hughes is Professor of Sociology at the University of Warwick and serves as Pro-Vice Chancellor. Her research focuses on equity and gender issues and her most recent work has been with jewellery designer makers. She has longstanding interests in methodological issues: see *Disseminating Qualitative Research* (2003); *Feminism Counts: Quantitative Methods and Researching Gender* (2011, with Rachel Cohen); *Researching Gender* (2013); Feminist Research Methods, *International Journal of Social Research Methodology* Virtual Special Issue, http://explore.tandfonline.com/page/bes/tsrm-vsi-feminist-methods (2015). She is co-editor (with Ros Edwards and Malcolm Williams) of the *International Journal of Social Research Methodology* and serves on the boards of *Gender and Education* and *Gender, Work and Organisation*.

Gabrielle Ivinson is Professor of Education at Manchester Metropolitan University. She is author of *Rethinking Single-Sex Teaching: Gender, School Subjects and Learning* (with Murphy), and co-editor of *Knowledge and Identity: Concepts and Applications in Bernstein's Sociology of Knowledge* and *Material Feminisms and Education, Gender and Education* (2013). As a social and developmental psychologist she researches the intergenerational transmission of knowledge as a social resource in places of poverty. Her recent projects (see www.productivemargins.ac.uk) involve working with a range of artists to co-produce art forms and artefacts to enable young people to communicate with persons in authority by drawing on the affective power of art to move.

Alecia Youngblood Jackson is Professor of Educational Research at Appalachian State University in Boone, NC, USA. She is co-author, with Lisa Mazzei, of *Thinking with Theory in Qualitative Research* (2012) and co-editor, with Lisa Mazzei Jackson, of *Voice in Qualitative Inquiry* (2009).

Alison Jones is Professor of Education in Te Puna Wānanga, School of Maori Education, University of Auckland, New Zealand. Her recent work focuses on settler–Indigenous educational relationships, in particular as they were played out at their beginnings in New Zealand in the early 19th century. She is a science graduate and her interest in posthumanist, or new materialist, theoretical work developed through her love of science, her long-standing critique of theory and methodology in social science, her enjoyment of poststructuralism and her encounter with Indigenous ontologies.

Liz Jones is Professor of Early Childhood Education at the Hong Kong Institute of Education, a position that she has held since April 2015. Prior to that, she was Professor of Early Childhood Education at the Manchester Metropolitan University, UK. Her research interests range across a number of theoretical locations including poststructuralism, deconstruction, feminism and queer theory. More recently, she has been working with new materialism, affect and activist philosophy in order to reconfigure children and childhood.

Hillevi Lenz Taguchi is Professor of Education and Child and Youth Studies and Director of Postgraduate Studies, Department of Child and Youth Studies, Stockholm University, Sweden. She has experience of trans- and interdisciplinary research specifically focusing feminist theories and continental philosophy in her studies of higher education, teacher education and early childhood practices. She is much involved with the theoretical development and transgressive methodologies as part of the posthumanist, new materialist and post qualitative turns. Her work has appeared extensively in international journals such as *Feminist Theory*, *Gender and Education*, *Qualitative Inquiry*, *International Journal of Qualitative Studies in Education*, and *Educational Philosophy and Theory*, and she is the author of the book *Going Beyond the Theory/Practice Divide in Early Childhood Education: Introducing an Intra-active Pedagogy* (2010). Nationally, she is a well-known author and Lecturer in Early Childhood Education and Gender Pedagogy, and as of 2015 a project leader of a large-scale educational neurology project with grants from the National Research Council.

Lisa A. Mazzei is Associate Professor of Education Studies at the University of Oregon, where she is also Affiliated Faculty in the Department of Philosophy. She is co-author, with Alecia Jackson, of *Thinking with Theory in Qualitative Research* (2012), co-editor, with Alecia Jackson, of *Voice in Qualitative Inquiry* (2009) and author of *Inhabited Silence in Qualitative Research* (2007).

Veronica Pacini-Ketchabaw is Professor of Early Childhood Studies in the School of Child and Youth Care at the University of Victoria in Canada. She is co-editor of the journal *Canadian Children*, the only peer-reviewed journal in Canada that expressly serves the early childhood community. In her edited collection *Flows, Rhythms and Intensities of Early Childhood Education Curriculum* (2010) and co-edited book *Re-situating Canadian Early Childhood Education* (2013), she worked with Canadian scholars to challenge normalizing perspectives in Canadian early childhood education.

Jocey Quinn is a professor at Plymouth Institute of Education, Plymouth University, UK, where she leads the Learning outside Formal Education research group and is Director of the Centre for Culture Community and Society. She has published widely in the field of higher education and lifelong learning. Her research monographs include *Powerful Subjects: Are Women Really Taking over the University?* (2003) and *Learning Communities and Imagined Social Capital: Learning to Belong* (2010). She has conducted a wide range of research projects including those funded by the ESRC, British Academy, Joseph Rowntree

Foundation and the Council of Europe. Her current research includes *Beyond Words*, a posthuman study of the role of the non-verbal in inclusive music making, funded by the Arts Council Research Grants Programme.

Emma Renold is Professor of Childhood Studies at the School of Social Sciences, Cardiff University. She is the author of *Girls, Boys and Junior Sexualities* (2005) and *Children, Sexuality and Sexualisation* (2015), and the co-editor of *Routledge Critical Studies in Gender and Sexuality in Education*. Inspired by feminist and queer posthumanist theory, her research investigates how gender and sexuality come to matter in children and young people's everyday lives across diverse sites, spaces and locales. Recent projects (see www.productivemargins.ac.uk) explore the affordances of co-productive, creative and affective methodologies to engage social and political change on young people's experiences of gendered and sexual violence.

Jessica Ringrose is Professor of Sociology of Gender and Education at the UCL Institute of Education. Her work develops feminist poststructural, psychosocial, 'intersectional' and new materialist approaches to understanding subjectivity, affectivity and assembled power relations. Recent research explores teen feminism and young people's networked sexual cultures and uses of social media. Her current collaborative AHRC-funded project is 'Documenting Digital Feminist Activism: Mapping Feminist Responses to New Media Misogyny and Rape Culture'. Books and reports include *A Qualitative Study of Children, Young People and 'Sexting'* (2012); *Post-Feminist Education? Girls and the Sexual Politics of Schooling* (2013); *Deleuze and Research Methodologies* (2013); and *Children, Sexuality and Sexualisation* (Palgrave Macmillan, 2015).

Elizabeth Adams St. Pierre is a professor in the Educational Theory and Practice Department and affiliated professor of both the Interdisciplinary Qualitative Research Program and the Institute of Women's Studies at the University of Georgia, USA. Her work focuses on theories of language and the subject from critical theories and poststructural theories in what she has called post-qualitative inquiry – what might come after conventional humanist qualitative research methodology. She is especially interested in the new empiricisms/new materialisms enabled by the ontological turn.

Affrica Taylor is Associate Professor of the Geographies of Childhood and Education in the Faculty of Education, Science, Technology and Mathematics at the University of Canberra. Her background in Indigenous Australian education and her doctoral studies in cultural geography have shaped her abiding interest in the relations between Indigenous and non-indigenous people, land and other species in settler colonial societies. She explores these relations in her book *Reconfiguring the Natures of Childhood* (2013) and in the co-edited collection (with Veronica Pacini-Ketchabaw) *Unsettling the Colonial Spaces and Places of Early Childhood Education* (2015).

Carol A. Taylor is a reader in the Sheffield Institute of Education at Sheffield Hallam University, where she leads the Higher Education Research Group. Her research focuses on space, gender, bodies and materialities, and student engagement and ethics. She has recently co-edited two journal special issues: one on new material feminisms for *Gender and Education* (with Gabrielle Ivinson) and one on student engagement and ethics for the *Journal of Applied Research in Higher Education* (with Carol Robinson). Her work has been published in *Cultural Studies<=>Critical Methodologies, Studies in Higher Education* and *Gender and Education*. She has a forthcoming book: *Material Feminisms and Education*, co-edited with Gabrielle Ivinson (2016). She serves on the editorial boards of *Gender and Education, Journal of Applied Research in Higher Education* and *Student Experience and Engagement Journal*.

Introduction

Carol A. Taylor and Christina Hughes

The post-qualitative turn, new empiricisms, and new feminist materialism, coupled with the interest in ecological perspectives, are all manifestations of a rapidly growing engagement with posthumanism. However, in such a theoretically and philosophically rich field, insufficient attention has been paid to the specifically methodological import of these debates. What do empirically grounded explorations of posthumanism look like in practice? How can they be designed? What sorts of 'data' are produced and how might they be analysed? And, importantly, what are the social, cultural and educational effects or impacts of empirically driven posthuman research?

Stemming, in rhizomatic ways, from the single term 'posthuman' are multiple genealogies, intents and concerns that create a rich landscape of debate and engagement. Putting posthumanism to work through concepts such as assemblage, thing-power, vital materiality, entanglement and nomadism, many of our contributors have been inspired by the work of Gilles Deleuze, Felix Guattari, Jane Bennett, Karen Barad and Rosi Braidotti. This demonstrates a powerful constellation of philosophical, political, ethical, ontological and epistemological deliberation. Taken together, the chapters illuminate how posthuman research requires, and is underpinned by, a fundamental recasting of ontology, epistemology and axiology. In doing so, this book identifies and unpicks the normalized and normative codes of dominant contemporary research and presents a series of radical, creative and innovative research engagements.

For those new to this area, the cacophony and complexity of voices within the field of posthumanism can be confusing as one works through the histories and implications of alternative arguments. Designed to be a framing for this text, Carol Taylor's opening chapter provides an initial sketch of this ground by situating posthumanism as both a reaction to humanism and an activation of new practices in educational research. Carol's chapter can be read as a mapping of key shifts from humanist to posthumanist modes of knowing, being and doing; and/or an introduction to the main contours of posthuman thought; and/or an introduction to the theories and concepts dealt with more largely in the chapters that follow.

Yet creating knowledge change is no easy task and, with clarity and analytic care, our contributors detail the dilemmas and complexities they have encountered, their approaches to, and experiments in researching differently. Because, if Cartesianism is totalizing, as Marc Higgins notes, it is never fully totalized. Elizabeth St. Pierre takes this issue up directly through a reflexive account of learning, doing and teaching qualitative methodology. As she points out, we are caught within the formative knowledge of our own academic histories and, indeed, as teachers we pass these on to our students. In doing so, we perpetuate the dominant approaches we critique. St. Pierre argues forcefully that what we need are not new methodologies and their knowledge practices but new concepts and new conceptual practices.

And so we see in this text. A key element of the posthuman is that it asks us to pay attention to a 'more-and-other-than-human' world (Hughes and Lury, 2013). And our contributors do this in a number of domains ranging from the brick (Luke Bennett), the mattress (Alecia Jackson and Lisa Mazzei), a Maori facial tattoo (Alison Jones and Te Kawehau Hoskins), doors (Rachel Holmes and Liz Jones), bear suits (Susanne Gannon), the sea (Jocey Quinn), the camera (Gabrielle Ivinson and Emma Renold), Portakabins and classrooms (Jessica Ringrose and Emma Renold) to dogs and earthworms (Veronica Pacini-Ketchabaw, Affrica Taylor and Mindy Blaise). The posthuman approaches they activate shift anthropocentric thinking by challenging presumptions of human exceptionalism.

In doing so, the chapters in this text change the parameters of research and what is counted as relevant. This requires us to think relationally with other beings/matter and to draw out the confederacy of objects, bodies and materialities. Many contributors employ the concept of assemblage to recognize such heterogeneous connections, each element having its own characteristics and dynamics and different temporal and spatial scales. Certainly, it is recognized that we are always in the realm of the not-known in terms of the indeterminacy of research and its effects. This serves to highlight an always becoming rather than a fixed state of being (Ken Gale), asking questions, and more questions, rather than seeking absolutist answers (Susanne Gannon) and contesting linear causality through, for example, fractal thinking (Alicia Jackson and Lisa Mazzei). Methodologically it requires us to operationalize the unself (Jocey Quinn), give focus to shadow stories (Rachel Holmes and Liz Jones), the co-implication, interdependency and entanglement of the researcher and research apparatus (Susanne Gannon). It also requires us to recognize the vitality and agency of other beings and materialities (Alecia Jackson and Lisa Mazzei). And it provides us with analytic tools such as rhizomatic readings and cartography mapping (Hillevi Lenz Taguchi), diffraction (Gabrielle Ivinson and Emma Renold), diffractive writing (Ken Gale), Indigenous storywork (Marc Higgins), intra-action (Jessica Ringrose and Emma Renold) affective pedagogy (Anna Hickey Moody), and the practice of Edu-crafting (Carol Taylor). The chapters demonstrate ways of reworking and transforming known methodologies, such as participatory research (Gabrielle Ivinson and Emma Renold), qualitative approaches (Jessica Ringrose and Emma Renold) and photo-voice (Marc Higgins) into posthuman frames.

As our contributors also detail, posthuman research provides a critique of the practices of 'othering' through, for example, an undoing of colonialism. Indeed, we still have much to unlearn in respect of Western assumptions of superior intellectual thought with respect to the entanglement of nature-culture. Thus, Alison Jones and Te Kawehau Hoskins detail how Maori ontology has never radically separated these spheres and indeed has much to say, and to which, we would suggest, we should humbly listen.

Central to the concerns in this text also are ethical accountabilities to human, more-than-human and other-than-human actors. Luke Bennett draws attention to what he refers to as bleak variants of posthumanism that suggest we should/can access a world without us. Luke demonstrates both the political reductionism of such an approach and its impossibility. Hillevi Lenz Taguchi also cautions that we should not 'go to war' based on judgemental attitudes or universal truth claims when, as we understand here, they are qualified, cultural and situated truths. And Jocey Quinn highlights how ethical responsibility shifts the time frame to thinking beyond our own lifetimes.

The concluding chapter in our text sets out a Femifesta (Anna Hickey Moody), written with passion and verve to argue the case of how art teaches in ways we are only beginning to see. We would extend this point to posthuman research practices more generally. For us, and our contributors, posthuman research provides more engaged ways to do, write about and present research. It focuses on the co-connections – or articulations to use Haraway's (1988) phrase – between practices and being in the production of knowledge. It requires us to 'dream along with' other disciplines in constructive ways (Stenger, 2000) and integrates issues of ethics, power and politics with ontological and epistemological concerns.

We trust you will gain much from the chapters in this text and that they help support your own research or encourage you, if you have not done so already, to experiment and innovate with our entanglement with the world around us. Do let us know.

September 2015

References

Haraway, D. (1988) 'Situated Knowledges: The Science Question in Feminism and the Privilege of Partial Perspective', *Feminist Studies*, 14(3), 575–599.

Hughes, C. and Lury, C. (2013) 'Re-turning Feminist Methodologies: From a Social to an Ecological Epistemology', *Gender and Education*, 25(6), 786–799, http://dx.doi.org/10.1080/09540253.2013.829910.

Stengers, I. (2000) 'God's Heart and the Stuff of Life', *Pli*, 9, 86–118, http://web.warwick.ac.uk/philosophy/pli_journal/pdfs/stengers_pli_9.pdf, accessed 17 January 2013.

1
Edu-crafting a Cacophonous Ecology: Posthumanist Research Practices for Education

Carol A. Taylor

Introduction: Posthumanism and educational research

Doing posthumanist research in education is a challenge. At the present time, education operates within a largely performative context, in which regimes of accountability, desires for a quick and easy relay from theory to practice, and the requirement that 'evidence' – the most valorized form of which often comes in the shape of large-scale randomized controlled trials – ought to inform pedagogic interventions, constitute the dominant ways of thinking and modes of inquiry. Posthumanist research practices in education engage a radical critique of some of the fundamental assumptions underpinning these dominant ways of doing educational research.

Posthumanism proposes different starting points for educational research and new ways of grasping educational experience than those afforded by humanism. Posthumanism calls into question the essentializing binary between human and nonhuman on which humanism relies; it throws anthropocentrism into doubt along with the categories and identities it underpins. These different starting points are located in a different set of epistemological presumptions about the forms of knowing that produce valuable knowledge about educational experiences, and in different ontological presumptions about the modes of being through which humans and nonhumans inhabit the world. More than that, posthumanist research practices offer a new ethics of engagement for education by including the nonhuman in questions about *who matters and what counts* in questioning the constitutive role played by humanist dominant paradigms, methodologies and methods in working as actualizers of normative procedures. Feminisms and post-structuralism have also, of course, long been interested in the politics of knowledge production but a posthumanist approach includes the 'others' that feminism, post-structuralism and postmodernism routinely excluded: nonhumans, other-than-humans and more-than-humans. Posthumanism, therefore, offers a 'theoretical rapprochement with material realism' (Coole and Frost, 2010, p. 6) to find new ways to engage with the immanent vitality of matter.

This chapter discusses various arrivals at the posthuman 'now'; it maps how posthumanism undoes humanist assumptions about research methodology and methods; and it signals some of the ways in which posthumanism is currently reshaping how educational research gets done. While the chapter's ambit is both broad and theoretical in dealing with the recasting of ontology, epistemology and ethics under the impress of posthumanism, its purpose, in illuminating how posthuman thinking can be put to work in research practices, is practical. Putting posthuman theory to work is both exciting and daunting. Posthumanism invites us (humans) to undo the current ways of doing – and then *imagine, invent and do the doing differently*. Readers will find many examples throughout this book of the innovative forms of doing invoked, indeed necessitated, by posthumanist thinking. This first chapter provides an initial sketch of the ground by situating posthumanism as both a reaction to humanism (Wolfe, 2010) and an activation of new practices in educational research (Snaza and Weaver, 2015). It can, therefore, be read as (a) a basic mapping of key shifts from humanist to posthumanist modes of knowing, being and doing; and/or (b) an introduction to the main contours of posthuman thought; and/or (c) an introduction to the theories and concepts dealt with in the chapters that follow.

Shiftings: Humanist centrings <> Posthumanist profusion

Posthumanism is a mobile term and the field of posthumanist thought in education is characterized by heterogeneity, multiplicity and profusion. Posthumanism is perhaps best considered as a constellation of different theories, approaches, concepts and practices. It includes (in no particular order): animal studies; 'new' material feminism; affect theory; process philosophy; assemblage theory; queer theory; speculative realism; thing theory; actor network theory; the nonhuman; the new empiricism; posthuman disability studies; object-oriented ontology; alien phenomenology; ecological relationality; decolonial and indigenous theories, plus others I don't know about. Posthumanism in its various incarnations is resolutely interdisciplinary, post-disciplinary, transdisciplinary and anti-disciplinary, which vastly expands the range and variety of conceptual resources available to educational research. In its current state as an unsettled and unsettling terrain – as an emergent field in flux that is continually concretizing, dispersing, flowing and mutating in unforeseen ways – posthumanism opens ways of researching that seek to undo tired binaries such as theory/practice, body/mind, body/brain, self/other, emotion/reason, human/nature, human/animal, producing instead multiple and heterogeneous knowledge pathways that are radically generative for educational research. In doing so it intersects with the anti-foundational insights of feminism and poststructuralism concerning the multiplicity of identity, the mobility of meaning, and the contestability of knowledge, supplementing those earlier insights by including nonhumans, things and materialities. The chapter charts various shiftings which seek to understand the complicated process of how we got from 'there' (humanism) to 'here' (posthumanism). The first shifting circumnavigates the im/possible task of describing how we arrived at the posthuman 'now'. The subsequent shiftings focus on subjectivity, relationality and ethics, and enfold these with discussions of ontology and epistemology.

Shifting <> Im/possible genealogies

The drawing of any single or straight line from humanism to posthumanism is tempting but probably illusory. One possible narrative begins with Foucault's (1970) pronouncement in *The Order of Things* – 'man is an invention of recent date. And one perhaps nearing its end' – moves through Derrida and deconstructionism, traverses poststructuralism and postmodernism, continues via the many facets of feminism, towards Deleuzian rhizomatics, interspecies interfaces (Haraway) and Massumi's virtual-real, to arrive (perhaps) at the swirl of Stewart's affects, Meillassoux's *post* human world without us, or Downey's neuroanthropology, or somewhere else instead, as long as that somewhere is 'recognizably' posthuman. That is, somewhere where the 'old' certitudes regarding identity and subjectivity, binaries and boundaries, language and representation, methodology and methods have been utterly displaced. The problem, though, in tracing this narrative line is that it has no one starting place and certainly no end in sight. We are already in the middle of the posthuman condition, its forces already entangled in the humanist fibre of our lives and thinking. Being intermezzo like this troubles the concepts of 'ends' and 'beginnings' and undermines the notion of lineage.

On the other hand, we could, as Snaza (2015, p. 19) admirably attempts to do, conceptualize a genealogy of 'the human' through its relation to various 'constitutive outsides: the animal, the machine, the savage, the slave, nature, the thing'. These conceptualizations arise from and are (still) tied to particular historically educative processes and located in particular educational institutional practices. Thus, we move from humanism's putative 'origins' in Plato's 'carnophallogocentric' (Derrida's phrase) humanism, which constitutes the meat-eating, male, rational political citizen and subject as different from and innately superior to woman, the emotional and animal, to its incarnation in the medieval Trivium and Quadrivium, a liberal arts education which was a basis for the production of the educated 'man', through Renaissance Humanism with its focus on the development of man's artistic, literary and moral capabilities. The Western Enlightenment built on these earlier conceptions but, via colonialism and science, generated a version of humanism grounded in the separation of, and domination by, a small-ish section of 'mankind' from/of the 'rest of' nature, humanity, and nonhuman 'others' in accordance with its god-given civilizing mission. Postmodern, post-structuralist and feminist theorists worked, rightly, to destabilize the origin myths of humanism and reincorporate those inappropriate/d others. Much of this theorizing (although Haraway's critique of speciesism is an exception) did not sufficiently unsettle the primacy of the 'human' as a central category of political privilege, thus leaving the systematic oppressions and ontological erasures that earlier forms of humanism had instituted largely intact. It is this unsettling that posthumanism seeks to accomplish for good. The aim is, as Snaza (2015, p. 27) notes, to undo the *telos* of humanism and its 'humanizing project' so that posthumanist thought can engage 'a future politics not reducible to anthropocentric institutions and practices'. In essence, this involves replacing the idea that the human is a separate category from 'everything else' with an ethic of mutual relation.

Furthermore, like posthumanism, humanism is and always has been heterogeneous. As Braidotti (2013, pp. 50–51) notes, 'there are in fact many humanisms'. There are romantic, revolutionary, liberal, secularist, antihumanist humanisms (Davies, 1997); there are intellectualist, spiritualist and metaphysical humanisms (Derrida, 1972); and there are Renaissance, academic, catholic or integral, subjective, naturalistic and religious humanisms (Lamont, 1997), as well as various versions of critical humanism (Plummer, 2012). The philosophical foundations of humanism are varied, and some humanisms do away with universalizations and recognize the material, concrete, pragmatic and partial basis of human experience. That humanism, like posthumanism, never was (or is) singular is, according to Braidotti, part of the problem: as soon as we express the desire to 'overcome humanism', we very quickly realize how utterly entwined we are within humanism's affordances and problematics, as feminists and post-structuralists already know. Any dis-entangling, therefore, has to be a continuing and incisive critical practice, not one done easily or 'once and for all'. Yet the desire to 'overcome' humanism is urgent and necessary. One only has to think for a moment of the geopolitical suffering, ecological depredation, and epistemological violence that humanism, particularly in its alliance with neo-colonialism and hyper-capitalism, has given rise to, to appreciate the urgency of the task. Thinking for a moment longer, though, might bring to mind humanism's legacy of universal human rights, communitarian politics and disability equality legislation. These are things we humans would probably not want to do away with, albeit that they often work as positive guises beneath which humanism seeks to hide its wreckages. One can appreciate that the larger project of *becoming* posthuman is fraught with difficulty, just as inventing practices which *use* posthumanist frames of reference in educational research are contentious.

Shifting <> Subjectivity

Trippers and askers surround me,

People I meet...the effect upon me of my early life...of the ward and city I live in...of the nation [...] But they are not the Me myself.

Apart from the pulling and hauling stands what I am, Stands amused, complacent, compassionating, idle, unitary, Looks down, is erect [...]

Both in and out of the game, and watching and wondering at it.
   (Whitman, 1977, extract from *Song of Myself*, l., pp. 58–70)

Since each of us was several, there was already quite a crowd.
   (Deleuze and Guattari, 1987, p. 3)

I stood at the entrance...I also stood some forty meters away, in the temple itself...Outside the doors of the temple I also stood in the cyanophyte-stained plaza...I patrolled [the upper city] as well. When I walked the edge of the water I could see myself standing in the plaza...That accounted for almost half of my twenty bodies. The remainder slept or worked in the house Lieutenant Awn occupied.
   (Leckie, 2013, *Ancillary Justice*, pp. 12–15)

In 1855, Whitman wrote confidently of the 'Me myself' as a secure place of observation and knowledge, founded in the essentializing masculine ego of the Western Enlightenment modernist self. *Song of Myself* is an undoubtedly exuberant epic but one which exemplifies Descartes' *cogito*, the knowing subject who stands apart from the world to observe, describe, measure and know it. This knowing figure keeps his distance from the world and aims to keep himself, his 'essence', intact. He sometimes paradoxically desires to consume/subsume 'it' (the world, woman, all those 'others') into 'his' identity, but doing so would dissolve the foundations of t/his separate knowing, thinking, feeling and seeing self, and with it the ontological and epistemological presumptions on which it is founded. This separation of self/world, the division of self/other it inaugurates, is his triumph, his tragedy, and, through postcolonial, feminist, post-structuralist or posthumanist eyes, a principal cause of his demise. Such a self-centre cannot hold as many postcolonial, feminist and post-structuralist critics have shown, and as many indigenous peoples have perhaps always known. The Enlightenment ego cannot function (or, in some modes, can only function) through repression, violence and subjection.

Deleuze and Guattari (1997, pp. 3–4) play with the Enlightenment 'I', throw its basis for producing truth, facts, knowledge, into doubt, pluralize it, and multiply it. They do so, they say, 'not to reach the point where one no longer says I, but the point where it is no longer of any importance whether one says I'. The I they posit is immanent to the social field, world and nature. This I is an intensity, an affective meld, a convergence of forces, always unstable, mobile, emerging, becoming. There is no *cogito* to centre and stabilize this I as it gets plugged into temporary assemblages, themselves composed through heterogeneity and multiplicity. This I does not reproduce itself by constituting binaries, divisions, hierarchies or any distinctions that separate out human/other. This I is, instead, detachable, reversible, open and connectable. It makes maps not tracings of the terrain; that is, it does not seek to copy and reproduce what is already there but works via creative 'experimentation in contact with the real' (ibid., p. 13). The knowledge this I produces does not require succour from a system of logical, objective rationalism with its linear and root-based presumptions that the 'right' research methodology and methods will disclose the 'truth' of the subject under inquiry. Instead, it unpicks the Enlightenment package of teleology, progress and development, operating instead with an idea of knowledge as a machinic network for knowing, replacing arborescent, lineage- and root-based images of thought with rhizomic modes of knowing characterized by non-linearity, multiplicity, connectivity, dimensions (rather than a pivot), flatness (rather than depth) and ruptures which may (or may not) tie unforeseen things together so that they work. The rhizome as a-centred image of thought shifts the focus from knowledge 'about', procedures for producing knowledge, and concerns about what knowing 'is', to questions about what knowledge does, how it works, and how its effectivity may generate more (not less) of life.

The voice of the third extract above belongs to One Esk Eleven, AI ancillary and former human, who inhabits multiple bodies, and is also materially manifest as the troop carrier ship *Justice of Toren* who/which has a taste for antique choral and folk songs. Over 2,000 years old, *Justice of Toren* has more than five senses, vast memory powers, and a tact, courtesy and sensitivity which make her communicative powers exemplary. One Esk is called 'she' for convenience because the Radchaai, the 'race' that colonized her, don't recognize gender difference. She is a complicated more-than-human entity with a conscience, a consciousness and multiple identities. She is the cyborg we (humans) all already are, as Haraway (1991, pp. 150–151) reminded us a while ago: we are 'theorized and fabricated hybrids of machine and organism' which operate with 'partiality, intimacy, irony and perversity' to undo any origin stories that institute difference. Cyborgs, as oppositional and utopian entities, signal the breakdown of the three boundaries which have held in place our 'last beachheads of [human] uniqueness': human/animal; animal-human organism/machine; physical/non-physical. The posthuman possible the cyborg heralds and institutes works through alliance, coalition, relationality.

And yet. The dispersals, possibilities and polymorphous becomings offered by posthuman identities are not equally available to all. For some the same old striations operate along class, gender, 'race', able/bodied, sexualized lines. Consider the UK House of Commons vote (3 February 2015) to amend the 2008 Human Fertilisation and Embryology Act to enable mitochondrial transfer allowing 'three-person embryos' to be artificially produced. Medically justified by its supporters on the grounds that it will help eliminate one strain of mitochondrial disease – a cause of liver failure and brain damage at embryo stage – the amendment enables the development of new in vitro fertilization treatments in which the nucleus from the genetic mother's egg is transferred into a donor's egg either before or after the donor egg is fertilized with sperm. While the case for the alleviating of human suffering is (perhaps) worth considering, the most striking concern is the commodification, invasion and appropriation of women's bodies as the primary genetic matter for this technological experimentation (mitochondria are passed on genetically by women, not men) and their genetic exploitation under the ruthlessly competitive conditions released by the flows of global capital, illuminating how 'market forces [now] happily trade on Life itself' (Braidotti, 2013, p. 59). Also consider the recent film *Ex Machina*, which features a contemporary-posthuman future ruthlessly gendered along binary lines in which (perennial) masculine fantasies of sexual compliance and desire for a beguiling female robot possessing youth and beauty play out alongside fears of the return of the monstrous feminine, the true possessor of the phallus, the castrating 'other' to the vulnerable male human. In the posthuman now-and-to-come, whose future matters more? And if, as Braidotti (2013, pp. 80–81) hopes, posthuman feminism provides a rebel stance against 'the political economy of phallogocentrism and of anthropocentric humanism', then how might this work in education?

For many, the posthuman promise of human dis-placement brings with it profound anxieties in contemporary conditions of rapid social, cultural, economic and technological change. Braidotti (2013, p. 9) comments on how unmanned drones have brought a form of 'necro-politics' to posthuman global armed warfare which profoundly transform the practice of war by distancing human decision-making from the act of killing. Shiny, clean, easy death by machine: we (humans) have no part in it and, therefore, no messy guilt or shame to deal with. And if our collective conscience/individual consciousness is momentarily troubled by the thought that 'real' people, animals, plants, things and buildings are destroyed, we can always comfort ourselves with the fact that the 'war on terror' is a necessary thing carried out on our behalf to safeguard democracy from those not quite as politically-morally-civically-educationally 'advanced' as 'us' that is, those 'others' who don't share 'our' commitment to human life and the attendant civilized Enlightenment values that follow. If 'death by drone' illuminates how ethics are being recast under posthuman conditions, it also sharply highlights how (particular versions of) humanism are entwined with posthumanism.

Shifting <> Relationality

> Nature has been given a baton and she is conducting musical interpretations of the forest's creatures and plant life as they interact with each other, resulting in a 'live' and 'ever-changing' performance in response to the atmosphere.
>
> (Barber, 2014)

> The animal looks at us, and we are naked before it. Thinking perhaps begins there.
>
> (Derrida, 2002, p. 397)

> The 90-minute performance [of *Cloakroom*] sees [Tilda] Swinton taking clothes that have been checked in by audience members on arrival, and treating them as her co-stars. She nuzzled a red mohair coat, buried her face in a suit jacket and had a conversation with a gilet.
>
> (Singh, 2015)

New material feminism, eco-philosophy, object-oriented ontology and other posthuman approaches emphasize an ecology of human-nonhuman relations in which we (all) are embedded and entangled. They undo easy/old notions of the 'we' in order to move beyond the speciesism and anthropocentrism of humanism (Wolfe, 2010) towards modes of interbeing, interspeciesbeing and worlding. Manning (cited in Springgay, 2015, p. 76) refers to 'ecologies of encounter' which unfix agency with its humanist ontological grounding in individuality and instead recognize a plurality of interrelationality. The posthuman promise of ecologies of encounter has been articulated in a variety of ways. For example, Braidotti's (2013, p. 100) affirmative posthuman feminism leads her to propose a materialist, vitalist, embodied and embedded politics of/for Life itself which gives priority to the 'irrepressible flows of encounters, interactions, affectivity and desire'. Bennett's (2010, p. 6) concern is with the vitality of things and she praises 'the curious ability of inanimate things to animate, to act, to produce effects both dramatic and subtle'. For Bennett, thing-power reconceptualizes ontology as a distributed swarm and agency as 'congregational' and 'confederate'. Haraway (2008, p. 182) talks of her 'encounters in dogland, with people and dogs, that have reshaped my heart, mind, and writing'. She avows her love and desire for Cayenne, her dog, which motivates her 'to be good for and with her. Really good.' Forget distance, be-with the dog on the floor, in the grass, because these 'meetings make us who and what we are in the avid contact zones that are the world' (Haraway, 2008, p. 287).

Inspired by quantum physics, Barad's (2007) agential realism is a posthuman performative account of the onto-epistemological beings, becomings and knowings made possible when these differing modes and understandings of relationality are set in motion. Agential realism proposes that intentions are not the interior possessions of individuals but cohere and are expressed in human-nonhuman networks, that subjectivity is not the property and possession of a separately bodied individual but that all that exists comes to being through intra-active material processes of emergence (not as pre-existent separate entities), and that causality as a linear and traceable series of effects between isolated objects has to be rethought as a material practice in which who/whatever makes an agential cut – and in a classroom that doing could be done by a coat, a chair, a pen, an iPad, a computer screen, the atmosphere, the temperature, just as much as any human – generates ongoing and continually differentiating interconnections that constitute the mattering of the world. Causality, hence, 'is an entangled affair...of cutting things together and apart within and as part of phenomena' (Barad, 2007, p. 394). Proceeding from our material entanglement agential realism, as a posthuman practice of mattering, profoundly reworks ontology, epistemology and ethics.

Posthuman forms of hybrid human-natural-object-animal intermixing instantiate Derrida's (2002, p. 381) hoped-for 'multiple and heterogeneous border', which does away with 'the abyssal limit of the human'. Looking at his cat looking back at him, Derrida felt that 'everything can happen to me, I am like a child ready for the apocalypse'. In valuing the inhuman and ahuman, the posthuman opens an onto-epistemological opportunity space for that 'everything' to happen, but that doesn't mean we (humans) can content ourselves with the luxury of being wide-eyed/wild-eyed innocents. We (humans) are responsible for producing 'the human' as a separate political, ontological and epistemological category in the first place so, some posthumanists of the dark ecology movement (Morton, 2009) might argue, if there is a coming apocalypse perhaps it is both deserved and ought to be invited. Presumptions that the world is as it is *for us* are nothing other than an idealized myth of anthropocentric dominion. In this vein, Wallin (2015, p. 135) argues that the world we have made and now know is a world of contamination and decay; the earth is not the pristine blue planet but a planet gripped by geotrauma. This *post* human 'alter Eaarth' (ibid., p. 139) is utterly indifferent to human life, human action is futile and humans have to learn to deal with 'the superabundant material realities unthinkable by humans' (ibid., p. 140). Such narratives of human obsolescence provoke varying responses, from a recuperated cosmopolitan humanism grounded in our shared humanity (Skillington, 2015) to the mobilization of pessimism 'as an ethical force' (Wallin, 2015, p. 134) in thinking a posthuman world without privilege.

Shifting <> Ethics

Encounters, meetings, contacts. Responsibility, accountability, commitment. These are some of the key terms through which posthuman ethics are currently figured and which offer some ways out of the ethical cul-de-sac of humanism – with its phenomenal grounding of moral conceptions in the anthropos of individual bodies and its abstract and universalizing rights-based discourses – in which we have been rather too complacently and comfortably sequestered for too long (despite the fact that all along only some individuals and some peoples' rights count for anything at all). Thinking posthuman ethics, therefore, begins by re-thinking interdependence, by including nonhumans in an ethics of care, by understanding the human always and only in-relation-to nonhumans who are no longer 'others' but are, intimately and always, ourselves as the body multiple. Embodying and enacting ethics-in-relation is anxiety-provoking to the extent that it dispenses with the privileged position of human separability and the fantasy of distance it installs. So Barad (2007, p. 394) writes: 'Responsibility entails an ongoing responsiveness to the entanglements of self and other, here and there, now and then' in an emergent process that is, at one and the same time, the ongoing material co-constitution of the world *and* an instantiation of practices of mattering (i.e., agential cuts which mean that some bodies count for more than others). Posthuman ethics, from a 'new' material feminist perspective, is an ethic of 'worlding' and proceeds from the presumption that ethics is not about trying to see the world from inside someone else's shoes – which presumes individuated bodies. Rather, it means recognizing skin not as a barrier-boundary but as a porous, permeable sensorium of connectivity with/in a universe of dynamic co-constitutive and differential becomings.

MacCormack (2012), too, is interested in developing ethics as an incarnate relation. Whereas Barad looks to quantum entanglements, MacCormack tracks back beyond the Cartesian bifurcation of body and mind to Spinoza's conception of the corporeality of the mind. For Spinoza, there is 'no body without mind, no individuality without connection, no connection without another dividuated life with its own concomitant reality, no affect without expression, will as appetite beyond consciousness and, perhaps most importantly, no thought or theory without materiality' (MacCormack, 2012, p. 4). A posthuman ethics, therefore, must be situational, emergent and unique, located in capacity and action, play out in living bodies as the point of ethical address, and be oriented to practices that are a positive affirmation of life. Because in Spinozist ethics 'the gift of liberty is allowing the power of the other to expand toward unknown futures' (ibid., p. 1) ethics becomes a material practice of passion, difference and expansion.

Spinozan ethics are activated in Bennett's (2010) posthuman conceptualization of thing-power. Derived from Spinoza's account of *conatus* (a substance which is itself in its continuing and creative self-differentiation), conative bodies are associative, social and affective; they form alliances and enter into assemblages with all manner of other bodies, forming ad hoc groupings of vital materialities. For Bennett (2010, p. 23), these 'living, throbbing confederations', with their horizontal and heterogeneous ontological capacities and the distributed agentic dance they engage in, are the site for posthuman ethics. As Bennett (2010, p. 37) suggests: 'the ethical responsibility of an individual human now resides in one's response to the assemblages in which one finds oneself participating'. Such flattened ontologies and epistemologies of knowing-in-being not only recalibrate modes of responsibility and accountability, they also 'chasten our will to mastery' (Bennett, 2010, p. 15). Similar points are made by Braidotti (2013, p. 129), for whom our shared vulnerability provides the condition for an 'affirmative ethics based on the praxis of constructing positivity' which will enable new social conditions and productive relations to be forged 'out of injury and pain' (ibid., p. 130).

Braidotti says we need to be worthy of the present and time and again the words 'humble' and 'humility' appear as a desired goal in considerations of posthuman ethics. Perhaps the desire for a posthuman ethics which displaces the morality of man with interspecies relationality may be best and cautiously 'propelled by the tasty but risky obligation of curiosity among companion species, once we know, we cannot not know. If we know well, searching with fingery eyes, we care. That is how responsibility grows' (Haraway, 2008, p. 287). While this ethical project must be 'a permanent critique of ourselves' (Wolfe, 2010, p. xvi), the obligations it gives rise to will not be known in advance because each and every encounter keeps the matter of ethics open.

Unmoorings <> Method/ology undone

What happens to method/ology in the posthuman if, as Rotas (2015, p. 102) suggests, 'human beings are not the only "participants" within a research study?' The question is a profound one which destabilizes many, if not all, of the ways knowledge has been produced about education during the last few centuries. Snaza and Weaver (2015) point out that posthumanism hasn't yet had much impact on educational studies but even a cursory glance at the mundane aspects of everyday lives within educational contexts indicates the necessity of taking the nonhuman into account alongside and with the human. Think, for example, of the chains of techno-chemical processing which have already transformed the 'food' in children's school dinners before it enters their mouths; or the millions of other-than-human microbes, bacteria and parasites that circulate among school populations each day as young people touch computer keyboards, share iPads or books, and sit or play together; or the pervasive use of social media within schools, the peer cultures that require belonging through particular items of clothing and objects; as well as the ways in which schooling practices are integrated with technological apparatuses such as interactive whiteboards; and the surveillance regimes that deploy nonhuman actors including computerized registers, webcam security systems, and classroom video observatories. These examples are from schools but conceptualizing the co-production of further and higher education by posthuman-human agencies is also a necessary and urgent task.

Mapping the posthuman within educational research is a complicated and lively endeavour, given our location *after* method (Law, 2004) and already *in* post-qualitative research which seeks to dispense with all the presumptions and categories of humanist qualitative research (Lather and St. Pierre, 2013). Yet, as Brinkman (2015, p. 621) has recently indicated, 'good old-fashioned qualitative inquiry' (GOFQI) with its centrings in dialogue, voice, empathy, narrative, meaning, method, coding, data (and, I would add, rigour, trustworthiness and validity) 'lives by constant self-destruction and resurrection like a phoenix'. Which means that the presumptions it entails – that one can access, know about, and represent the 'experience' of an 'other's' 'reality' – are not so easily dispensed with, no matter how reflexively one tries, as various feminisms and 'posts-' have already shown. And which is why Lather (2013, p. 635) points out that 'there is no methodological instrumentality to be unproblematically learned', what we have instead is 'methodology-to-come' which means that we 'begin to do it differently' with every new project and 'wherever we are in our projects'.

Being methodologically in the mess (Law, 2004), in the middle (Deleuze and Guattari, 1997), and in the mesh (Ingold, 2007), makes the question many doctoral students (including myself) were invited to struggle with – 'do I choose a paradigm first within which to shape the research, or does the research question dictate paradigm choice' – now seem rather beside the point, because beginning in the *here* of posthuman research dis-places the whole panoply of what arrives with one's 'choice' of research paradigm. As Barad (2007) illuminates, practices, doings and actions are enactments of presumptions about ontology, epistemology and ethics. Taking this up in posthumanist research practices means we begin with immanence, relation, non-separability, values, partisanship, responsibility for each and every choice or cut, immersion, emergence. Beginning with the embodied idea that posthumanist research is an ethico-onto-epistemological practice of materially-emergent co-constitution, what emerges as 'research' cannot be 'about' something or somebody, nor can it be an individualized cognitive act of knowledge production. Rather, posthumanist research is an enactment of knowing-in-being that emerges in the event of doing research itself. In opening new means to integrate thinking and doing, it offers an invitation to come as you are and to experiment, invent and create both with what is (already) at hand and by bringing that which might (or might not) be useful, *because you don't yet know*, into the orbit of research.

Posthuman scholars such as Maclure, Lather, St. Pierre, Koro-Ljunberg and Mazzei and Jackson, among others, encourage researchers to track down the very many ways the human is enfolded within and intercedes in the research process, encouraging vigilance to the unwitting ways that humanist remnants smuggle themselves into posthuman research intraventions. You can't simply mix and stir posthumanism into a research design. Neither is it enough to 'adapt' a familiar method to posthumanist ends, as Kuntz and Presnall's (2012) reconceptualization of the interview as intra-view shows. Nor will it do to 'add' a posthuman analysis to the interpretation of data that has been conventionally collected. Instead, new analytic practices such as attending to moments of 'productive disconcertion' and the rebel becomings induced by data 'hotspots' are needed (MacLure, 2013). So, if the 'usual' methodological procedures are no longer possible in the posthuman, if we invite emergence and take the question '*can* posthumanist research be "planned" in advance' seriously, then how to proceed?

Many of those putting posthumanist research practices to work take up Deleuze and Guattari's (1987) invocation regarding 'the logic of the AND', developing rhizomic means to interrogate educational instances in their manifold multiplicity. Others take up Barad's (2007) agential realism, using the concepts of intra-action, entanglement, cut, apparatus, and phenomena to drive their research intra-ventions. Others, like Bennett (2010, p. xiii), propose following 'the scent' of the thing, where to follow means 'always to be in response to call from something, however nonhuman it may be'. For Bennett, following entails lingering in moments so as to avail oneself of the fascination of objects, of letting sense wander so that it may become attuned to things and their affects. Harman (2011), following Latour, offers the love of lists by which to adumbrate the beauty of the real that surrounds us which, he avers, cannot be known but can only be loved. Bogost (2012), also in speculative realist vein, prefers speculative fictions as a means to imaginatively capture alien phenomenology, that is, the trails left by things as they withdraw to pursue their thingly lives without us. Stewart (2007, p. 1) practises speculation and curiosity to provoke attention to the forces, resonances and impacts of moments, events and sensations of the 'weighted and reeling present' she seeks to approach.

These practices dis-place 'methodol/ogy' and call forth new ways of finding out. Springgay (2015) suggests that these new ways of doing may be better approached as 'techniques' than methods or research tools in that techniques are processual, emergent and continually reinvent themselves. As a way of leaning into a posthuman practice that is 'a mode of thought, already in the act' (Manning and Massumi, 2014, p. ix), techniques activate modalities of thought, rhythms, affects from inside the act, techniques activate a practice from within, thinkings-in-the act set practice in motion, so that practice *becomes* interference, always diffractive, multiple, uneasy and intense. And it is perhaps because of the profound questions posthumanism raises about what research is and how it may get done differently that posthumanist researchers lean towards arts-based, visual, sensory, movement, sonic and creative writing practices (as in some of the chapters in this volume). Such post-disciplinary conversations give rise to questions about what data are, how they matter, and how we may interpret the empirical materials (Denzin's phrase for those entities formerly known as 'data') generated in any act of research. These questions work as a practical means to push forward the open question about what constitutes educational research in the posthuman.

Edu-crafting <> The *potentia* of posthuman research practices in education

Immanent, vitalist, materialist, embedded, embodied, relational, sensory, affective, contingent, experimental. These are the modes of thinking-in-being which issue a call to those interested in posthumanist research practices in education. Such research cannot be 'done' or 'carried out', it may only be activated, enacted, instantiated, so that it strives to set in motion a 'cacophonous ecology' (Manning and Massumi, 2014, p. viii) of bodies, objects, materialities, affects, sensations, movements, forces. Posthuman research enactments are a practice of the plunge: letting go, diving, freefall, surfing, swimming, waving *and* drowning. They are a plunging into particularity that collapses scale, structure and level – to (try to) see a world in a grain of sand, indeed – and a committed ethico-onto-epistemological venture to (try to) do away with the binaries that have held 'man' and 'human' so securely in place as a means to other everything/everyone else. Plunging is a messy, ungainly and sometimes dangerous business: there are no methodological safeholds, handholds or niches for secure knowing. Yet one of the forces that traverse and propel us in the not-known of posthumanist research in education is *potentia*: energy, vitality, the constitutive desire to endure. *Potentia*, Braidotti (2013, p. 137) says, 'disintegrates the ego with its capital of narcissism, paranoia and negativity' and installs an affirmative power; it provokes experiments with posthuman modes of subjectivity; and it generates relational posthuman encounters productive of new forms of sociality. *Potentia* may also help activate modes of radical experimentation to propel posthuman research practices that the field of education can benefit from.

'Edu-craft' is a neologism I've made up to think about how to join the impulse behind craftivism (a movement which uses craft for critical thinking, questioning and considered creative activism) with 'new' material feminist/posthuman research practices. Edu-crafting, as a posthuman research experiment, puts bodies, things and concepts in motion. One example of an edu-craft intervention I've enacted with undergraduate students entails a collaborative investigation of how the curriculum is brought into being and enacted though a mutable range of posthuman materialities and spatialities. Activities include focusing on the nonhuman matter that textures the seminar room space, tuning into embodied enactments of space in classrooms, experimenting with noise, atmosphere and light. The challenge of working out how to describe these activities, account for their effects, and explain the passages of affect they make possible, draws us further into the human–nonhuman conjunctions within the 'fielding of the event' (Manning and Massumi, 2014, p. 14). From this, assessment becomes a practice of making some 'stuff' (a mood board, photos, poems, objects) as a spatio-material record of our immersion in educational spaces; of connecting these to a post-disciplinary analysis of the space and matter of educational experience which draws resources from a range of disciplines (sociology, education, organization studies, material culture studies); and of producing a collaborative journal to collect our texts and products. These emergent workings out of the affective, material and spatial happenings *as* curriculum practices interrogate inherited educational categories and knowledge boundaries, helping to foreground agency as a posthuman 'commotion of co-activity' (ibid., p. 14). This edu-craft intervention, as a *matter* of knowing-in-doing, draws theoretically on Barad's (2007, p. 170) view that 'bodies do not simply take their place in the world...rather "environments" and "bodies" are intra- actively constituted'. It also summons Debord's (1955) notions of the *dérive* (getting lost) and the *détournement* (re-routing or hijacking) by undoing the 'tight' modular package within which undergraduates' usual modes of knowing, learning and writing are normally contained. These edu-crafting activities sometimes produce profound discomfort and sometimes generate desires for greater risks. This particular example of edu-crafting sits uneasily on the boundaries between educational research, pedagogic practice and reflective practice; it blurs individuality by trying to think self in motion in spatio-material assemblages; it destabilizes student assessment by provoking the production of things and objects, not just written assignments; and it invites consideration of the confederate activity of all manner of bodies, not just human bodies, in the production of the curriculum. It is just one instance of how an experimental research/pedagogy/practice can open a way to think the unforeseen, temporary, unpredictable and contingent, and draw attention to the regimes of normalcy and oppressive institutional sedimentations that higher education spaces often entail and require us to embody.

Concluding <> Continuing

Posthumanism is a mobile term, a concept in motion, an active theoretical assemblage. As an itinerant constellation of differing intellectual vectors and scholarly convocations, it gives rise to a complex mix of anxieties and fears as well as pleasurable fantasies, hopes and dreams about the newly possible in educational research.

This chapter has introduced posthumanism as a theoretical field, explored some of its conceptual moorings, and considered how empirical research in education is recast when the implications of posthumanism are taken as a starting point. It has proposed that there is no one line *from* humanism *to* posthumanism but, rather, various complicated genealogies. What is not in question is that the exclusions, hierarchies and violences imposed by Eurocentric, colonialist and patriarchal forms of humanism have been instrumental in provoking new modes of posthuman thinking and doing to contest these denigrations.

Far from being a future event, posthumanist practices and ways of thinking and doing are already with us. Posthumanism is entangled with the philosophical and everyday frames of reference through which ethical judgements are filtered and reconstituted; it informs the cultural categories, biological framings and technological procedures by which we make ourselves up as individual humans and as humans in relation to our human and other-than-human Earthly cohabitants; and it is imbricated in the hyper-capitalist, neoliberal economic imperatives that have gained precedence in constituting and explaining who 'we' are at this moment in the world's history. The 'everydayness' of posthumanism supports Braidotti's (2013, p. 2) point that the posthuman condition has introduced a 'qualitative shift in our thinking about what exactly is the basic unit of common reference for our species, our polity and our relationship to the other inhabitants of this planet'.

The challenge for posthumanist educational research is how to produce knowledge about education which undoes the humanist presumptions that have thus far grounded educational research. The approaches and practices outlined in this chapter try in various ways to do away with method/ology-as-usual by opening a wider purview for transdisciplinarity, and by activating *potentia*, with its promise of more ecological modes of being, based on relationality and co-constitutive worlding. The innovative posthuman practices touched on here generate concerns which resonate throughout the book. I have included a brief mention of edu-crafting as an experimental approach I have developed in my own field of higher education to illuminate my own (here, now, emerging, provisional) response to the posthumanist challenge to (try to) do educational research and pedagogy differently.

References

Barad, K. (2007) *Meeting the Universe Halfway: Quantum Physics and the Entanglement of Matter and Meaning* (London: Duke University Press).

Barber, M. (2014) 'Thetford Forest Wildlife "Performs" Living Symphonies' Premier', http://www.bbc.co.uk/news/uk-england-27256881, date accessed 22 August 2014.

Bennett, J. (2010) *Vibrant Matter: A Political Ecology of Things* (London: Duke University Press).

Bogost, I. (2012) *Alien Phenomenology, or What It's Like to Be a Thing* (Minneapolis: University of Minnesota Press).

Braidotti, R. (2013) *The Posthuman* (Cambridge: Polity Press).
Brinkman, S. (2015) 'GOFQI and the Phoenix of Qualitative Inquiry', *Qualitative Inquiry*, 21(7), 620–622.
Coole, D. and S. Frost (2010) *New Materialisms: Ontology, Agency, Politics* (Durham, NC: Duke University Press).
Davies, T. (1997) *Humanism* (London: Routledge).
Debord, G. (1955) 'Introduction to a Critique of Urban Geography', *Les Levres Nues*, 6, http://library.nothingness.org/articles/SI/en/display/2, date accessed 12 December 2013.
Deleuze, G. and F. Guattari (1987) *A Thousand Plateaus: Capitalism and Schizophrenia* (London: Continuum).
Derrida, J. (1972) *Margins of Philosophy* (Chicago, IL: University of Chicago Press).
Derrida, J. (2002) 'The Animal That Therefore I Am (More to Follow)', *Critical Inquiry*, 28(2), 369–418.
Foucault, F. (1970) *The Order of Things: An Archaeology of the Human Sciences* (New York: Vintage/Random House).
Haraway, D. (1991) *Simians, Cyborgs and Women: The Reinvention of Nature* (London: Free Association Books).
Haraway, D. (2008) *When Species Meet* (Minneapolis: University of Minnesota Press).
Harman, G. (2011) *The Quadruple Object* (Alresford, Hants: Zero Books).
Ingold, T. (2007) *Lines: A Brief History* (Abingdon: Routledge).
Kuntz, A. and M. Presnall (2012) 'Wandering the Tactical: From Interview to Intraview', *Qualitative Inquiry*, 18(9), 732–744.
Lamont, C. (1997) *The Philosophy of Humanism* (Amherst, NY: Humanist Press).
Lather, P. (2013) 'Methodology-21: What Do We Do in the Afterward?' *International Journal of Qualitative Studies in Education*, 26, 634–645.
Lather, P. and E. St. Pierre (2013) 'Post-qualitative Research', *International Journal of Qualitative Studies in Education*, 26(6), 629–633.
Law, J. (2004) *After Method: Mess in Social Science Research* (Oxon: Routledge).
Leckie, A. (2013) *Ancillary Justice* (London: Orbit).
MacCormack, P. (2012) *Posthuman Ethics: Embodiment and Cultural Theory* (Surrey: Ashgate).
MacLure, M. (2013) 'Classification or Wonder? Coding as an Analytic Practice in Qualitative Research', in R. Coleman and J. Ringrose (eds.) *Deleuze and Research Methodologies* (Edinburgh: Edinburgh University Press).
Manning, E. and B. Massumi (2014) *Thought in the Act: Passages in the Ecology of Experience* (Minneapolis: University of Minnesota Press).
Morton, T. (2009) *Ecology without Nature: Rethinking Environmental Aesthetics* (Harvard: Harvard University Press).
Plummer, K. (2012) 'A Manifesto for Critical Humanism in Sociology', http://kenplummer.com/manifestos/a-manifesto-for-a-critical-humanism-in-sociology/, date accessed 17 July 2015.
Rotas, N. (2015) 'Ecologies of Praxis: Teaching and Learning Against the Obvious', in N. Snaza and J. Weaver (eds.) *Posthumanism and Educational Research* (London: Routledge) pp. 91–103.
Singh, A. (2015) 'Tilda Swinton's Latest Performance Art: Licking Coats', http://www.telegraph.co.uk/news/celebritynews/11350653/Tilda-Swintons-latest-performance-art-licking-coats.html, date accessed 16 January 2015.

Skillington, T. (2015) 'Theorizing the Anthropocene', *European Journal of Social Theory*, 18(3), 229–235.

Snaza, N. (2015) 'Toward a Genealogy of Educational Humanism', in N. Snaza and J. Weaver (eds.) *Posthumanism and Educational Research* (London: Routledge) pp. 17–29.

Snaza, N. and J. Weaver (eds.) (2015) *Posthumanism and Educational Research* (London: Routledge).

Springgay, S. (2015) 'Approximate Rigorous Abstractions: Propositions of Activation for Posthumanist Research in Education', in N. Snaza and J. Weaver (eds.) *Posthumanism and Educational Research* (London: Routledge) pp. 76–88.

Stewart, K. (2007) *Ordinary Affects* (Durham, NC: Duke University Press).

Wallin, J. (2015) 'Dark Posthumanism, Unthinking Education, and Ecology at the End of the Anthropocene', in N. Snaza and J. Weaver (eds.) *Posthumanism and Educational Research* (London: Routledge) pp. 134–147.

Whitman, W. (1977) 'Leaves of Grass', in M. van Doren (ed.) *The Portable Walt Whitman* (Harmondsworth, England: Penguin).

Wolfe, C. (2010) *What Is Posthumanism?* (Minneapolis: University of Minnesota Press).

2
Rethinking the Empirical in the Posthuman

Elizabeth Adams St. Pierre

The concept 'posthuman' appears to imply an understanding of human being different from Descartes' invention that helped launch the Western Enlightenment: his spectacular *cogito*, the knowing, epistemological subject who, through the right use of reason, can produce foundational truth. Rorty (1979) called Descartes' approach to philosophical thinking 'methodological solipsism' (p. 192) because it invents and then installs a particular description of human being, the 'I think' and 'I know', ahead of the world, separate from the world. Then, in a feat of magic, this *cogito* invents the world – a stunning onto-epistemological project. It could be argued that such arrogance inevitably calls into existence its own resistance; and, indeed, a counter tradition in Western thought has always resisted Descartes' knowing subject. In the 20th century, his description of human being was refused by scholars we have labelled 'postmodern' because of its devastating epistemological projects in the name of *progress* and *science*. Over time, *to be* became equated with *to know*, and empirical science was privileged as the superior path to true knowledge. Lyotard (1979/1984) critiqued the supremacy of scientific knowledge with his statement 'Knowledge is not the same as science' (p. 18), a critique supported by those whose knowledge has been deemed unscientific and then dismissed.

In these first decades of the 21st century, the critique of the *cogito* has gathered strength and produced various 'new' approaches to thinking about what counts as human being. Perhaps fatigued by an over-abundance of epistemological projects, scholars in a variety of disciplines have shifted their focus to ontology, intensifying the decentring of the epistemological subject. This new work organizes itself differently as affect theory (Gregg and Seigworth, 2010), thing theory

(Brown, 2001), actor network theory (Latour, 2005), assemblage theory (De Landa, 2006), the new materialism (Coole and Frost, 2010), the new empiricism (Clough, 2009), the nonhuman (Grusin, 2015), the posthuman (Braidotti, 2013) – the project of this book – and other formations I have no doubt missed or that are in the making. This is an exciting time as some of us try to make the 'ontological turn' and to think differently about the nature of being and so to live differently.

This new work promises educators a way out of theoretical, material and empirical structures that seem to strangle us. The new approaches listed above offer different descriptions of human being and of the nature of being more broadly. They also offer different approaches to inquiry informed by different descriptions of ontology and of empiricism.

What I have learned in the last few years, however, is that making the ontological and empirical turns required to be/live/do something different is not easy. Our ambitions seem to exceed our capacities. Why are these turns so hard? Why is it so difficult to think of ourselves differently – as posthuman, as assemblage? And, given that I am an educational researcher, I wonder why it is so difficult to inquire differently? What is the relation between a focus on scientific method and methodology and difficulty in making these turns?

My trajectory as a qualitative methodologist in the US from 1991 to the present is illustrative, I think, of the inadequacy of an empiricism grounded in Cartesian theories of epistemology and ontology. Preoccupations with particular epistemologies and their empiricisms (empiricism and rationalism are two branches of epistemology) as well as the rush to application (to methodology), especially in applied fields like education, can sideline ontology. I would argue that, in general, doctoral training in educational research in the US not only bypasses the relation between ontology and epistemology (and empiricism) as well as the philosophy and history of science and social science and, instead, leaps to methodology, to the 'doing', to 'practice', as if practice is not always normed by theories of knowing and being.

When I began my doctoral studies in 1991, qualitative methodology had just been invented as an interpretive critique of and alternative to positivist educational research methodologies. What I've been calling 1980s qualitative methodology in the US (e.g., Denzin, 1989; Erickson, 1986; Lincoln and Guba, 1985) seemed to offer radical possibilities to, as I wrote in 1997, 'produce different knowledge and produce knowledge differently' (p. 175). Over the years, qualitative methodology became popular and was elaborated and structured in journal articles, textbooks and university curriculums. Journals and conferences devoted to qualitative methodology also helped to legitimate and formalize it.

In much of this empirical work in educational research, methodology served epistemology in an effort to uncover subjugated knowledges. Early interpretive efforts in qualitative research projects to describe everyday lived experiences often shifted to critical work when researchers were not content with mere description and moved to the identification and critique of structures of oppression in which such lived experiences were possible. However, those of us who studied postmodern and post-structural approaches increasingly found the structure of what I've called 'conventional humanist qualitative methodology' unable to accommodate the 'posts', which refuse that methodology's Cartesian epistemological subject, its ontology and its empiricism. Deconstruction of that methodology's organizing concepts followed – e.g., voice, data, validity, authenticity, reflexivity, the interview, the research process, the human. Working the ruins (St. Pierre and Pillow, 2000) of the structure preoccupied us, perhaps for too long.

I was increasingly dissatisfied with the hegemony of a qualitative methodology that could not rethink human being, a methodological structure I suspected could not exist without that human. I began concluding conference presentations with sentences like 'Perhaps qualitative methodology will become unintelligible' and eventually 'Perhaps we can leave it behind and do something different from the beginning.'

Just what that was I didn't know, but I did know that qualitative methodology had failed me decades earlier in my first study, my dissertation research (1994), which used postmodern theories to think about the subject. Once I had studied Foucault's, Butler's, Braidotti's, Nietzsche's, and Deleuze and Guattari's refusal of the Cartesian *cogito*, nothing about the structure made sense. Concepts like *fold, haecceity and assemblage* opened up a plane of thinking on which I could neither think nor do conventional humanist qualitative methodology, grounded as it is in the *cogito*.

Nonetheless, over a period of 18 years, I taught my university's introductory course in conventional qualitative methodology 19 times, but with increasing difficulty. During those years, I also developed a survey course on theoretical frameworks for doctoral studies (2001) and courses in postmodern theories (2003), Foucault (2006) and Derrida (2008). Students who studied the 'posts' had the same troubles with conventional humanist qualitative methodology that I'd had, and so, in 2003, I developed another new course, 'Post Qualitative Research', to support them. We didn't know what post-qualitative research was, what it 'meant', or how to 'do' it, but it sounded promising. I advised students to read theory before they studied methodology and to use those theories to 'inquire', much as one might do in philosophy. I no longer thought inquiry could be reduced to the methodologies of qualitative, quantitative and mixed methods research, which had become the three chief alternatives for empirical educational research in the US. I reminded students that the 'posts' opposed method because it is prescriptive, always comes too late, and is immediately out of date. In 2010, a colleague then at my university, Mark Vagle, and I began an initiative in our college we called 'philosophically informed research' in an effort to reconnect educational research, too attached to the positivism of the social sciences, to its roots in philosophy. We organized a well-attended session at the 2011 American Educational Research Association on that topic. In 2013, Bronwyn Davies, who visited my institution, and I taught a new course we called 'Feminism, Poststructuralism, and the New Empiricisms/New Materialisms'.

In a sense, my teaching, described above, maps my slow understanding that for me, at least, making the ontological turn would mean abandoning the conventional humanist qualitative methodology in which I had been so well trained. That particular empirical project could not accommodate the ontology of the new work that refused the *cogito* – the posthuman, more-than-human, nonhuman, inhuman and so on. During those years, my students encouraged me to write papers they could cite to justify their own 'post' work – they needed citational authority to inquire differently. In 2011, I wrote a chapter on 'post qualitative inquiry' for that purpose.

This long trek has taught me several things. The first is the need to return to philosophy, which I first studied as an undergraduate decades ago. Second, we learn what we're taught. If we teach methodology without first teaching ontology and epistemology (and their empiricisms), without teaching the philosophy and history of science and social science, then we reduce inquiry to conventional empirical scientific method that is saturated through and through with the humanist subject and, in large part, with logical empiricism, which denies the speculative, exactly what these new turns ask us to engage. Third, it's very difficult to escape our training. Those of us well trained in qualitative methodology may find it difficult to think outside its normalized, formalized, taken-for-granted structure. It's difficult not to think, 'What research design should I use for this project – is this an interview study, an ethnography, a grounded theory study?', 'Who will I interview?', 'How many times should I observe that classroom?', 'I wonder if I should buy that new software for coding data?' It's not so easy to put aside those ordinary methodological questions that assume the *cogito* and do something different from the beginning – to realize, in fact, that we are always already entangled in inquiry, that there is no beginning.

At this point, I refuse the concepts *method* and *methodology* as they are used in most empirical educational research. That means I also refuse the empiricisms that enable those methods and methodologies. This ontological turn, which does not assume that to be is to know, demands a different empiricism that is not grounded in the humanist subject.

What might an empiricism for the posthuman look like? In the following section, I briefly describe Deleuze and Guattari's transcendental empiricism, in which, I believe, neither the humanist subject nor conventional social science empirical inquiry is thinkable.

Transcendental empiricism

About classical empiricism, Deleuze and Parnet (1977/1987) wrote the following:

> Empiricism is often defined as a doctrine according to which the intelligible 'comes' from the sensible, everything in the understanding comes from the senses. But that is the standpoint of a history of philosophy: they have the gift of stifling all life in seeking and in positing an abstract first principle. Whenever one believes in a great first principle, one can no longer produce anything but sterile dualisms. (p. 54)

Instead of first principles, which he called masks, Deleuze was interested in the 'concrete richness of the sensible' (p. 54) as it exists *for-itself*, not *for-us* after mediation by language, reason, or our a priori categories into which it must fit.

Deleuze's *transcendental empiricism* appears odd because it seems to unite the incompatible philosophies of empiricism (Hume) and transcendentalism (Kant). Kant's transcendental idealism posits a priori categories, pure concepts, that provide the conditions of possibility of objects in general. For Kant, a category is a characteristic or property that can be predicated of a thing, and he called categories *ontological predicates*. On a transcendental level, the human subject, using those categories and its judgement, synthesizes for itself the manifold of the sensible, empirical world, which for Kant was disordered chaos. In this image of thought, the function of the transcendental is to ground the empirical world; therefore, as Bryant (2009) explained,

> If the transcendental is traced from the empirical, if it is conceived in *resemblance* to the empirical, we have only engaged in a strange doubling of the empirical that risks essentializing the recognized, rather than truly grounding that which it seeks to ground. We have not established that the empirical is truly a necessary structure in the sense asserted, rather than something that is simply contingent and could be otherwise... Deleuze argues that Kant ends up valorizing *recognition* [emphasis added] as a model of what it is to think in a way that ends up defending orthodoxy and prohibiting the emergence of the new. (p. 20)

In his radical empiricism, Deleuze removed the subject from its transcendental position as the synthesizing, unifying agent of judgement who recognizes (identifies) and orders the world using a priori categories and concepts, thereby *knowing* it, producing it as an object of knowledge. Deleuze insisted that the empirical has to be taken into account in all its peculiarities not as it appears *for-us* but as it is *for-itself* in its difference, with no mediation by the human. Deleuze (1966/1991a) believed we must go beyond the human condition, which is the 'meaning of philosophy, in so far as our condition condemns us to live among badly analyzed composites, and to be badly analyzed composites ourselves' (p. 28). His focus then is on the *difference* of the empirical. 'Difference is not diversity. Diversity is given, but difference is that by which the given is given, that by which the given is given as diverse' (Deleuze, 1968/1994, p. 28). In this way, Deleuze's philosophy is a philosophy of difference. In his transcendental empiricism, the given is not the origin but that which must be actualized, made. Here, human consciousness is removed from the dominant position of intentionality which can recognize an always already pre-given essence.

Though he moved the human out of a transcendental realm, Deleuze did retain the differentiation of a virtual transcendental field he called variously the *plane of consistency, plane of immanence* and *body-without-organs*, which is composed of *singularities* or *haecceities* – unformed (but determinable) matter of pure speeds and intensities at the limits of deterritorialization. The plane of consistency is 'everywhere first and primary, always immanent' (Deleuze and Guattari, 1980/1987, p. 70). Deleuze (1968/1994) emphasized that it is virtual rather than possible:

The virtual could be confused with the possible. The possible is opposed to the real; the process undergone by the possible is therefore a 'realisation'. By contrast the virtual is not opposed to the real; it possesses a full reality by itself. The process it undergoes is actualisation. (p. 211)

So the virtual and the actual are both real. The transcendental field does not resemble or mirror the actual but allows for an actual that creates itself by differentiating itself from the virtual field in a process of individuation of intensities. The event of an actuality occurs when existing forces, intensities and relations converge *by chance*, leave behind the actuality in its difference, and then erase themselves. That chance movement by which an entity is produced, then, gives it its genetic history, its difference. Bryant (2009) explained that 'the transcendental field is a set of genetic conditions presiding over the individuation of individuals' (p. 46). Here 'individual' could be a rock, a person, a colour, or five o'clock in the afternoon. So the entity comes into existence not through an internal act of synthesis by the transcendental ego (no human needed here) but by the external, chance intersection and divergence of series through external relations or associations on the plane of consistency. Deleuze did not, however, create two different ontological realms – the transcendental field and the empirical field. Rather, the transcendental field is composed of *relations* of the unformed that are expressed in empirical states of affairs.

Deleuze borrowed the idea of *external relations* from Hume, and they exist not only in the transcendental field as described above but also in the empirical field. The *relation of actualities* is external, not internal, not governed by the logic of identity by being included within an a priori concept that unites them in their prior identity. The relation of actualities employs the logic of difference. 'Everything separable is distinguishable and everything distinguishable is different' (Deleuze, 1953/1991b, p. 87). Baugh (1992) wrote that 'it is the empirical actuality of instances that makes multiplicity possible, since it is through the empirical actuality that a non-conceptual difference, and hence the purely additive and external relation of the AND, is made possible' (p. 137). The external relation marked by AND offered Deleuze a different logic, a logic of movement and *becoming*, of *assemblage*, of *difference* instead of the logic of stasis, the logic of 'to be', the logic of identity that enables 'recognition'.

In transcendental empiricism, then, we have no pre-existing categories, no existing order actualities have to fit into. In Deleuze's empiricism, order is not opposed to disorder, which is how Kant described the empirical that required ordering. Deleuze believed there can be different kinds of order and that the empirical has its own immanent ordering principles.

Most important, the humanist subject does not exist on Deleuze's transcendental field. 'Impersonal and pre-individual nomadic singularities constitute the real transcendental field' (Deleuze, 1969/1990, p. 110). A singularity is not the same as a 'particular' subsumed under a generality as in Kant. A singularity on the plane of consistency does not have a unique essence that can be recognized so it can be put into a category with other things that have the same essence. Singularities, always found in relation to each other, are aconceptual, impersonal, pre-individual, unformed, nonobjectival and capable of self-organization. They do not have a direct relation to the entities they form in states of affairs, so, again, there is no transcendental Idea of the Actual to which the actual refers. As noted earlier, singularities – the unformed – exist in external relations on the virtual plane of consistency and are understood in their iterability, in their repetition in series (not linear sequences) that continue and join other series and are always breaking off and then starting up again in the middle (like rhizomes and haecceities). Both the actual (states of affairs) and the virtual (plane of consistency) realms are organized as series that are stretched out, fluid, changing, connecting and intersecting – independent of human observers, human consciousness, intentionality, or a faculty of representation.

In this empiricism, space doesn't *contain* series, actualities and events but is constituted by them. Deleuze (1969/1990) explained that 'to reverse Platonism is first and foremost to remove essences and to substitute events in their place' (p. 53). Events are characterized by the infinitive form of the verb, as in 'to green', and are never present – they are 'something which has just happened and something about to happen, never something which is happening' (Deleuze, 1969/1990, p. 63). Events have a specificity, a mode of individuation that is singular 'but very different from that of a person, subject, thing, or substance' (Deleuze and Guattari, 1980/1987, p. 261). They are incorporeal relations of movement, 'jets of singularities' (Deleuze, 1969/1990, p. 53) 'deployed in a problematic field, in the vicinity of which solutions are organised' (p. 54). In *The Logic of Sense*, Deleuze's (1969/1990) two primary series are states of affairs (bodies and things) and expression (language). An event is not a rupture, a break, something completely new that occurs. 'As an event, a beginning must be understood as a novel selection in ongoing and continually altering series...a set of animals altering course due to climatic change, or politically disinterested citizens woken from apathy by events' (Williams, 2008, p. 2). The event runs along the series – which is not passive or static but always connecting with other series, breaking off, starting up again – and both the event and the series are changed. Events, then, resonate through the ongoing variations of different series that are transformed by the event that has selected them. 'Where the series diverge, another world begins, incompossible with the first' (Deleuze, 1969/1990, p. 111).

So Deleuze does not adopt the classical understanding of empiricism that uses experience as the origin and source of true knowledge. Again, Deleuze's radical empiricism is not in the epistemic register, it does not follow the classical epistemological model of empiricism premised on a conscious human subject who has access to the given (lived experience, brute data) as the origin and justification of knowledge. Knowledge is not primary in transcendental empiricism, and we do not think in terms of knowledge or of a knower who can know the world. The word *epistemology* rarely appears in Deleuze's work. *Transcendental empiricism, then, does not have the status of an epistemology, and knowledge is not its concern.*

Boundas (1991) wrote that Deleuze followed Hume in substituting belief for knowledge. Deleuze's questions were not questions of knowledge; rather, as Rajchman (2000) explained, 'the question of empiricism is found in the identification of a new problem...the problem of belief in the world' (p. 25).

> It is not so much a matter of being optimistic or pessimistic as of being realistic about the new forces not already contained in our projects and programs and the ways of thinking that accompany them. In other words, to make connections one needs not knowledge, certainty, or even ontology, but rather a trust that something may come out, though one is not yet completely sure what.
> (Rajchman, 2000, p. 7)

In their book, *What Is Philosophy?*, Deleuze and Guattari (1991/1994) wrote about 'people yet to come' (p. 176), 'still-missing people' (p. 109), 'people that do not yet exist' (p. 109) who might be able to attend to all those external relations in the empirical we continue to force into old categories. We will have to invent a people, always a minor people, who can think the unthought.

Thoughts about posthuman research practices

I believe there is much 'old' work to read (e.g., Spinoza, Leibnitz, Nietzsche, Pierce, Whitehead, James) and much prior reading (especially about conventional empirical research methodologies) to distance ourselves from if we want to engage new material, new empirical, posthuman work after the ontological turn. In this paper, I provided a sketch of empirical transcendental empiricism, which is, of course, not an epistemological project. My point here is that we will be unable to think the posthuman and to invent posthuman research practices as long as we continue to employ conventional empirical research methodologies grounded in the *cogito* whose purpose is knowledge production. I believe we will have to resist *the idea of methodology itself*, which will prevent us from producing the new that is everywhere, immanent and inexhaustible, that we might actualize.

To move into a different image of thought, I repeat that I believe we need new concepts and new conceptual practices – *not new methodologies and their knowledge practices* – to do this new work that is not interested in recognizing conventional epistemic objects but in the 'concrete richness of the sensible' (Deleuze and Parnet, 1977/1987, p. 54) as well as in the encounters of events 'in the context of the problem whose conditions they determine' (Deleuze, 1969/1990, p. 54).

But concepts and practices cannot be determined in advance. If we suspend our belief in a human being who should know what to do before she does it and if we can be 'realistic about the new forces not already contained in our projects and programs and the ways of thinking that accompany them' (Rajchman, 2000, p. 7), we might move towards the 'new' that is everywhere. In the posthuman, *life is no longer personal*. As we help each other think about that startling claim, we must trust that something will come out, the 'nonthought within thought' (Deleuze and Guattari, 1991/1994, p. 59) that will enable new practices and new lives. Whether and how inquiry (not methodology) figures in that work is not, I believe, our primary concern at this time. 'First, it is necessary to read' (Lacan, as cited in Ulmer, 1985). I suspect it may take a great deal of reading to get a concept like transcendental empiricism – an empiricism adequate to the posthuman – in our bones so that we can think differently about the nature of being, the posthuman and people yet to come. Appropriate practices will follow as we do the next thing the concept enables.

References

Baugh, B. (1992) 'Transcendental Empiricism: Deleuze's Response to Hegel', *Man and World*, 25, 133–148.
Braidotti, R. (2013) *The Posthuman* (Cambridge, UK: Polity Press).

Boundas, C. V. (1991) 'Translator's Introduction', in G. Deleuze (eds.) *Empiricism and Subjectivity: An Essay on Hume's Theory of Human Nature* (C. V. Boundas, Trans.) (New York, NY: Columbia University Press) (Original work published 1953), pp. 1–19.

Brown, B. (2001) 'Thing Theory', *Critical Inquiry*, 28(1), 1–22.

Bryant, L. R. (2009) 'Deleuze's Transcendental Empiricism: Notes Towards a Transcendental Materialism', in E. Willatt and M. Lee (eds.) *Thinking between Deleuze and Kant: A Strange Encounter* (London, UK: Continuum), pp. 28–48.

Clough, P. T. (2009) 'The New Empiricism: Affect and Sociological Method', *European Journal of Social Theory*, 12(1), 43–61.

Coole, D. and Frost, S. (eds.) (2010) *New Materialisms: Ontology, Agency, and Politics* (Durham, NC: Duke University Press).

De Landa, M. (2006) *A New Philosophy of Society: Assemblage Theory and Social Complexity* (New York, NY: Continuum).

Deleuze, G. (1990) *The Logic of Sense* (C. V. Boundas, ed., Mark Lester, Trans.) (New York, NY: Columbia University Press) (Original work published 1969).

Deleuze, G. (1991a) *Bergsonism* (H. Tomlinson and B. Habberjam, Trans.) (New York, NY: Zone Books) (Original work published 1966).

Deleuze, G. (1991b) *Empiricism and Subjectivity: An Essay on Hume's Theory of Human Nature* (C. V. Boundas, Trans.) (New York, NY: Columbia University Press) (Original work published 1953).

Deleuze, G. (1994) *Difference and Repetition* (P. Patton, Trans.) (New York, NY: Columbia University Press) (Original work published 1968).

Deleuze, G. and Guattari, F. (1987) *A Thousand Plateaus: Capitalism and Schizophrenia* (B. Massumi, Trans.) (Minneapolis, MN: University of Minnesota Press) (Original work published 1980).

Deleuze, G. and Guattari, F. (1994) *What Is Philosophy?* (H. Tomlinson and G. Burchell, Trans.) (New York, NY: Columbia University Press) (Original work published 1991).

Deleuze, G. and Parnet, C. (1987) *Dialogues* (H. Tomlinson and B. Habberjam, Trans.) (New York, NY: Columbia University Press) (Original work published 1977).

Denzin, N. K. (1989) *Interpretive Interactionism* (Newbury Park, CA: Sage Publications).

Erickson, F. (1986) 'Qualitative Methods in Research on Teaching', in M. C. Whitlock (ed.) *Handbook of Research on Teaching* (3rd ed.) (New York, NY: Macmillan), pp. 119–161.

Gregg, M. and Seigworth, G. J. (eds.) (2010) *The Affect Theory Reader* (Durham, NC: Duke University Press).

Grusin, R. (ed.) (2015) *The Nonhuman Turn* (Minneapolis, MN: University of Minnesota Press).

Latour, B. (2005) *Reassembling the Social: An Introduction to Actor-Network-Theory* (Oxford, UK: Oxford University Press).

Lincoln, Y. S. and Guba, E. G. (1985) *Naturalistic Inquiry* (Newbury Park, CA: Sage Publications).

Lyotard, J. F. (1984) *The Postmodern Condition: A Report on Knowledge* (G. Bennington and B. Massumi, Trans.) (Minneapolis, MN: University of Minnesota Press) (Original work published 1979).

Rajchman, J. (2000) *The Deleuze Connections* (Cambridge, MA: The MIT Press).

Rorty, R. M. (1979) *Philosophy and the Mirror of Nature* (Princeton, NJ: Princeton University Press).
St. Pierre, E. A. (1995) *Arts of Existence: The Construction of Subjectivity in Older, White Southern Women.* Unpublished doctoral dissertation (Columbus, OH: The Ohio State University).
St. Pierre, E. A. (1997) 'Methodology in the Fold and the Irruption of Transgressive Data', *International Journal of Qualitative Studies in Education*, 10(2), 175–189.
St. Pierre, E. A. (2011) 'Post Qualitative Research: The Critique and the Coming After', in N.K. Denzin and Y.S. Lincoln (eds.) *Sage Handbook of Qualitative Inquiry* (4th ed.) (Los Angeles, CA: Sage), pp. 611–635.
St. Pierre, E. A. and Pillow W. S. (eds.) (2000) *Working the Ruins: Feminist Poststructural Theory and Methods in Education* (New York: Routledge).
Ulmer, G. L. (1985) *Applied Grammatology: Post(e)-Pedagogy from Jacques Derrida to Joseph Beuys* (Baltimore, MD: John Hopkins University Press).
Williams, J. (2008) *Gilles Deleuze's Logic of Sense: A Critical Introduction and Guide* (Edinburgh, UK: Edinburgh University Press).

3
Deleuzo-Guattarian Rhizomatics: Mapping the Desiring Forces and Connections between Educational Practices and the Neurosciences

Hillevi Lenz Taguchi

Introduction

We live in a time of multiple neuro-ontologies where one academic discipline after the other adds on the prefix 'neuro-' to emphasize a new awareness of the significance of neuroscientific findings to their specific field of study: neuro-economics, neuro-marketing, neuro-architecture, neuro-psychology, neuro-education, and on and on (Rose and Abi-Rached, 2013; Satel and Lilienfield, 2013). A growing number of politicians and policymakers urge educators to take an interest in the advances of the neurosciences for it to apply to practice. Moreover, for over a decade researchers in the emerging discipline of *educational neurosciences* have aimed to create a new *trans*disciplinary field of research, where knowledge from the neurosciences and education can be integrated (Battro et al., 2011; Fischer et al., 2007; Samuels, 2009).

Cognitive psychologists regard their discipline as the link between the fields that might provide the necessary *two-way street* between neurology and education, while dismissing a simple idea of applying the neurosciences to education (Geake, 2011; Ansari et al., 2011). With the main aim of researching the connections between brain and mind, cognitive psychologists have launched theories of the extended brain and concepts such as the *embodied brain* and *mindbrain* (Campbell, 2011, p. 11). There is a profound interest among some of these neuro-cognitive researchers in the philosophies of mind and sometimes even educational philosophy (Campbell, 2011; Geake, 2011; Howard-Jones, 2011). However, when the chips are down, the taken-for-granted position within this new transdiscipline is to focus on how neurology as a 'basic research' might contribute to and improve educational practices (Bruer, 1997; Ferrari, 2011). The field of education at large is thus recognized as the passive recipient of 'real' and 'hard' scientific knowledge (Ferrari, 2011, p. 32). Given this standpoint, we should not be surprised by the intensive discussions of the many difficulties in getting practitioners interested in the neurosciences (e.g., Bruer, 2011). In a conversation between the neuro-educational researcher Helen Immordino-Yang and educational theorist Howard Gardner at the USC Rossier School of Education on 11 February 2013, these difficulties were brought to the surface. Gardner concludes that we cannot – and maybe shouldn't even try to – build bridges between the neurosciences and educational practices. This is, he states, because they are entirely different enterprises, based on different forms of creativity. Gardner declares that education is *neither* a science, *nor* an arena for applying scientific knowledge, but is rather an *art* which is built on and saturated with humanly constructed values (Gardner and Immordino-Yang, 2013).

Yet, alongside those who are uninterested, disengaged and indeed antithetical, there is also evidence of the opposite response (Pickering and Howard-Jones, 2007). However, for those working in inter- and transdisciplinary studies, where researchers from the humanities, education, social sciences and the cognitive and neurosciences aim to collaborate and translate knowing between disciplines, there is a recognition of the sometimes extensive problems that such research brings in the different phases of the research process (e.g., Fitzgerald et al., 2014). Irrespective of what various researchers in the different disciplines might think or do, want or desire, something is nevertheless already being produced in the encounters and connections taking place between these fields of thinking and practising. How then might it be possible to study this particular field of encounter between these different fields?

In concert with growing inter- and transdisciplinary developments, which strive to connect the knowledge and theories of social, natural and humanist sciences, various kinds of *posthumanist* empirical research have grown rapidly (see Introduction and Chapter 1). However, when the social sciences and humanities have engaged with the neurosciences, the research performed (whether it is framed as posthumanist research or not) often seems to get caught in a classical binary division. As Fitzgerald and Callard (2015) write, it tends to be driven by either ebullience or critique. With an ambition not to get stuck in either of these, the aim of this chapter is to make some initial explorations of the possibilities of investigating this field by putting to work Deleuzo-Guattarian inspired *rhizomatic readings* and *cartography mapping* (Deleuze and Guattari, 1987). This choice is made due to the qualities inherent in such a methodological strategy, which aims to perform a doubled movement of critique and innovative creation. This, I have claimed, is also what distinguishes posthumanist research from critical and post-structuralist accounts (Lenz Taguchi, 2012, 2013, forthcoming). A doubled movement means performing both a critical tracing of normative articulations and practices on a field of thinking, as well as an experimental mapping exercise that might help us narrate the reality in question differently (Stengers, 2008). Martin and Kamberelis (2013, p. 671) write that the methodology of mapping, the way they conceive it, not only brings...

> ...into high relief the dominant discursive and material forces at play (i.e. lines of articulation); but the map also discloses those forces that...might have the power to transform or reconfigure reality in various ways (i.e. lines of flight). Ultimately, mapping discloses potential organizations of reality rather than reproducing some prior organization of it.

Hence, a Deleuzo-Guattarian rhizomatic reading and cartography mapping can be understood to take us beyond critique, and thus to ask what new possible realities for education might be envisioned on this particular plane of interacting desiring discourses and material practices. In terms of a posthumanist empirical research study, this chapter asks not only how this ongoing production can be studied, but what a posthumanist study in itself might be productive of in terms of constructing new possible narratives (Stengers, 2008). The primary focus of this chapter, as of this book, is that of methodology, although some of the productive forces in the connections between the fields of (cognitive) neurosciences and education are also proposed in the enactment of this example. Before outlining the methodology, I will provide a brief overview of this particular plane of thinking and its various dominant lines of articulation that can be traced and put back onto this map. The second half of the chapter provides a preliminary outline of some of the tracings of the desiring forces that have been mapped in order to perform some initial experimentation.

A plane of multiple, evolving and transforming neuro-ontologies

Various neuro-ontologies can be laid out as a map of interacting strata (Deleuze and Guattari, 1987). I want to emphasize that this map is not a representation of the field or plane, but involves a tracing and creative construction of the articulations that these strata are made of. Descriptions of realities based on neurology – neuro-ontologies – connect in very different ways to problems of learning and education (Vidal, 2011). Some of these ontologies turn to the brain itself as a distinct entity to understand how *it* shapes learning and culture, and thus how we as humans, in turn, are shaped by *it* (Wexler, 2008). Others, who promote the force of *affect* in learning, turn instead to the social environment of interpersonal relations in order to understand how the brain is shaped by these relations and how we, as a consequence, can shape *it*: 'human connections shape neural connections', as the founder of interpersonal neurobiology – Daniel Siegel – has claimed (Siegel, 2012, p. 3). Yet others turn to the dynamism of *plasticity*, which in terms of neuro-plasticity refers to the ability the brain has to change throughout life, for better or worse (Stevens and Neville, 2009, p. 165).

In a wider perspective, plasticity refers to the process from which all living beings, brains and thoughts and ideas are generated: *a brain of bodily interaction* (Cutler and MacKenzie, 2011, p. 69). The anti-Cartesian neuro-philosopher Andy Clark writes that 'human thought and reason is born out of looping interactions with material brains, material bodies and complex cultural and technological environments. [...] We exist as the thinking beings we are, only thanks to a baffling dance of brains, bodies, and cultural and technological scaffolding' (Clark, 2003, cited p. 10 in Colebrook, 2011). However, as in most other anti- or post-Cartesian neuro-philosophies, this thinking eventually refers to a turning back to the body and the material stuff of which we and the world are made (Alaimo, 2010). Colebrook (2014, pp. 34–51) critically refers to this as what is taken as the (true) meaning of life, as well as part of (the) '*one* ecology and system of interconnected life', from which we somehow forgot we emerged.

Cartography mapping as building on but transgressing critical discourse analysis

Deleuze's philosophical project has sometimes been described in terms of taking a philosopher 'from behind' (Colebrook, 2008, p. 12). This can be read as a methodology of an encounter, engaged in critically tracking a theory or thinking. It can be described, writes Colebrook (2008, p. 16), to – ex post facto – *queer* that thinking by critically deterritorializing it. However, my first attempt to perform tracing and mapping on this particular plane constituted something like an insolent feminist rebellion against the dominant neuroscientific discipline. As an educational feminist researcher, I completely aligned myself with the critical feminist neuroscience community (Dussauge, 2014; Fine, 2010, 2014; Schmitz and Höppner, 2014; Vidal, 2005, 2014), which – from within the realm of the life sciences themselves – has been at enmity with the persistent research that for so long has made it their cause to sustain fundamental gender differences. Such research has thereby reproduced an irreconcilable representational gender dualism with effects far beyond the realm of the sciences themselves (Pinker, 2003). The differences implied in this dualism are permeated by a cultural logic where they become productive of a negative ontology and relationality: a difference that means to be 'different-from' but also to be 'less than', or 'to be *worth* less than' as woman as compared to man (Braidotti, 1994, p. 147; original emphasis, in Dolphijn and van der Tuin, 2012, p. 27).

The very idea, however, of reading and taking a philosophy, or a discipline, 'from behind' extends, as Colebrook (2008, pp. 13–14) points out, the problematic masculinism inherent to philosophy, psychoanalysis and the academy as a rebellion against the father, which simply restores an emasculated position of knowing from a feminist point of view. To get away from such a weakened position, Colebrook (2008) suggests we read Deleuze and Guattari's philosophy as a methodology of a certain mode of reading that is not simply preoccupied with tracings, and especially not tracing the master or dominant discourse as a wicked scapegoat or straw man to put the blame on. It is due to this tendency to get stuck in the critical aspect of tracing that Deleuze and Guattari explicitly tell us: 'Make a map, not a tracing' (1987, p. 12). Although mapping does indeed entail rigorous performances of tracing the lines of the regimes of signs, these tracings must always be put back on the map at a different entry point, in order to form new relations and thus to restore a multiplicity of connections and a state of heterogeneity: 'It is a question of method: *the tracings should always be put back on the map*' (ibid., p. 13, original italics), at least if we want to achieve that practice of queering and deterritorializing that Colebrook (2008, p. 16) suggests feminist researchers engage in.

Deleuze and Guattari's mapping thus extends to a practice of what Colebrook (2008) has described as reading the intensive, creative and transformative *chatter* on a particular plane of thinking. This chattering can be understood to transpose and creatively transforms the dominant lines of articulation that have been traced. Colebrook describes such chattering as putting in motion a multiplicity of voices that create 'a pattern, a field of forces, but does so *without* external justification'

(Colebrook, 2008, p. 16, italics added), i.e. not referring back to an original root nor the origin of the tracings. Hencethese are what Mazzei (2013) would call voices without organs. This means that they do not refer to specific, fixed and positioned organic bodies, but constitute an assemblage of interrelating voices or chatter: sometimes in strong unison and harmony, sometimes in dissonance. Reading the transformative chatter means a style or mode of reading that, instead of reading in order to trace and reveal the underpinning structures, aims instead to read in dissonance with, and to be productive of 'difference as shown differing' (Dolphijn and van der Tuin, 2012, p. 86). Hence, reading the intensive chattering aspires to produce new ways of thinking that render the masters – old and new – 'indiscernible and imperceptible behind creative productions', as Colebrook writes (2008, p. 17).

In other words, we trace the desiring forces where neurosciences and education connect in order to establish the contours of the multiple intensive forces that produce a preliminary 'map' of intensities and flows of narratives articulated from the chatters produced by regimes of signs, but without trying to discover some general or prior ground (Bonta and Protevi, 2004). In this way, the methodology of cartography mapping is more about what Colebrook (2008, p. 14) talks about in terms of practising an *internal pragmatics*: 'to look at the ways styles of position create fields and modes of force' and to 'look at how modes of argument, concept-creation and problem-production effect ways of living' (ibid., p. 8).

The constructive mapping of this plane of different ways of thinking and practising, which together constitute the larger machinic assemblage of – in this case – articulations of neuro-ontologies and their material practices in education, can be illustrated with a drawing by Ramon y Cajal. He produced the first known neuro-images of, as in this case, neuro-connections of the retina, meticulously drawn over 100 years ago.

Hence, the 'map' and the process of mapping is not about representing a field of forces, but should be understood as a process of 'cartography' preoccupied with both tracing and mapping by laying out the lines (both the articulating lines and lines of flight) and thus 'the longitude and latitude of an intensive body' (Bonta and Protevi, 2004, p. 126). Deleuze and Guattari (1987) refer to this body and its particular plane of thinking and practising as forming a complex *rhizome* (ibid., pp. 4–25) of multiple threads and lines of articulation that together form a larger assemblage that works in machinic and power-producing ways, thus constituting a *machinic assemblage* which Figure 3.1 can be imagined as.

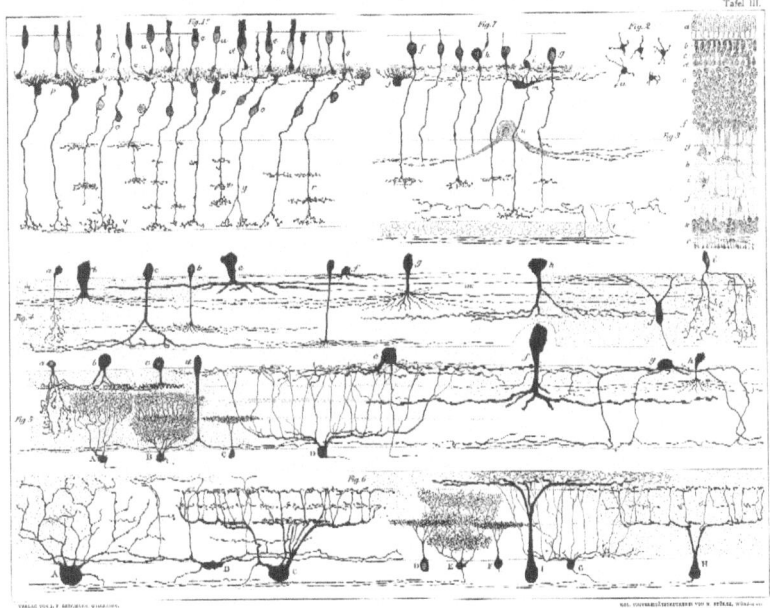

Figure 3.1 Santiago Ramón y Cajal. Line drawing of the retina

The principles and process of rhizomatics and mapping

As researcher, you trace and put onto your constructed map some of the intensive chattering of various loud and dominant (molar) *lines of articulation*, in terms of ways of thinking, talking and practising particular ways of knowing. You observe how different forms of chatter harmonize, converge and stretch their root threads into stronger circles of convergence. Other intensive chattering might instead stretch out towards other circles or make offshoots in completely other directions to become deterritorialized. These are the *lines of flight*: the escaping forces away from those articulating molar lines. Deleuze and Guattari (1987, p. 11) describe the process as following the root threads of a rhizome in the following way.

> Follow the plants: you start by delimiting a first line consisting of circles of convergence around successive singularities; then you see whether inside that line new circles of convergence establish themselves with new points located outside the limits and in other directions.

The above description can be connected to a more detailed drawing of cell morphologies by Fernando de Castro Rodríguez, Cajal's contemporary and co-researcher (Figure 3.2).

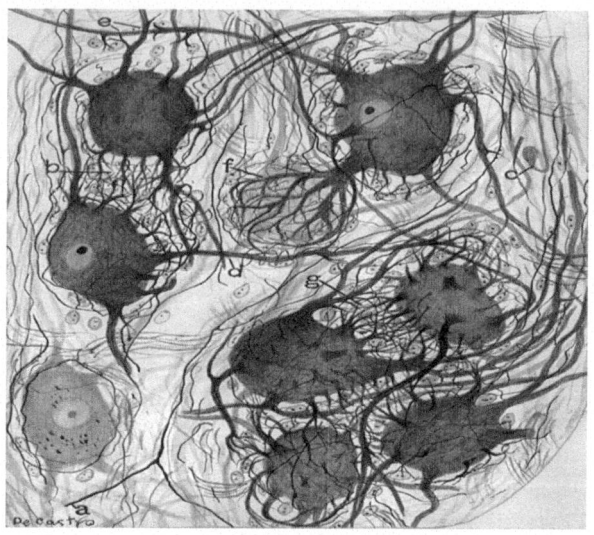

Figure 3.2 Fernando de Castro Rodríguez, 1896–1967. Cell morphologies within a typical sympathetic ganglia

To give a simplified example: we can listen to the intensive articulations from the renewed forms of Bowlby's and Ainsworth's attachment-theories, connected to both psychoanalysis and the neurosciences (Howard et al., 2011; Mayers et al., 2007). We observe how their lines of articulation swirl into their circle of convergence the articulations of various conservative political lobbying groups that privilege stay-at-home parenting and schooling over tax-funded day care and/or Head Start preschooling (Howard et al., 2011; mercatornet.com; loving-attachment-parenting.com/stay-home-mom). However, when we follow one of those intensive threads of interpersonal attachments, we can also observe how one of those lines of articulations makes an offshoot to establish new circles of convergence on a different part of the map. Here, it connects to and converges with those lines of articulation that in contrast to the former would claim that it is due to unhealthy attachments with stay-at-home parents that children instead need the interpersonal relations and attachment provided by educated staff in day care and early childhood education (Cozolino, 2013). At this location on the map, we can trace the lines of articulations of economic research, showing that good-quality early childhood education will have long-term effects on employment and income (e.g., Chetty et al., 2011; Cunha and Heckman, 2007). Such lines converge smoothly with the advocates of universal high-quality early childhood services.

Hence, in the enactment of mapping, you actively follow or put in motion the four principles of rhizomatics: *connection, heterogeneity, multiplicity* and the *asignifying rupture* (Deleuze and Guattari, 1987, p. 9), as you trace the lines of articulation to see whether they converge into molar lines, or become deterritorialized to form new molecular lines at a different space of the map. It is the exploration of the deterritorializing flows and the possible 'lines of flight', according to which the rhizome can transform and expand, that is key to Deleuzo-Guattarian rhizomatics and mapping. The critical tracing where the rhizome operates by capture and conquest to form dominant molar lines of articulations is simply one aspect of the doubled movements of this exercise, the primary aim of which is to explore the variations, offshoots and expansion of the rhizome.

In order to explore those variations and lines of flight that diverge from the segmentary (molar) lines, you sometimes need to enact the fourth principle of the rhizome: the *asignifying rupture*. This means actively engaging in a practice of estrangement to get away from taken-for-granted and common sense significations (ibid., p. 11). In other words, it is the enactment of creative ruptures and following the *lines of flight* to new connections, or to something omitted, left out, or silenced, which might evoke something completely new, that this methodology of rhizomatics or mapping is trying to achieve. Deleuze and Guattari (1987, p. 12) write: 'What distinguishes the map from the tracing is that it is entirely oriented towards an experimentation in contact with the real' [...] '[We] experiment with the opportunities and find potential movements of deterritorialization and possible lines of flight' (ibid., p. 161). As Martin and Kamberelis (2013, p. 271) emphasize, 'even the most intensely territorialized landscape have some lines of flight, testifying to the potentials within them for deterritorializing and reterritorializing activity'.

In relation to the example above, what might such an asignifying rupture entail? The 10 last years of gay, lesbian, queer and transsexual rights, have illustrated the possibilities of multiple other ways of constructing parenthood, family, attachment and early care and education. The possibility of a transgender man carrying and giving birth to a child (Thomas Beatie), and the construction of extended families where gay and lesbian couples constitute a multiple-parental unit to form attachments with, care for and educate their shared children, can disrupt and be performative of an asignifying rupture in the above example. It can be ruptured in various ways, depending on what socio-historical and geographical space we inhabit.

The enactment of rhizomatics is thus driven by another kind of desire than the desire to find or know the 'essence' or 'truth' of underlying structures and dominant discourses, but without trying to disrupt or re-signifying them. Posthumanist research inspired by Deleuze and Guattari's rhizomatics and cartography mapping is instead driven by the desire to become part of a creative, innovative, impersonal and transformative chatter that might be productive of new and multiple ways of knowing, which can transform lived and actualized realities (c.f. Martin and Kamberelis, 2013; Lenz Taguchi, 2012, 2013).

Mapping some of the connections and desiring forces of the neurosciences and education

What, then, are the contours of the intensive processes (Bonta and Protevi, 2004, p. 64) on the rhizomatic plane of thinking where the neurosciences connect to and traverse philosophies of the mind, cognitive psychology and educational practices? On this map we can spot two exceptionally strong lines of desiring production and articulation that swirl into their respective circles of convergence a multiplicity of successive singularities (Deleuze and Guattari, 1987). They join together a multiplicity of singular lines of thinking into two strong opposing segmentary and molar lines of articulation that have become productive of a 'common sense' and normalizing power-producing binary (see also Lenz Taguchi, forthcoming).

Thus, the field of neuro-ontologies and philosophies of thinking seems to be caught up in a classical binary closure (c.f. Howard-Jones, 2011). On the one side we have a *Cartesian mind-body dualism*, celebrating the unique humanness of the mind and the self in terms of an autonomous human, who can transform the material world (Dennett, 2007; Searle, 2007). On the other side we can spot a humanness reduced to sheer and extended brain matter, or, if you will, an 'organic monism' (Colebrook, 2008, p. 9). The latter constitutes, as has already been noted above, a materialist ontology of relations, or play, between the firing of transmitting neurons, connecting and interacting with each other and extending outside of the embodied brain (Bennett and Hacker, 2007; Clark, 2011). On the plane of thinking, where these polarized neuro-ontologies become articulated, there seem to be educational theories and practices, underpinned by specific values, drawn into their respective circles of convergence.

Circles of convergence on dualist ontological territory

At one binary end, we find ourselves on a territory where an anthropocentric dualist neuro-ontology seems to converge educational discourse with neuroscientific arguments of specific *windows of opportunity* (Singer, 2011). A Cartesian mind-body split underpins the molar lines of thinking in its connection with practices of education. These lines of thinking draw into their circle convergence a classical developmental discourse, with normative assertions about how these windows of developmental possibilities might be more or less closed, in the case of experience deprivation in families or day care/preschool (ibid.). But they also converge with constructivist learning theories based on cognitive psychology, especially those interested in the teaching and learning strategies of conceptual change (c.f. de Freitas and Palmer, 2015). The neurological concept of plasticity here ties into the notion of 'use-it-or-lose-it', meaning that if you do not develop an ability or skill in a specific period you will have a hard time developing it at all (Singer, 2011).

When a classical child-development approach traverses neuroscientific knowledge based on research methodologies relying on average statistical outcomes, this might produce an uncritical applying of neuroscience to educational practices in a reductionist fashion, as Ferrari notes (2011). In early childhood education a particular line of signification reactivates previously dominant developmentally appropriate practices that outline *a* normal development with specific deviances from the norm. This segmentary line of thinking plays on values of the golden opportunities of childhood and early development, vis-à-vis the risk and fear of missed opportunities. In contrast to this, a number of educational neurologists (e.g., Ferrari, 2011; Stein and Fischer, 2011) and neurodidactic educationalists (Olivestam and Ott, 2010; Wilson and Coyers, 2013) advocate a reactivation of previous signifying lines of articulation, produced by cognitivist psychology (Piaget), socio-cultural learning theory (Vygotsky), and progressive educational philosophy (Dewey), etc. But the way they are reactivated, in terms of ontological, epistemological underpinnings with respective adhesive cultural values, will determine how these practices will come to matter for children in preschools and schools.

These reactivated value-based ontological underpinnings risk aligning themselves with stagnant unimaginative educational practices-as-usual, thus cementing rather than challenging already existing molar lines and normative practices in education, emphasizing learning as a development that will always progress from concrete to abstract and from simple to complex (Wilson and Conyers, 2013, p. 13). This is specifically apparent in the neuro-didactic interpretations of various examples of educational practices (Olivestam and Ott, 2010) and the directions for early years' education (Wilson and Conyers, 2013). Despite the possibilities that neuroscientific findings might entail for the development of educational practices, they cling on to the same molar lines of a progressive step-wise cognitivist maturation of the learning content, although informed by neurological findings on the importance of positive emotions and interpersonal exchange in learning, which is said to simply confirm old behaviouristic and socio-cultural knowledge on learning (Olivestam and Ott, 2010, p. 110).

If however, we look more closely into those circles of convergence, is it possible to find lines that aspire or struggle to depart or escape the dominant regime of signs? Interestingly, neurobiological findings are often contradictory, complex and do not always comply with the philosophical or otherwise value-charged progressive models as some would like them to do. When seriously taking into consideration the recent findings of plasticity and epigenetics, it is possible to see how brain growth and learning are taking place in complex processes of interaction and interrelated change. Moreover, although learning and cognitive development generally occurs through what we consider recurring cycles, tied to different age spans, these cycles can be observed to jump and drop in complex and unpredictable patterns (Fischer, 2011). Consequently, neurocognitive development should *not* be conceived as a ladder of successive stages, but as a complex network of interactions, nested cycles and clusters of discontinuities: a web of many strands (Bailey, 2002; Fischer, 2011).

Hence, it is the complex variations in these patterns that are of interest for practitioners. This implies that rather than reactivating established educational theories, and judging the extent to which they might 'fit' neuroscientific findings, we should instead try to construct new kinds of educational theories. Connecting to other scientific disciplines, other ontologies and epistemologies, it is actually possible to think about learning and education differently. The construction of an *intra-active pedagogy* (Lenz Taguchi, 2010), based on feminist physicist Karen Barad's *agential realism* (Barad, 1999), constitutes one such attempt. Here, learning and the learning-subject are mutually constituted. Learning is produced in the intra-active connections not only between human discursively inscribing agents, but also in the entanglements of matter and discourse (ibid.). 'Connections are a matter of coming into existence', as Stengers (2008, p. 39) writes. Any form of learning is an effect of connections that can start in the most abstract of metaphysical problems that small children might pose – as it were, *in the middle of things* – or that might emerge as a result of observing what happens in the connections between different forms of matter, or practices, affects or semiotic expressions (Lenz Taguchi, 2010).

Circles of convergence on monist ontological territory

Let us now place ourselves onto the monist ontological territory of the map, where an anti- or post-Cartesian thinking refers to one single ecology or system of interconnected life. Here it is possible to hear an intensive chattering of various rhizomatic fine root threads and lines of articulation, which sometimes swirl together into a strong circle of convergence that can be labelled *affective and social neuroscience* (e.g., Damasio, 2000; Immordino-Yang, 2011). On closer inspection it is possible to spot lines that draw into their respective circles of convergence teaching and learning practices, such as the Social Emotional Learning practices (SEL). SEL is presently recommended by the American National State Board of Education and can be understood as one of a growing number of what Dorthe Staunæs (2011) has called *affective-management strategies*. SEL is the process through which children (and adults) develop skills needed to effectively manage themselves and their relationships with others (Durlak et al., 2011; Yoder, 2014).

SEL has emerged as a result of several different lines of articulation converging, where the social and emotions are the main desiring forces understood to shape the human brain. The neuron, write Rose and Abi-Rached (2013, p. 9), used to be seen as genetically fixed and deteriorating, but it is now seen as 'exquisitely adaptable to human interaction and sociality'. The brain is hereby construed as an embodied social brain and thus an effect of interpersonal relations in the new interdisciplinary science called interpersonal neurobiology, or the even more widespread social neurology. These interdisciplinary new sciences have emerged because, as Siegel (2012, p. 3) claims, 'Human connections shape neural connections', not the other way around.

Affective neuroscience, as an umbrella term for the various disciplines mentioned above, can be identified as a style of thinking underpinned by a monist ontology of interdependence between the body, brain and mind. Conceived as the 'Holy Grail' of human development and learning (Immordino-Yang, 2011, p. 102), *affect*, in the social and affective neurosciences, has, as exemplified above, already had very specific impact on and material implications for teaching and learning practices in preschools and schools all over the world. When emotion and cognition, body and mind, are understood to be working together, learning practices can be designed to influence the individual student's subjective and emotional status, each according to its own predispositions and personal history. In these practices, 'the student's body, brain and mind are seen to come together to produce cognition and emotion, which are subjectively intertwined as the student constructs culturally relevant knowledge and makes decisions about how to act and think', as Immordino-Yang (2011, p. 101) concludes.

Initial readings in dissonance to achieve estranging and creative ruptures

On this field of forces we have traced some loud and intensive articulating lines, materializing as specific stratifying practices where the neuroscience and educational practices connect and interact. What happens if we put that tracing back onto the map in a different territory, to read it in 'dissonance', and thus perhaps achieve an estranging asignifying rupture? How might that already dominant or emerging regime of signs be deterritorialized?

Given that children's bodies, brains and minds are understood to work together in accordance with an affective neuroscientific logic (Immordino-Yang, 2011), this can, of course, take place in any kind of cultural and educational context. That is, educational practices that draw from affective educational neuroscience will not only occur in liberal arts, democratic teaching and learning environments. If we read the previously presented circle of convergence in dissonance, following a line of flight to a – in a Western context – silenced territory of a more traditional and authoritarian educational practice, is it possible that the same measurable effects on learning might be achieved, as an effect of the emotive potential in learning, but on other emotional grounds? Perhaps we might find that the same learning outcomes, at least those that can be measured by PISA (Program for International Student Assessment) tests, are achieved just as effectively but under entirely different emotional circumstances for the students.

What I am suggesting is that the same molar lines that articulate social and affective neuroscience can converge with very different lines of articulation, in terms of teaching and learning practices. Instead of engaging children in topics of their own interest in order to increase the emotive responses, the desire for learning might also be triggered by the success of submitting to rules and conventions, which might provide a predictable and perhaps a more emotionally 'safe' learning environment than what can be provided in a more liberal, open-ended, collaborative and explorative learning environment. In other words, the neuro-biological emotional reward produced in the brain, whether it depends on successful compliance with authoritarian teaching practices and the finishing of prescribed tasks, or on the rewards of explorative learning processes driven by the student's own interests and suggestions, might be the same. Hence, the desiring forces of what some consider to be the 'Holy Grail' of educational practices – affect – might, in fact, converge with a wide range of educational and societal value system and practices, which make use of the force of affect and emotion in learning but in completely different ways: ways that might enhance learning better for some children even within a Western neoliberal educational context.

Another example of reading the chatter in the circles of convergence in dissonance, or rather in a simple move of a reversal, can be experimented with on the map. Here, educational neurosciences suggest that students with attention deficit hyperactivity disorder (ADHD) can learn to self-manage their intake of Ritalin depending on the kind of school activity they are required to engage in (Richardson, 2002, in Ferrari, 2011). That is, the students are encouraged to take the medication when doing routine school activities that require that they sit still and listen or work by themselves. On the other hand they are encouraged to refrain from taking their medication when engaged in a creative or artistic activity, and in group activities with other students, where their intensive creativity can be put to use (ibid.). When experimenting with an asignifying rupture, we might read the example in a reversal mode. Instead of succumbing to the 'seductive allure' of neurosciences (Weisberg et al., 2008, in Ferrari, 2011, p. 32) 'calling the shots' to regulate and manage children who do not fit into our educational practices-as-usual, we make a reversal rupture in order to get away from the commonsense signification that desires to make deviant children increasingly normalized within existing preschool and school systems. What is omitted from such segmentary molar lines of thinking is a serious engagement with thinking differently about education itself and thus engaging with the neurosciences in a different way, and perhaps establishing new circles of convergence in another direction on the map (Deleuze and Guattari, 1987). On a deterritorialized space of the map, we can invite the neurosciences to experiment with us in order to know more about how these ADHD students, as well as all other students, might benefit in different ways from a learning environment which is based on creative, explorative and artistic practices of knowledge production (de Freitas and Palmer, 2015; Lenz Taguchi, 2010; Olsson, 2008). As we experiment with these opportunities, other ontologies of learning, underpinned by other values, can become part of the desiring production. But of course, we need always to be aware of how how such ways of thinking and living will be actualized and materialized in ways that risk *re*territorialization and turning into yet another molar line of signification creating the need for subsequent escape (Lenz Taguchi, 2013).

Concluding discussion

In this chapter, I have performed some initial movements of Deleuzo-Guattarian rhizomatics, tracing some of the connections, specific articulations and 'formalizations of expression' (Deleuze and Guattari, 1987, p. 111) as the neurosciences and education connect and traverse each other. I have traced the articulations of some of the strongest lines of articulation, being attentive of the heterogeneity and multiplicity that always makes up a rhizomatic assemblage (Deleuze and Guattari, 1987). Moreover, as a vital aspect of the doubled movements of rhizomatics, I have also listened to the intensive chattering (Colebrook 2008) of some of the intensive and transformative articulations that has enabled some estranging asignifying ruptures. This has been done by putting the tracings of the signifying articulations back on the map at a different entry-point, in order to disrupt their taken for granted ways of reading the rhizome (ibid). As a posthumanist methodology, Deleuzo-Guttarian rhizomatics thus aims to be creative of new potential ways of knowing and producing a multiplicity of realities in ways that might entail more flourishing aspects of being and becoming, whether this concerns humans or the more-than-human (Lenz Taguchi, 2012).

I have argued that findings from the neurosciences can be drawn into other disciplinary circles of convergence, and intensify the force of that particular discipline as a consequence. Even if knowledge based on neuroscientific findings adds nothing to the general arguments, a study of how people relate to and take up an argumentation that includes neuroscientific evidence shows that an argument supported by neuroscientific findings was always taken as the better argument (Weisberg et al., in Ferrari, 2011). What Wisenberg et al.'s study refers to as the 'seductive allure of neuroscience explanations' can in the present study rather be spotted as a hijacking of the seductive desiring force of the neurosciences by other disciplinary desiring forces, often with the ambition to reactivate their respective ontological and value-based ideas and practices.

In relation to the above, Gardner's argument that 'bridging the gap' between the neurosciences and education is impossible, since education is a value-based discipline and the neurosciences are not, seems only to confuse the discussion. Rather, what we can learn from this preliminary mapping exercise is that *all* disciplines and sciences are based on ontological underpinnings which are also cultural and value-based. And so are the views of a *Cartesian dualism* and an *organic monism*, as well as the claimed division between them (Colebrook, 2014). What the methodology of cartography mapping can help us do is to move away from seeking *any kind* of external justification. Instead, we should be engaged in the practice of what Colebrook (2008) talks about as an *internal pragmatics*, spotting lines that make an offshoot or experimenting by enacting queering ruptures that might make us think differently. What we need is, in fact, as Stengers puts it, with references to Haraway (2008), new or '*other kinds of narratives*, narratives that populate our worlds and imaginations in a different way' (2007, p. 4, italics added). This might prevent us from getting stuck in any kind of taken-for-granted, molar or reterritorialized way of thinking or doing.

To conclude: a posthumanist and Deleuzo-Guattarian approach is simultaneously about intervention and invention, responsibility and ethics (Lenz Taguchi, 2012). It means being responsively engaged in shaping the future in our production of knowledge, because production of knowing is always also a production of reality that has material consequences (Barad, 1999, pp. 7–8). As posthumanist and Deleuzo-Guattarian inspired researchers, we need to be aware of this responsibility of taking our research practices further than critique, in order not to 'go to war' based on judgemental attitudes or universal truth claims that are most probably qualified, cultural and situated truths. Rather, as posthumanist researchers, we need to learn how to embrace multiple ontologies and differing ways of knowing the world, before deciding upon what necessary, but provisional, claims, choices and decisions to make in a specific situated socio-historical and geographical context.

References

Alaimo, S. (2010) *Bodily Natures: Science, Environment, and the Material Self* (Bloomington, IN: Indiana University Press).

Ansari, D., D. Coch and B. De Smedt (2011) 'Connecting Education and Cognitive Neuroscience: Where Will the Journey Take Us?' *Educational Philosophy and Theory*, 43(1), 37–42.

Bailey, D. B. (2002) 'Are Critical Periods Critical for Early Childhood Education? The Role of Timing in Early Childhood Pedagogy', *Early Childhood Research Quarterly*, 17, 281–294.

Barad, K. (1999) 'Agential Realism: Feminist Interventions in Understanding Scientific Practices', in M. Biagioli (ed.) *The Science Studies Reader* (New York: Routledge), pp. 1–11.

Battro, A. M., K. W. Fischer and P. J. Léna (eds.) (2011) *The Educated Brain: Essays in Neuroeducation* (Cambridge: Cambridge University Press).

Bennett, M. and P. Hacker (2007) 'Selections from Philosophical Foundations of Neuroscience', in M. Dennet, D. Dennett, P. Hacker and J. Searle (eds.) *Neuroscience & Philosophy: Brain, Mind, & Language* (New York: Columbia University Press).

Bonta, M. and J. Protevi (2004) *Deleuze and Geophilosophy: Deleuze Connections* (Edinburgh: Edinburgh University Press).

Braidotti, R. (1994) *Nomadic Subjects: Embodiment and Sexual Difference in Contemporary Feminist Theory* (New York: Colombia University Press).

Bruer, J. T. (2011) 'Building Bridges in Neuroeducation', in A. M. Battro, K.W. Fischerand P. J. Léna (eds.) *The Educated Brain* (Cambridge: Cambridge University Press).

Bruer, J. T. (1997) 'A Bridge Too Far', *Educational Researcher*, 26(8), 4–16.

Campbell, S. R. (2011) 'Educational Neuroscience: Motivations, Methodology, and Implications', *Educational Philosophy and Theory*, 43(1), 7–16.

Chetty, R., J. N. Friedman, N. Hilger, E. Saez and D. Whithmore Schanzenback (2011) 'How Does Your Kindergarten Classroom Affect Your Earnings?' *The Quarterly Journal of Economics*, CXXVI(4), 1593–1660.

Clark, A. (2011) *Supersizing the Mind: Embodiment, Action, and Cognitive Extension* (Oxford/New York: Oxford University Press).

Clark, A. (2003) *Natural-Born Cyborgs: Minds, Technologies, and the Future of Human Intelligence* (Oxford: Oxford University Press).

Colebrook, C. (2014) *Sex after Life: Essays on Extinction*, Vol. 2 (Open Humanities Press, http://openhumanitiespress.org/essays-on-extinction-vol2.html).

Colebrook, C. (2011) 'Time and Autopoesis: The Organism Has No Future', in *Deleuze and the Body* (Edinburgh: Edinburgh University Press), pp. 9–28.

Colebrook, C. (2008) 'Introduction Part I.', in C. Colebrook and J. Weinstein (eds.) *Deleuze and Gender* (Edinburgh: Edinburgh University Press).

Cozolino, L. (2013) *The Social Neuroscience of Education* (New York: Norton & Company).

Cunha, F. and J. J. Heckman (2007) 'The Economics of Human Development. The Technology of Skill Formation', American Economic Association (AEA) Papers and Proceedings.

Cutler, A. and I. MacKenzie (2011) 'Bodies of Learning', in L. Guillaume and J. Hughes (eds.) *Deleuze and the Body* (Edinburgh: Edinburgh University Press).

Damasio, A. R. (2000) *The Feeling of What Happens: Body and Emotion in the Making of Consciousness* (New York: Harcourt).

de Freitas, E. and A. Palmer (2015) 'How Scientific Concepts Come to Matter in Early Childhood Curriculum', *Cultural Studies of Science Education*, published online 13 February 2015, DOI:10.1007/s11422-014-9652-6, Online ISSN, 1871-1510.

Deleuze, G. and F. Guattari (1987) *A Thousand Plateaus: Capitalism and Schizophrenia*. (Minneapolis: University of Minnesota Press).

Dolphijn, R. and I. van der Tuin (2012) *New Materialism: Interviews & Cartographies* (Ann Abor: Open Humanities Press/University of Michigan Library).
Dennett, D. (2007) 'Philosophy as Naïve Anthropology: Comment on Bennett and Hacker', in M. Dennet, D. Dennett, P. Hacker and J. Searle (eds.) *Neuroscience & Philosophy: Brain, Mind, & Language* (New York: Columbia University Press).
Durlak, J. J., R. P. Weissberg, A. B. Dymnicki, R. D. Taylor and K. B. Schellinger (2011) 'The Impact of Enhancing Students' Social and Emotional Learning: A Meta-Analysis of School-Based Universal Interventions', *Child Development*, 82(1), 405–432.
Dussauge, I. (2014) 'Brains, Sex, and Queers 2090: An Ideal Experiment', in S. Schmitz and G. Höppner (eds.) *Gender and Neurocultures: Feminist and Queer Perspectives on Current Brain Discourses* (Vienna: Zaglossus).
Ferrari, M. (2011) 'What Can Neuroscience Bring to Education?' *Educational Philosophy and Theory*, 43(1), 31–36.
Fine, C. (2014) 'Explaining, or Sustaining, the Status Quo? The Potentially Self-Fulfilling Effects of "Hardwired" Accounts on Sex Differences', in S. Schmitz and G. Höppner (eds.) *Gender and Neurocultures: Feminist and Queer Perspectives on Current Brain Discourses* (Vienna: Zaglossus).
Fine, C. (2010) *Delusions of Gender: How Our Minds, Society and Neurosexism Create Difference* (New York: WW Norton).
Fischer, K. W. (2011) 'Dynamic Cycles of Cognitive and Brain Development: Measuring Growth in Mind, Brain, and Education', in A. M. Battro, K.W. Fischer and P. J. Léna, (eds.) *The Educated Brain* (Cambridge, UK: Cambridge University Press).
Fischer, K. W., D. B. Daniel, M. H. Immordino-Yang, E. Stern, A. Battro, H. Koizumo (2007) 'Why Mind Brain and Education? Why Now?' in *Mind, Brain and Education*, 1(1), 1–2.
Fitzgerald, D. and F. Callard (2015) 'Social Science and Neuroscience Beyond Interdisciplinarity: Experimental Entanglements', *Theory, Culture and Society*, 32(1), 3–32.
Fitzgerald, D., M. M. Littlefield, K. J. J. Knudsen Tonks and M. Dietz (2014) 'Ambivalence, Equivocation and the Politics of Experimental Knowledge: A Transdisciplinary Neuroscience Encounter', *Social Studies of Science*, 44(5), 701–721.
Gardner, H. and M. H. Immordino-Yang (2013) USC Rossier School of Education, Institute for Visual History and Education, arranged by The Shoah Foundation, Recorded discussion on 11 February 2013, https://sfi.usc.edu/news/2013/02/multiple-intelligences-theorist-howard-gardner-digital-media-learning-and-empathy.
Geake, J. (2011) 'Position Statement on Motivations, Methodologies, and Practical Implications of Educational Neuroscience Research: fMRI Studies of the Neural Correlates of Creative Intelligence', *Educational Philosophy and Theory*, 43(1), 44–47.
Haraway, D. (2008) *When Species Meet* (Minneapolis: University of Minnesota press).
Howard, K., A. Martin, L. J. Berlin and J. Brooks-Gun (2011) 'Early Mother-Child Separation, Parenting, and Child Well-Being in Early Head Start Families', *Attachment & Human Development*, doi: 10.1080/14616734.2010.488119.

Howard-Jones, P. A. (2011) 'A Multiperspective Approach to Neuroeducational Research', *Educational Philosophy and Theory*, 43(1), 24–30.

Immordino-Yang, M. H. (2011) 'Implications of Affective and Social Neuroscience for Educational Theory', *Educational Philosophy and Theory*, 43(1), 98–103.

Lenz Taguchi, H. (forthcoming) 'The Concept as Method': Tracing-and-Mapping the Problem of the Neuro(n) in the Field of Education', *Cultural Studies <=> Critical Methodologies*.

Lenz Taguchi, H. (2013) 'Images of Thinking in Feminist Materialisms: Ontological divergences and the production of researcher subjectivities', *International Journal of Qualitative Studies in Education*, 26(6), 706–716.

Lenz Taguchi, H. (2012) 'A Diffractive and Deleuzian Approach to Analysing Interview Data', *Feminist Theory*, 13(3), 265–281.

Lenz Taguchi, H. (2010) *Going Beyond the Theory/Practice Divide in Early Childhood Education: Introducing an Intra-active Pedagogy* (London and New York: Routledge).

Mayers, L., P. Fonagy and M. Target (eds.) (2007) *Developmental Science and Psychoanalysis: Integration and Innovation* (London: Karnac Books).

Mazzei, L. A. (2013) 'A Voice without Organs: Interviewing in Posthumanist Research', *International Journal of Qualitative Studies in Education*, 26(6), 732–740.

Martin, A. D. and G. Kamberelis (2013) 'Mapping Not Tracing: Qualitative Educational Research with Political Teeth', *International Journal of Qualitative Studies in Education*, 26(6), 668–679.

Olivestam, C. E. and A. Ott (2010) När hjärnan får bestämma. Om undervisning och lärande: Inflytelserika didaktiska traditioner, Nyorienterande neurodidaktik [When the Brain Gets to Decide. Teaching and Learning: Influencial Didactic traditions, Reorienting Neuro-didactics], www.remusforlag.se; www.laromedia.se.

Olsson, L. M. (2008) *Movement and Experimentation in Young Children's Learning: Deleuze and Guattari in Early Childhood Education* (London/New York: Routledge).

Pickering, S.J. and P. Howard-Jones (2007) 'Educator's Views on the Role of Neuroscience in Education: Findings from a Study of UK and International Perspectives', *Mind, Brain, and Education*, 1, 109–113.

Pinker, S. (2003) *The Blank Slate: The Modern Denial of Human Nature* (NY/London: Penguin Books).

Richardson, C. A. (2002) A Look at Adolescent Attention Deficit/Hyperactivity Disorder Form the Inside: How medication is perceived to affect one's sense of self, unpublished Master's thesis, University of Toronto.

Rose, N. and J. M. Abi-Rached (2013) *Neuro: The Brain Sciences and the Management of the Mind* (Princeton, New Jersey: Princeton University Press).

Samuels, B. M. (2009) 'Can the Differences Between Education and Neuroscience be Overcome by Mind, Brain, and Education?' *Mind, Brain and Education*, 3(1), 45–55.

Satel, S. and S. O. Lilienfeld (2013) *Brainwashed: The Seductive Appeal of Mindless Neuroscience* (New York: Basic Books).

Searle, J. (2007) 'Putting Consciousness Back in the Brain: Reply to Bennett and Hacker, Philosophical Foundations of Neuroscience', in M. Dennet, D. Dennett, P. Hacker and J. Searle (eds.) *Neuroscience & Philosophy: Brain, Mind, & Language* (New York: Columbia University Press).

Schmitz, S. and G. Höppner (eds.) (2014) *Gender and Neurocultures: Feminist and Queer Perspectives on Current Brain Discourses* (Vienna: Zaglossus).
Siegel, D. J. (2012) The Developing Mind (2nd ed.) (New York & London: The Guilford Press).
Singer, W. (2011) 'Epigenesis and Brain Plasticity in Education', in A. M. Battro, K.W. Fischer and P. J. Léna (eds.) *The Educated Brain* (Cambridge: Cambridge University Press).
Staunæs, D. (2011) 'Governing the Potentials of Life?: Interrogating the Promises in Affective Educational Leadership', *Journal of Educational Administration and History*, 43(3), 227–247.
Stein, Z. and K. W. Fischer (2011) 'Directions for Mind, Brain, and Education: Methods, Models, and Morality', *Educational Philosophy and Theory*, 43(1), 56–66.
Stengers, I. (2007) 'Diderot's Egg: Divorcing Materialism from Eliminativism', Radical Philosophy conference, *Materials and Materialisms*, London, 12 May, 2007, http://philpapers.org/rec/STEDED-3.
Stengers, I. (2008) Experimenting with Refrains: Subjectivity and the Challenge of Escaping Modern Dualism, *Subjectivity*, 22, 38–59.
Stevens, C. and H. Neville (2009) 'Development and Plasticity in Human Neurocognition', in M. S. Gazzaniga, (ed.) The Cognitive Neurosciences (4th ed.) (Baskerville/Hong Kong: Massachusetts Institute of Technology).
Wexler, B. E. (2008) *Brain and Culture: Neurobiology, Ideology, and Social Change* (Cambridge, MA: The MIT Press).
Weisberg, D. S., F. C Keil, J. Goodstein, R. Rawson and J. R. Gray (2008) 'The Seductive Allure of Neuroscience Explanations', *Journal of Cognitive Neuroscience*, 20, 470–477.
Vidal, C. (2014) 'Neuro-pedagogy and the Gender Theory', in S. Schmitz and G. Höppner (eds.) *Gender and Neurocultures: Feminist and Queer Perspectives on Current Brain Discourses* (Vienna: Zaglossus).
Vidal, C. (2005) 'Brain, Sex and Ideology', *Diogenes*, 52, 127–133.
Vidal, F. (2011) 'Historical Considerations on Brain and Self', in A. M. Battro, K.W. Fischer and P. J. Léna (eds.) *The Educated Brain* (Cambridge: Cambridge University Press).
Wilson D. and M. Conyers (2013) *Flourishing in the First Five Years: Connecting Implications from Mind, Brain, and Educational Research to the Development of Young Children* (Lanham, Maryland: Rowman & Littlefield Education).
Yoder, N. (2014) Teaching the Whole Child Instructional Practices That Support Social-Emotional Learning in Three Teacher Evaluation Frameworks. Center on Great Teachers & Leaders at American Institute for Research. Revised Edition.

4
Thinking like a Brick: Posthumanism and Building Materials

Luke Bennett

Introduction

Posthumanism exhorts us to pay more attention to nonhuman things, but can we actually engage any more 'deeply' with non-sentient objects, and in a way that detaches our investigations from human concerns and positionality?

Much of posthuman writing and research thus far has been focused on animals or advanced technology. It is time now to explore the non-sentient: things that are truly inert, and which cannot speak, move or die. Therefore this chapter's analysis will be pursued by reference to construction materials: brick, concrete and rock. As Bjørnar Olsen (2013) notes, this classically 'dumb brute' matter makes up the built environment, it is all around us, it creates the very conditions by which modern life and social systems are sustained and yet *these* things rarely get noticed in contemporary social science research, given its preoccupation with language, identity and human-to-human power relations.

The guiding question for what follows, then, is how can we know of bricks, blocks and slabs in a posthuman way? Exploring this will necessarily engage posthuman pedagogy, because it will require us to examine how we learn about, and pass on, the materiality of the world around us.

Posthumanism and the world with or without us

In considering this question this chapter will examine the motives and methods by which posthumanists reach for the nonhuman. In doing so it will characterize two directions of posthuman enquiry, one which aspires to access the world beyond us for its own sake (*the world without us*), and the other which remains anchored in an appreciation of human positionality and projects (*the world with us*). This chapter seeks to explore the motivations and implications of these tendencies, and the thing-focused methodologies that can be derived from them. This analysis is pursued in order to consider what assistance either formulation of posthumanism might productively contribute to educational research around human-built environment materiality.

All posthumanists would agree that posthumanism seeks to de-centre humans from the world. This is in conscious reaction to the 'correlationist' (Meillassoux, 2008a, p. 5) model that takes all knowledge of, and engagement with, the world as deriving from humans – from our thoughts, needs, actions and perspectives (both cultural and somatic), and in which 'objects' are human perceptual compositions, the mere epiphenomenon of language and culture. Posthumanism, in its varieties of forms and intensities, aspires to engage the 'other' aspects of reality that get missed or marginalized by a human-centred model. But the motivations and intended destination for that journey towards the posthuman are diverse and not always compatible with each other.

For example, transhumanist posthumanists, such as Julian Huxley (1957), Robert Ettinger (1972) or Max More (2013) have optimistically seen technology and human-machine hybridity, as the key to the next phase of human evolution and progress. Here is a clear and unapologetic 'world with us' posthumanism which celebrates human attachment to the world. For these posthumanists learning about our place in the world is key to finding a sustainable human-world fellowship, and overcoming the limitations of human embodiment. But while some posthumanists are optimistic about the improvement of mankind by working with the things around us, some certainly are not. For example, Ray Brassier draws out from anti-correlationist realism a nihilism based upon a realization that the world exists without us, that it is indifferent to our existence 'and oblivious to the "values" and "meanings" which we would drape over it in order to make it more hospitable' (2007, p. xi).

There has been a tendency in discussion of posthumanism within educational research to figure posthumanism as optimistic – as aligned to a desire for human advancement (even though some such posthumanists, like Rosi Braidotti (2013), have felt the need to distinguish their progressivism from that encapsulated in the Enlightenment's formulation of humanism, with its linear view of what progress and human subjectivity should look like). But there are other – more nihilistic – formulations of posthumanism that rarely get a mention within an educational context. Helena Pedersen provides a rare glimpse of this alternative emphasis when she writes: 'taken to its extreme, posthumanism thus implies a dystopic, literal posthumanism, reaching beyond the specific notion of the "death of the subject" to a scenario where actual extinction is at stake' (2010, p. 246).

A preoccupation with humanity's crisis of survival does not automatically render such posthumanists misanthropic. Indeed a sense of such crisis can be the epitome of a 'world with us' concern to improve human-nonhuman relations now that humanity's effect upon and embeddedness in the world has been pointed out to us in the form of industrial pollution and climate change. However, hovering sometimes within the outer fringes of an ecologically inspired posthumanism is a latent human self-loathing, one which at times appears to yearn for a 'world without us', an implicit desire to eradicate the human, which echoes the antihuman loathing of Friedrich Nietzsche's aetiology: 'The earth has a skin; and this skin has diseases and one of them is man' (2003, p. 153). This is a bleak 'disanthropy' (Garrard, 2012), traceable in various intensities to the 'apocalyptic affect' Peter Gratton (2014, p. 52) finds in the work of philosophers like Quentin Meillassoux and Ray Brassier whose speculative realism is fuelled by visions of the insignificance of humanity. These works resonate with the post-apocalyptic work of writers such as Alan Weisman, whose 2008 book, *The World without Us*, gives us an account of how the world might fare if humankind were to suddenly disappear. Specifically his concern is how the 'natural' environment would assail – step by step – the remains of our built environment. Weisman paints a compelling portrait of our (human) insignificance in doing so. The world would soon, and very effectively, recover from our demise. Slavoj Žižek (quoted in Gratton, 2014, p. 52) castigates Weisman's book, for its 'world without us' portrayal of 'the Earth itself regaining its pre-castrated state of innocence', anchored around a conceit of desiring to witness one's non-existence. It is thus, Žižek concludes, a 'fantasy at its purest'.

In such work, the built environment's materiality becomes visible (in an apocalyptically foregrounded way) only in the moment of its destruction. Indeed, the presence of the rubble signifies the collapse of human civilization, it is a terminal index of human *absence*. Such visions of the 'world without us' (and preoccupations with human-induced ecocide, and the resurgent properties of matter beyond the human) have their origins in the 'deep ecology' movement, and in particular in the work of Arne Næss (1973). They embody a reverence for the separateness and pureness of the nonhuman (usually characterized as 'nature'). Such discourse is often characterized by proud talk of nature's resilience and of its beyond-human temporalities, of a 'deep time' that emphasizes the insignificance and precariousness of human existence, with mankind imperilled by 'nature's capacity to be a great deal more or a lot less than what we would ask of it' (Clark, 2011, p. xiii).

A posthumanism that yearns for the ascendancy of the nonhuman is of limited use for studies of human education; it is also a posthumanism that oddly perpetuates a key Enlightenment binary (which posthumanism is supposed to transcend), namely the separateness of (nonhuman) 'nature' and (human) 'culture'. But posthumanism of all shades poses a conundrum around how distant from humanism it is actually capable of being, for many posthumanists would be uncomfortable with the suggestion that the baby should be thrown out *instead of* the bathwater. Facing this dilemma, Rosi Braidotti (2013, p. 29) concludes that, if it is to be 'progressive', posthumanism cannot escape the foundational goals of humanism entirely. In her view it remains committed to human needs and perceptual scales, social justice and a notion of human 'becoming'. It therefore retains a notion of human advancement, at least in so far as it aligns to a 'world with us' direction of enquiry.

This chapter now turns to consider the methodological formulations of posthuman attempts to reach out to both 'the world without us' and the 'world with us'. In the argument that follows I will contend that posthuman approaches that prioritize accounting for 'the world without us' have little productive to offer any human-centric endeavour like human education and in contrast suggest that posthumanism can best challenge the hubris of anthropocentricism when the investigation is framed as an attempt to account for 'the world *with* us'. This is attainable if researchers balance an attentiveness to human purpose and positionality with a holistic and appreciative 'more than human' (Whatmore, 2006) access to the nonhuman aspects of the world. Unlike 'world without us' posthumanism's tendency towards an (implicit or desiring; apocalyptic or analytical) erasure of the human, this approach to posthumanism pursues a collaborationist agenda: for it is people that make things matter to us, and matter that makes us (Barad, 2007), and that is particularly true of how we learn to bend rock, clay and sand to our will as building materials.

On taking a brick to work: A thwarted journey towards 'the world without us'

In pursuit of a taste of the 'world with us' approach towards posthuman research, and of its limitations, I will now tell the short story of an encounter with a discarded house brick found one morning in my garden.

I was set to give a lecture that day and decided to co-opt that brick as a surprise feature in a presentation about the underacknowledged links between art and work. Standing at the lectern, I announced to my audience that I had brought a friend with me to help with the session. Explaining that he was shy, I named the undisclosed assistant as 'Frank', and then let anticipation build for a few moments more, before finally pulling the dirty brick, complete with dripping soil and tendrils of spiders' webs, out from the carrier bag and into the clean, ordered and ideational milieu of the lecture theatre.

Following this, I'm now known to members of that day's audience as 'the brick man'. Indeed, I was subsequently commissioned on the back of this idle breakfast thought to research and write an account of tracing 'my' brick back to its birthplace (Bennett and Hock, 2013). That brick moment has served me well – but did it do anything for the brick? Did this performative event actually reveal anything about the brick, over and above what I made it reveal about myself and the aims of my presentation?

Was the effect – the unsettling appearance inherent in the event – simply a semiotic one, a semantic frisson caused by two objects (dirty brick + lecture theatre) colliding in an unanticipated way? Was it just contextual dissonance that rendered the unfurling of this brick an 'event'; that it was only (to paraphrase Mary Douglas (2002)) the presence of the dirt that made this brick out of place in a lecture theatre?

Or, alternatively – and in the spirit of the object-oriented theorists to be discussed below – can we confront matter in a way that (as Jane Bennett claims occurred to her in coming upon a glove, a dead rat, a bottle cap and a stick entrained in a storm drain) 'can command [...] attention in its own right, as existents in excess of their association with human meanings, habits, or projects' (2010, p. 4)? Here, Bennett's passage hints at some deeper existence for the glove, the dead rat, the bottle cap and the stick above and beyond her cultural projection onto them, signifying them as 'trash' or 'worthless'.

This figuring of a separate essence to such mundane matter, independent of human perception or use, is the crux of the 'thing with us' vs 'thing without us' divide posited above. This is not to claim that Bennett is a misanthropic nihilist, but rather that the (neo) realist ontological assumptions found in her work have an important role to play in (ultimately) supporting a position that privileges the 'world without us', and which in turn poses awkward questions for ontology, epistemology and ethics. Posthumanism advocates flat ontologies in which humans are treated no differently from bricks, rocks or plants (Marder,

2013), but what are the political consequences of this, if the human is no longer privileged? As Peter Gratton (2014) warns, the proliferation of flat ontologies may have as-yet uncharted moral ramifications, for how can the 'rights' of rocks and people be adjudicated if a flat ontology produces a flat ethics?

And then an epistemological question appears: even if this nonhuman, independent existence is real, how can it be known of by us, except through human perception (and the cultural projections onto matter that Bennett is seeking to dismiss as an inadequate account of those things)? Here an 'ontoepistemological' (Barad, 2007, p. 43) divide between an extreme and a mild posthumanism opens. If we believe it possible to step outside of ourselves, then we can aspire to know 'the world without us' (a strong – if not necessarily an extreme – posthumanism), but if we decide that this is simply not possible then we can only contemplate 'the world with us', via a mild posthumanism. But even that – seemingly modest – posthumanism may still have significant ethical implications, for through its lens we must learn how to notice the things around us, and work out how to share our world equitably with them.

The question for us to work through here thus becomes – returning to our materials of choice – is there a deeper brick-ness waiting to be discovered by the 'right' posthuman method of enquiry?

Bricks without us

Jane Bennett (2010) calls for an embrace of the 'vibrancy' of matter, but where is the vibrancy of brick? What and where is its agency, mystery and will-to-life? Perhaps there is something wrong in the formulation of this question – it is too anthropocentric; for an extreme 'world without us' posthumanist bricks should not be judged by whether they have human qualities, or damned to the 'dumb brute' sidelines because they lack sentience, mobility or even organic qualities. No, the challenge to be pursued by them would be to 'know' bricks in and of themselves, to understand brick-ness without reference back to human needs or preconceptions, to (somehow) see the 'brick without us'.

In his seminal 1949 book *A Sand County Almanac*, Aldo Leopard (1968, p. 132) urged generations of future US environmentalists to 'think like a mountain'. Reflecting on this in his 1996 book *A Moment on the Earth*, US eco-optimist journalist Gregg Easterbrook (Easterbrook, 1996) remarked on how Leopard's 1949 call had actually left unexplored precisely how a mountain might indeed think. Easterbrook took up that challenge and co-opted mountain-think in his presentation of a counter-reading of environmental change and nature's resilience. For Easterbrook the key point was that a mountain exists across an entirely supra-human timescale. If a mountain could think, its horizon of consideration – the timescales that would be of concern to it – would be the truly long term, for rock is born, exists and eventually decays in deep time.

Trying to think like a mountain is humbling and puts us back in our place – but a mountain is a mountain and we are human. There are limits to how much we can grasp the full reality of being a mountain, no matter how hard we try (and whether by contemplative thought or hard empiricism). Here's where 'world without us' posthumanism hits difficulties.

Timothy Morton can help illustrate the cognitive limits of our attempts to think like either a mountain or a brick, or to access their own essences rather than our human-centric phenomenal rendering of them, through his imagined account of a deep-time study that seeks to orient ourselves to an object, rather than the object to our human whims, temporalities and sensate abilities. In a splendidly playful passage, Morton laboriously charts the futility of attempts to fully know a concrete construction block:

> Maybe if I sit here and wait patiently, I will see the real block. I wait. I become impatient. I develop all kinds of contemplative practices to stay here looking at the block. I become enlightened. The block still refuses to spill the beans. I train a disciple to take over from me when I die. She sees nothing of the real block, which now has a large crack across the top, inside of which you can see right through it. She starts a religious order that carefully transmits my instructions about how to monitor the block. For tens of thousands of years, cultures, peoples, robots study the block, which is now looking pretty gnarly. A hundred thousand years later, a fully enlightened robot sits monitoring the faint traces of dust hanging in the air where the block used to sit. Still no dice.
>
> (2013a, p. 28)

Perhaps to glimpse the 'brick without us' we have to embrace the nonhuman temporality of brick (or at least of the clay, sand and other matter comprised within the localized and temporary stabilization that we humans recognize as a brick), to learn to see grains of sand, beds of clay, weathered brick in gardens, landfills or ancient building sites 'watching' us over far longer timescales than we can watch them. But – the truth is – *we* can't wait and watch that long. We can't even *think* in deep time, because it is not *our* time. Thus this glacial perception of brick-ness is doomed to lie beyond us.

I do not deny the creative value of speculation – and poetry and other expressive arts do well to conjure an independent sense of nonhuman things. However, it is precisely because object-oriented ontologists such as Morton doubt the possibility of any access to the essences that they claim lie beyond an ever changing surface crust of accessible-to-us 'purely accidental sensual qualities' (Harman, 2011, p. 48), that this variant of posthumanism fails to deliver upon its rebellious commitment to ultra-flat ontologies. Graham Harman has been the most prolific of the object-oriented ontologists, and that label signals that for thinkers in Harman's oeuvre the world is made up of objects, objects which are 'out there' in the world and which exist independently of us and our perception (or ignorance) of them. Harman's work takes Martin Heidegger's (correlationist) existential phenomenology as its starting point, adopting – but then radically extending – Heidegger's notion of 'tool-analysis' (Harman, 2002, p. 2). For Heidegger (1978), a large part of the reality of things lies – iceberg-like – beneath the surface of our perception or attention. Thus the hammer only reveals itself to consciousness if instead of hitting a nail it misses its target and connects with the user's thumb instead. At that moment – as pain sets in – the hammer suddenly becomes noticed as very real indeed. But Heidegger's was not a flat ontology; for him only humans have true being (total existence). In Heidegger's hierarchy of existence rocks were specifically dismissed as totally lifeless and without being – latent or otherwise.

But Harman took Heidegger's notion of the everyday alienation of people from the things that they use in the world, and extended it to all objects, arguing that all objects have being, and that that being is inaccessible to all other beings. Therefore the world of things is an atomized one – there are myriad objects, all of which caricature (and simplify) all other objects with which they interact. Thus – for Harman – all objects are equally 'real', but also every object is locked within itself, interacting only approximately with any other.

Harman's writing is deceptively easy to read, and his continual anchoring of his ideas by reference to amusingly juxtaposed lists of everyday objects suggests a down-to-earth connection which is deceptive, for Harman's principle of an object's inevitable withdrawal leaves little that can be operationalized in research terms. If a stone has being, but is inaccessible, then that doesn't move us very far towards accessing 'the world without us'. Indeed, others writing within the broad field known as speculative realism take Harman's notion of the perceptual qualities of objects being in flux even further away from the realm of empirical deployment – with others aligning to an ontology based, even more so than Harman, upon the creative agency of accident and unpredictability, such as the chaotic potentiality figured in the work of Ray Brassier (nihilism) and Quentin Meillassoux (auto-genesis and waiting for 'the god yet to come' (Meillassoux, 2008b, p. 261)).

If this strand of posthuman research methodology equates to sitting and intently staring (and/or waiting for the improbable to spontaneously occur) then where does it take us as a contribution towards educational research? Despite their fondness for foregrounding instances of 'everyday' materiality in their writings, object-oriented ontologists like Ian Bogost (2012), Graham Harman (2010) or Timothy Morton (2013a, 2013b) have written little on how this new-found fascination with a mute, unknowable materiality can be pursued beyond the confines of scholarly reflection; thus there is still no actual methodological road map for taking the journey beyond – or away from – the human. Furthermore, the epistemological pessimism of this new school rather undermines the hope of its mission, asserting that the access to the 'essences' of a brick may be very difficult indeed. For, as Morton (2013b, p. 11) puts it – in the eldritch horror register so characteristic of the object-oriented ontologists – all entities 'are shy, retiring octopuses that squirt out a dissembling ink as they withdraw into the ontological shadows'.

Morton's attempt to access the 'world without us' flounders upon ontoepistemological concerns around the impossibility of an unmediated access to the inner being of *any* object of enquiry, but it is a difficulty compounded by the fundamental alien-ness of non-sentient, 'dumb brute' materiality. It is no surprise that posthuman scholarship has found it easier to access the nonhuman – but at least sentient – being of other animals, and even plants (e.g., in Pedersen, 2010 and Kohn, 2013).

Meanwhile, Ian Bogost (2012) has written of his own search for techniques for pursuing an 'alien phenomenology'. Bogost's book is subtitled enticingly 'what it's like to be a thing', and yet in the end he also falls short of finding a path of access to 'the thing itself'. Instead his exhortation is that to know things in a post-relational way, we (humans) would need to find a way to write the 'speculative fictions' of nonhuman things (2012, p. 34) – to write as best we can of what the world and its interactions must seem like to a nonhuman object. But this tumbles us back towards an (inevitable) anthropocentrism for it is us (humans) trying to use our senses and experience to portray the beyond-human essence of a nonhuman thing. Bogost advocates:

> writ[ing] the speculative fictions of their processes, of their unit operations. Our job is to get our hands dirty with grease, juice, gunpowder and gypsum. Our job is to go where *everyone* has gone before, but where few have bothered to linger.
>
> (2012, p. 34, emphasis in original)

Whether Bogost intends it or not, this formulation acknowledges the human presence within this reading/writing: 'our job' (i.e., us, as humans desiring to widen our engagement with the nonhuman realm) is to go 'where few have bothered [previously] to linger'. Thus the endeavour does not aspire to the eradication of human positionality, and even hints at a good old-fashioned empirical colonialism, in which the human moves to occupy and, through knowing, 'claim' previously uncharted object-territories. Thus here we are travelling back in the (human) direction of impressions, phenomenological reductions, representations – and ultimately of the view of (in our case) bricks from a human standpoint. We seem to tumble back to a very familiar position, in which knowing bricks involves animating them anthropomorphically.

But how could it be otherwise? How could we ever escape (or bracket out) our humanness anyway? We might each be able to – via introspection and triangulation with others – identify and thereby account for our *individual* subjectivity and positionality. But could the generic perceptual and conceptual baggage of being human ever be left at check-in?

Bricks with us

We are now travelling back from the outer – bleak – theoretical reaches of extreme posthumanism towards a mild posthumanism which, more modestly, wants us to notice the nonhuman realm more, and to understand our entanglement with it (Hodder, 2012; Olsen, 2013). And the difference – compared to extreme posthumanism – is that it actually has some methodology to offer, in that it hooks back into the humanities and social sciences (rather than into writing evocative poetics and horror fictions that seek to report the shimmering unknowability of a reality beyond perception, which is the method of choice for the speculative realists).

As Bruno Latour puts it, while the desired summoning of objects may be achieved imaginatively through the arts, it can also still be achieved via more traditional interpretive routes:

> when objects have receded into the background for good it is always possible – but more difficult – to bring them back to light by using archives, documents, memoirs, museum collections etc., to artificially produce, through historians' accounts, the state of crisis in which machines, devices, and implements were born.
>
> (2005, p. 81)

As he then argues, it is not inaccessibility of data that prevents us from studying objects and their network relations with us humans, but rather a lack of will.

In its own terms Latour's Actor Network Theory (ANT) is a pretty heretical position when viewed against the canon of mainstream social theory, although set against the machinations of the hardcore 'world without us' posthumanists it starts to looks rather tame (and surprisingly sane and useful). Like Morton, Latour finds cause to meditate upon bricks, as part of his attempt to reinsert matter into social theory. Starting with the simple (but still quite challenging for the vested interests of conventional social theory) observation that the process of building a wall entails the intermixing of the social and the physical, Latour moves on to note that the physical dimension is a mute one, particularly after the construction phase has ended: 'Once built, the wall of bricks does not utter a word – even though the group of workmen goes on talking and graffiti may proliferate on its surface' (2005, p. 79).

The task therefore (for ANT) becomes one of how to *'make* [objects] *talk,* that is, to offer descriptions of themselves, to produce *scripts* of what they are making others – humans or non-humans – do' (2005, p. 79, emphasis in original). This at first glance appears to echo Ian Bogost's call for a speculative object-fiction, but the difference is that ANT is not seeking to eliminate the human from the picture. Instead ANT's call is for social science to analyse the co-constitutive effects of humans and things in their network relations. It is not an approach that seeks (as do the object-oriented ontologists) to emphasize the isolation of every object from every other object, but instead foregrounds the dynamic flux of interaction, and co-dependence between loosely bounded things. Here we reach a vision of posthumanism closer in spirit to that of the materialist feminists. It is a position that is concerned with mapping local situations and which doesn't see it as too late or fruitless to try to improve human–thing relations. It is a position that has a concern with furthering (human) social justice and equitable (and sustainable) allocation of access to earthly resources, and which sees the productive power of 'situated knowledges' (Haraway, 1988) in constructing efficacious – and locally valid – understandings of human–thing relations. It is a position in which both people and things matter, and are found to be entangled co-constitutively. It is a position in which existing methodologies can be adopted and adapted in order to reveal (pedagogically) and examine (via research) the entanglement of things, people and relations. It is also a position that sees these objects and their relations as in a dynamic state of ever-becoming.

Here we can start to think about situational engagements with supposedly 'dumb brute' matter, and how those who need to find a way of engaging the matter that they are working with achieve this (in other words, how they come to know and to co-constitute their actions with such matter). Thus David Paton (2013) describes the intimate relationship formed between the apprentice stonemason and the Cornish granite that he selects and hews from the quarry face, showing how familiarity (a sense of knowing a material) is a function of processes of engagement: that a knowing comes from a process of exchange, of experiencing the stone's affordances and resistance to the mason's attempts to change it, and to the stone's acting back upon the body of the mason (via its weight, the vibration of working it and the development of muscle memory through such labour).

Similarly, Lieven Ameel and Sirpa Tani (2012) introduce us to the 'parkour eyes' developed by Finnish traceurs as they gaze purposefully upon the concrete surfaces of Helsinki's built environment that they assail in their adult play, finding through their *need to know* features and qualities in the urban landscape that are beyond the perception of most passers-by. We can also encounter similarly heightened human–thing communion in the Swedish underground tunnellers studied by Alexander Styhre (2008), whose on-the-job experiential learning forms an aesthetic knowledge founded upon tactile, aural and olfactory engagement with their task. Here, deep underground, the application of sprayed cement to tunnel walls is perfected by operatives listening to, smelling and feeling their spraying machine and its issuance. Here is human–machine synchronization forming an embodied, intimate – near instinctive – learning of materiality. As one operative describes it,

> Quite often, you hear various sounds... You may see the movements of the machine... You notice that it [the machine] doesn't do too

well, the spray concrete just bubbles and hisses by the mouth-piece, and then something's wrong... You can listen to the pump-beats whether machine works as it should.

(quoted in Styhre (2008, p. 407), ellipses in original)

In contemplating such human-matter relationships we can helpfully adopt Tim Ingold's (2010) critique of any approach that subdivides the world into discrete objects. Ingold argues that the term 'materiality' actually works inadvertently to preserve a humans-separate-from-the-world binary because it implies that we are somehow separate from the matter that comprises the world, and yet we and everything else are made of flows of matter. Ingold urges humans to engage with the world in a way that creatively inhabits it – a disposition that sees nothing as fixed, solid or given. Thus matter for Ingold is neither dumb, brutally unchangeable nor separable from the life-world that it processes through, in a flux of ever changing assemblages. Through Ingold's eyes we move to the potentiality of even seemingly inert matter like bricks, stone blocks or concrete; of the impermanence of walls, and the co-dependence of all matter and energy.

Posthumanism helpfully questions anthropocentrism, and reminds us that we (humans) are part of the world that we, and other things, exist in. But to be productive for educational research posthumanism must keep sight of the human, and seek to explicate bricks, blocks and *béton brut* precisely because they are meaningful and necessary (or at least useful) to us. A posthumanism that desires to access 'the world *without* us', as has been shown, is thwarted by our own positionality and perceptual ranges. In contrast, a posthumanism that embraces 'the world with us' can – by decentring but not abandoning the human entirely – sensitize our attention towards the entanglement of us, our ideas and the material world in which we are enmeshed. Such a posthumanist research agenda would address both that which is 'of us' (representation; practices of use) and that which is not 'of us' (the physical properties and alien temporalities of the nonhuman around us), in each case showing how a 'social materiality' (Dale, 2005) operates through human engagements with the world, and the intermixing of the human and the nonhuman.

Therefore how we come to 'know' the world, and learn how to frame it and use it, is important, and that – ultimately – is a matter of education in its widest sense. This relationship with things is 'semiotic-material' (Haraway, 1988, p. 585), and as such is both embodied, and learnt and transmitted. Posthumanism's methodological contribution to educational research is thus its holistic attentiveness to our entanglement with nonhuman things, and to both the being of *and* our storying of those things – the narrative and other practices through which we learn to live within the world, its resistances and affordances.

For Ingold, accounting for matter is about telling the stories of the flow, mix and mutation of materials, alongside describing the normative and affective impressions they leave upon any (human) spectator. It is also about attempts to vicariously engage with matter, and the processes and techniques, through which it was worked at other times, both by humans and by other agents (rain, frost, salts and soot in the case of bricks) within its 'total surroundings' (Ingold, 2007, p. 15). For Tim Edensor (2013, p. 450) in similar vein, in his study of the materiality of Manchester's urban stone, it is about using multiple methods – archives, interviews, site visits and sensations to seek out the 'multiple traces of other time-spaces… [amidst]… an affective and sensual encounter with materiality that promotes empathy with other times, people, events and non-human agents' (p. 450).

But for all its ingenuity, Edensor's is ultimately a sense-making through a multi-stranded storying. And how could it be anything else? We cannot help but seek to contextualize, to narrate and to fit encounters with matter into a 'human interest' framework. Yes, we can bring matter into the analytical grid, by decentring the human, but we can't (fully) throw the human out. But who would listen to the story of 'stone without us'? Indeed, can the stone itself be said to have an independent (i.e., 'stone without us') story? ANT and Ingold (2012) would argue that Paton's quarry stone and his stonemason only exist (in those forms, and as discrete entities) in their interrelationship. The process of quarrying makes vast, indeterminate strata divisible, parsing into discrete chunks and exposed surfaces that render vast rock beds tangible (to us) as localized objects, within specific temporalities and for specific purposes. Likewise a stonemason is a spatio-temporal localization of his task – but that's only one identity fragment of many (father, brother, lover, Elvis impersonator) that may make up his shimmering, multifaceted 'posthuman' subjectivity.

Conclusion

In contemplating the bleak extremes of posthumanism and the awkward ontoepistemological status of bricks, stone blocks and sprayed concrete, this chapter has ventured far from the traditional territories of educational research. The purpose of this strange journey has been to introduce a note of caution into any embrace of posthumanism. That warning has been two-fold. First, to be clear about what posthumanism is intended to mean in any educational research project. If it denotes a sensitivity to the presence of nonhuman agents within learning situations, then what is in play is a mild notion of the posthuman, and that type of posthumanism is interested in 'the world *with* us', for it retains a link both to the human and to fundamental commitments to human advancement. Second, few if any methods exist whereby we might aspire to connect with 'the world *without* us'. Milder variants of posthumanism that acknowledge that nonhuman things are being studied because of their influence or relevance to human concerns are more viable, and mild posthumanism represents an ecumenical rebalancing of both humanist pedagogy and humanist epistemology, rather than a fundamental break with either.

In mines and quarries humans in their quest for building materials seek to apply labour and ingenuity to 'dumb brute' matter, in order to change its form in accordance with human will. But in the process they change themselves too: the miners die young or become wise, experienced operatives, their bodies moulded to the daily tasks, their senses attuned to the subtle 'voices' of the machines and matter that they are working with. Work thus is shown to be a co-creation of the resistances and affordances of matter and of ideas enacted upon it. Institutionalized education likewise is a co-creation of matter and ideas. Both are embodied activities that take place in distinct locations at which human and nonhuman matter is engaged in constant exchanges, through which meaning emerges. Both are instigated by humans, but act out through semiotic-material processes which are never entirely within human control or understanding.

Enmeshed within such processes of becoming (the brick being made, the rock hewn, the cement being sprayed) humans are ever entwined and entwining in the world around them, and in the consequences of their and others' actions. This flux becomes understood by processes of meaning-making; in other words, processes of learning. That learning is achieved through engagement with the stuff of the world.

Following Ingold, we can better understand our (human) being-in-the-world by understanding how we are constantly caught up in flows of matter and energies. We will also better understand our learning in the world by reflecting upon how we compose and circulate our stories by which we make sense of the situations we find ourselves in, how we 'join the dots'. Thus studying our material relations is centrally a matter of studying how we learn to accommodate to tasks and the things we work upon (and which act back upon us) in those tasks. A posthuman approach to education can chart these semiotic-material connections (in the manner of Latour's ANT), strive to account for all dimensions (after Edensor), *and* (but not exclusively) consider the point of view of the objects we manipulate and depend upon (in the spirit of Bogost and Harman).

All such attempts are about learning and teaching at its most primal level: it is about investigating how humans build their competency to know and to act in a 'more than human' world, while being already in (and part of) that world.

References

Ameel, L. and T. Sirpa (2012) 'Everyday Aesthetics in Action: Parkour Eyes and the Beauty of Concrete Walls', *Emotion, Space and Society*, 5, 164–173.

Barad, K. (2007) *Meeting the Universe Halfway: Quantum Physics and the Entanglement of Matter and Meaning* (London: Duke University Press).

Bennett, J. (2010*) Vibrant Matter: A Political Ecology of Things* (London: Duke University Press).

Bennett, L. and K. Hock (2013) *Scree* (Sheffield: Tract Publishing).

Bogost, I. (2012) *Alien Phenomenology, or What It's like to Be a Thing* (London: University of Minnesota Press).

Braidotti, R. (2013) *The Posthuman* (Cambridge: Polity).

Brassier, R. (2007) *Nilhil Unbound: Enlightenment and Extinction* (London: Palgrave Macmillan).

Clark, N. (2011) *Inhuman Nature: Sociable Life on a Dynamic Planet* (London: SAGE).

Dale, K. (2005) 'Building a Social Materiality: Spatial and Embodied Politics in Organizational Control', *Organization*, 12, 649–678.

Douglas, M. (2002) *Purity and Danger: An Analysis of Concepts of Pollution and Taboo* (London: Routledge).

Easterbrook, G. (1996) *A Moment on the Earth* (London: Penguin).

Edensor, T. (2013) 'Vital Urban Materiality and Its Multiple Absences: The Building Stone of Central Manchester', *Cultural Geographies*, 20, 447–465.

Ettinger, R. (1972) *Man into Superman* (New York: St. Martin's Press).

Garrard, G. (2012) 'Worlds without Us: Some Types of Disanthropy', *SubStance*, 41, 40–60.

Gratton, P. (2014) *Speculative Realism: Problems and Prospects* (London: Bloomsbury Academic).

Haraway, D. (1988) 'Situated Knowledges: The Science Question in Feminism and the Privilege of Partial Perspectives', *Feminist Studies*, 14, 575–599.

Harman, G. (2002) *Tool-Being: Heidegger and the Metaphysics of Objects* (Chicago: Open Court Publishing).

Harman, G. (2010) *Towards Speculative Realism: Chapters and Lectures* (Ropley: Zero Books).

Harman, G. (2011) *The Quadruple Object* (Alresford: Zero Books).

Heidegger, M. (1978) *Being and Time* (J. Macquarrie and E. Robinson, Trans.) (Oxford: Blackwell).

Hodder, I. (2012) *Entangled: An Archaeology of the Relationships between Humans and Things* (London: Wiley-Blackwell).
Huxley, J. (1957) *New Bottles for New Wine* (London: Chatto & Windus).
Ingold, T. (2007) 'Matter against Materiality', *Archaeological Dialogues*, 14, 1–16.
Ingold, T. (2010) *Bringing Things to Life: Creative Entanglements in a World of Materials*, Working Paper 15 – ESRC National Centre for Research Methods (Manchester: University of Manchester).
Ingold, T. (2012) 'Toward an Ecology of Materials', *Annual Review of Anthropology*, 41, 427–442.
Kohn, E. (2013) *How Forests Think: Towards an Anthropology Beyond the Human* (London: University of California Press).
Latour, B. (2005) *Reassembling the Social: An Introduction to Actor Network Theory* (Oxford: Oxford University Press).
Leopard, A. (1968) *A Sand Country Almanac* (Oxford: Oxford University Press).
Marder, M. (2013) *Plant-Thinking: A Philosophy of Vegetal Life* (Chichester: Columbia University Press).
Meillassoux, Q. (2008a) *After Finitude: A Chapter on the Necessity of Contingency* (London: Continuum).
Meillassoux, Q. (2008b) 'Spectral Dilemma', in R. Mackay (ed.) *COLLAPSE IV* (Falmouth: Urbanomic), pp. 261–275.
More, M. (2013) 'The Philosophy of Transhumanism', in M. More and N. Vita-More (eds.) *The Transhumanist Reader: Classical and Contemporary Essays on the Science, Technology, and Philosophy of the Human Future* (Chichester: John Wiley & Sons), pp. 3–17.
Morton, T. (2013a) *Realist Magic: Objects, Ontology, Causality* (London: Open Humanities Press).
Morton, T. (2013b) *Hyperobjects: Philosophy and Ecology after the End of the World* (London: University of Minnesota Press).
Næss, A. (1973) 'The Shallow and the Deep, Long-Range Ecology Movement', *Inquiry*, 16, 95–100.
Nietzsche, F. (2003) *Thus Spoke Zarathustra* (R. J. Hollingdale, Trans.) (London: Penguin).
Olsen, B. (2013) *In Defense of Things: Archaeology and the Ontology of Objects* (Plymouth: AltaMira Press).
Paton, D. A. (2013) 'The Quarry as Sculpture: The Place of Making', *Environment & Planning A*, 45, 1070–1086.
Pedersen, H. (2010) 'Is "the Posthuman" Educable? On the Convergence of Educational Philosophy, Animal Studies, and Posthumanist Theory', *Discourse: Studies in the Cultural Politics of Education*, 31, 237–250.
Styhre, A. (2008) 'The Aesthetics of Rock Construction Work: The Beauty of Sprayed Concrete, Rock Reinforcement and Roof Bolting', *Culture and Organization*, 14, 401–410.
Weisman, A. (2008) *The World without Us* (London: Virgin Books).
Whatmore, S. (2006) 'Materialist Returns: Practising Cultural Geography in and for a more-than-human World', *Cultural Geographies*, 13, 600–609.

5
A Mark on Paper: The Matter of Indigenous–Settler History

Alison Jones and Te Kawehau Hoskins

Here is an object of research, found in the archives: a piece of 'data', an ink-on-paper mark. It exists on the bottom right-hand side of a sturdy square of parchment. The intriguing drawing (Figure 5.1) represents the unique tā moko or facial tattoo of a Maori leader, Hongi Hika. The central whorls are the lines from either side of the bridge of Hongi Hika's nose and the curved lines below frame his mouth – all shapes from the most sacred part of the body: the head. This ink-on-paper mark played a significant role in the earliest Indigenous–settler (Maori–Pakeha) relationships in Aotearoa-New Zealand. Hongi Hika drew his tā moko on 4 November 1819 on the second New Zealand land deed: 13,000 acres at Kerikeri in the Bay of Islands, sold to the Church Missionary Society for 48 axes.

This mark, seen as a signature, is generally understood today as evidence of Hongi Hika having sold land to Pakeha (European) purchasers. As a result of this sale, the land, on which the town of Kerikeri now stands, shifted permanently into Pakeha ownership. Hongi Hika's people, the Ngāpuhi people, who once lived there, now largely inhabit the outskirts of the town and the rural surrounding area.

This is a simple description of our 'object of research' and its usual place in New Zealand history, as typically understood by Pakeha. Our description makes sense within the rules of common-sense observation. The scientific imperative suggests and encourages this description: repeating the facts, all of which are empirically true.

Now, if we were interpretivist scholars, suspicious of common sense, we would automatically bring to this object the question of *meaning*. The usual meaning to many Pakeha has been outlined above. But what might the inked representation of the tā moko signify to Hongi Hika and his people? Does it carry the same meaning as a signature on a land

76 *A Mark on Paper*

Figure 5.1 Hongi Hika's tā moko drawn on paper by him in 1819
Source: Hocken Library, University of Otago. Ref: S08-122 – MS-0070/A

deed in a European context, where the owner sells an area of land to purchasers, into their independent ownership? In modern critical social research it has become possible, even necessary, to argue that Hongi Hika's tā moko has *many possible meanings*: for instance, as his agreement that the Kerikeri land is sold for ever (the 'standard' view); as an artefact in the history of European land alienation and robbery; as the act of a naïve native leader going along with a peculiar European ritual that he did not fully understand; as the act of a shrewd Maori strategist recruiting 'his' Pakeha into his territory.

At this point, an interpretivist position gets into trouble. What can be said next about this 'web of conflicting definitions' (Stengers, 2008, p. 38)? We usually remain enchanted, or satisfied, or paralysed, or irritated, with such multiplicity. And/or we debate the politics and effects of dominant discourses, and point to subordinated meanings of Indigenous peoples. Such is the business of critical social science. Interpretivist engagement in the interminable and necessary struggle between interpretations is done 'against' the old limitations of empirical objective science, and 'for' the inevitability of human subjectivity in meaning making. Paradoxically, perhaps without realizing it, at the same time as we seek to *reject* the old subject–object dualism implied or insisted on by science, we nevertheless *reiterate* that dualism as we come down on one 'side' – the side of the subject, discourse and meaning. We repeat the dualism in order to reject it; in rejecting it, we repeat it.

This book suggests a different (posthumanist) approach to data objects. It voices a set of philosophical arguments in recent social research that give critical attention to the stubborn repetition of the subject–object dualism. By revealing shared ontological assumptions that underlie both empirical and interpretive analysis, posthumanist arguments radically collapse the subject–object dualism, thereby tracing a 'line of flight' to new patterns of inquiry, new ways of doing research. In this chapter, we take up the invitation offered by these debates experimentally to relook at Hongi Hika's tā moko on paper. In joining attempts by posthumanist arguments to fold back into itself the subject–object dualism, we encounter the drawn tā moko – our 'object of study' – as an organic, speaking subject. What might this creative experiment add to our understanding of the object? In other, less dualistic terms, what might be possible when we, as researchers, encounter this empirical text, the inked outline of a tattoo on an old land deed, as *having something to tell us*?

'We' who speak to 'you'

Te Kawehau is Ngāpuhi, a descendent of Hongi Hika who traced his tā moko on the Kerikeri land deed, and a scholar working in the field of Maori governance (see Hoskins, 2010, 2012; Hoskins et al., 2011; Hoskins and Jones, 2012). Alison is a Pakeha researcher who works on Indigenous–settler educational engagement (see Jones, 1999, 2012; Jones and Jenkins, 2008). We evoke these ethnic-cultural identities as a necessary element of our encounters with the tā moko on paper. It is worth noting that we are very conscious of the difficulties of usefully addressing non-Indigenous *and* Indigenous audiences in one chapter. In our experience, the ontological assumptions and political emphases of these two audiences (if we can binarize and homogenize here for a moment!) tend to differ such that we might follow a different path of argument for each. Aware of the fact that this book is published in Europe, written largely by Europeans, we steer a careful course in this chapter. We always keep Indigenous thinkers in mind, and try to offer something of use to both Indigenous and non-Indigenous audiences.

In our experiment we do not try to find or to enact a 'better way of knowing' than science (see Colebrook, 2010; Stengers, 2008, for a critique of new materialist or posthumanist claims to truth). Nor do we claim radically to move beyond/outside the rules of science as we approach this piece of data, which is a material and textual object. The inky fragment acts here as a catalyst, an opportunity for our engagement with each other, with you and with it, as we tentatively talk our way into a creative research conversation framed by our shared interest in settler–Indigenous relationships.

We could not have found a better object-partner with which to carry out this experiment. This tā moko on paper is already an object of engagement. Although it was drawn for/in a Maori landscape 200 years ago, it was clearly drawn for/in a Pakeha setting as well. To provoke the signature to speak to us, we approach it located in the Maori material and knowledge context in which Hongi Hika made it – a context that continues to underpin what counts as Maori knowledge and experience today.

Maori ontology

The Indigenous ontological world in which the mark on paper was made, took (and still takes) it for granted that objects could speak, act and have effects independently of human thought and will. This ontology – like all ontologies – was developed in a particular context of knowing that was itself moulded out of the problems of living, acting and thinking in specific natural and social environments. Indigenous peoples, just as did European peoples before/outside the dominance of science (the Enlightenment) and the Church, engaged with an environment that was always already formed by powerful and weak forces and objects, where human beings had to negotiate with a capricious natural world on a daily basis. Developing outside European science, Indigenous ontologies never *had* a nature-culture dualism, never truly differentiated 'culture' and 'nature'. Indigenous people's everyday entanglement of nature and culture has produced lasting ontologies and epistemologies that identify humans in and with nature, and vice versa. This is easily observed. Maori regularly engage in invocations that address and welcome, say, the plants or the sea when food or other resources are collected. Much of Maori everyday life is shaped by awareness of the human-nonhuman dynamic, as humans (*as* Maori) constantly negotiate with the natural world, endeavouring to meet its dispositions and participate in its balances. It is widespread among Maori today to talk about a river, a mountain, an entire tribe, or an ancestor that lived hundreds of years ago, as yourself: 'ko au te awa, ko te awa ko au' ('I am the river and the river is me').

This sort of statement is not simply metaphor, but a deep visceral identification as the animated embodied river, mountain, or ancestor (an observation well-known to Western research; see, for instance, Thomas, 1991; Clammer et al., 2004). It remains common in Maori and other Indigenous thinking for 'objects' – whether Hongi Hika's tā moko on paper, a dead body, a forest or a piece of greenstone – to be understood as determining events, as exerting forces, as volitional, or as instructing people, as speaking to us, and people being able to hear what they might tell. Beyond Maori examples, one does not need to look far into other Indigenous ontologies to see evidence of the world not as nature/object and culture/subject in interaction, but as a form of related sociality. For instance, Indigenous scholars such as North American Indian academic Vine Deloria (Deloria et al., 1999, p. 37) remind us that in Sioux metaphysics all human and nonhuman beings are interrelated, and each form of being has its own character: sunflowers 'engage in purposeful action' by using buffalo as a transport mechanism for their seeds; stones' character or personality is stillness. The Ojibwa people know that all things, as beings, express themselves in movement or personality: thunder can speak intelligibly; the natural world is full of signs that may or may not be interpreted by humans (see Ingold, 2004). In the Ahnishinahbæóᵖjibway language 'there is no subject acting upon object', objects exist in equal relation to others including humans: so a person 'meets the Lake' rather than 'goes to get water' (Wub-e-ke-niew, 1995, pp. 225, 218). While in post-Enlightenment Western ontologies, objects such as tools and stones are typically experienced and known as inanimate matter, it is possible to say that for Indigenous peoples 'the liveliness of matter is grasped as quite ordinary' (Horton and Berlo, 2013, p. 18). Within an Indigenous ontological frame, all beings and objects are experienced as having mana, a form of presence and authority, and a 'vigour, impetus and potentiality' which Maori call *mauri* (Durie, 2001, p. x). *Te mauri o te whenua* – 'the life force of the land', or *te mauri o te tā moko o Hongi Hika* – 'the life force of Hongi Hika's tā moko' on the paper fragment, are perfectly mundane ideas to Maori. Terms such as 'mauri' and 'mana' name the intra-connections of the people-world.

So within an Indigenous ontological world, the tā moko on the land deed lives; it is alive. It is not something old, inert, flat on a page, but something present, vibrant and lively. The tā moko is not merely an inked shape traced on a slice of paper, but a taonga, a sacred object holding Hongi Hika's presence, his mana, his authority and chiefly power, co-present with the mana of his ancestors. His face and its embodied authority is before us, it encounters us; we are face to face with Hongi Hika. His presence carries an invitation to engage: to mihi – to speak greetings and make genealogical connections; to tangi – to remember and lament this dead relative and others; to hongi – to press noses and intermingle hau, breath, in a solemn enactment of a relationship, a joining of forces. These invitations by the tā moko assume and take seriously the idea that the object is animate and therefore always already in an active relationship with those who encounter it. In this sense, the object *acts*. The object speaks, it makes demands and it draws forth from us a response.

And here is the key point. In Indigenous ontologies, all beings and things have particular qualities and capabilities by virtue of their taking form always and only in a *relational* context. The identity of 'things' in the world is not understood as discrete or independent, but emerges through, and as, relations with everything else. It is the relation, or connection, not the thing itself, that is ontologically privileged in Indigenous Maori thought. Indeed, the general term for Maori people, 'tāngata whenua', refers literally to land-earth-placenta-human: each forms the other. So, the vitality of things is possible not because of the intrinsic qualities of one object alone but because of 'its relationship with the mauri [vigour, impetus and potentiality] of others' (Durie, 2001, p. x). This ontology – or, to use Salmond's (2012) useful phrase, ontological style – produces a necessarily mutually constituting relationship between all things, including human beings (see also Henare, et al., 2006).

Lest such ontological assumptions be considered merely theoretical, or unusual within the modern world of scientific research, it is worth pointing out that modern, ordinary Maori research practice entails such elements as: karakia – to invite nonhuman forces to enable the research to proceed well, to enfold forces (bodies, spaces, ancestors, earth and sky) into productive engagement; mihi – connections made to others and the earth-place from which they come; hongi – the pressing of noses in an exchange of breath that binds the parties together in a relationship of trust; kai – sharing of food that both seals a relationship between 'researcher and participant' as they work together in research conversations and, because food is noa (non-sacred), also counteracts the tapu or sacredness of the exchange of knowledge that is the basis of a research encounter. In other words, it is commonplace for Maori in the academy today to practice ontological understandings of the world in its 'ongoing processes of becoming' (Marsden, 2003). It is worth mentioning here that in Aotearoa-New Zealand, these ontological practices are not only 'cultural', but also political acts. The phrase 'kaupapa Maori' provides an umbrella term for the critical decolonizing project that nurtures theorizing and researching with Indigenous Maori ontologies and practices (Hoskins, 2012; Pihama, 2010; Roberts and Wills, 1998; Smith, 2012; Smith et al., 2012).

The matter of language

We have summarized some ontological points about the human-world relationship at the heart of Maori encounters with the world. Similar ontological moves are at the centre of posthumanist discussions in Western social analysis, arising from different origins and therefore quite different in character. Posthumanist critics of the 'linguistic turn' in Western social science point out that the dominance of discourse and meaning has left the object-world necessarily alienated from us. Philosopher of science Karen Barad in *Meeting the Universe Halfway* (2007) asserts that 'language has been granted too much power... even materiality is turned into a matter of language or some form of cultural representation' (p. 132). She and others such as Jane Bennett in *Vibrant Matter: A Political Ecology of Things* (2010) invite us to foreground 'the material' – objects and things – which, they maintain, have been largely relegated to the shadows of modern social theory, 'behind' language.

Some have pointed out that the position of objects 'behind' or at least 'separated' from discourse is embedded in the very logic of European languages such as English. The usual logic of English grammar (object: passive; subject: active) reflects and reproduces a Western subject–object dualism, and the ontological assumption that nature/object is a priori passive and culture/language is the source of active differentiation (Salmond, 2012; Viveiros de Castro, 2004). So, for instance, the simple descriptive statement that 'a shape *is traced* in ink. The shape *represents* the facial tattoo' is ontological in that it places the act of drawing and the act of representation between the inked shape (nature or object) and its author (culture or human actor). The ink is *being* traced; the tattoo is *being* represented. Is it possible, on this dualist logic, for the ink to have/conduct/channel mauri (an energetic force), or for the tattoo to *be* the force of a person? Even these questions seem awkward and strange; our thinking is already shaped for us by the logic contained within the language in which we write and speak.

Foregrounding the material, posthumanist or new materialist arguments posit the object as having character, as able to 'speak back' to its observers; matter appears as 'a self-disclosing activity' (Massumi, 2002, p. 228). As Clough puts it, such arguments 'address the movement, potentiality or virtuality immanent to matter' (2009, p. 44). Or in Maclure's (2013, p. 660) words: 'we are obliged to acknowledge that data have their ways of making themselves intelligible to us'. Rather than only passive products of language, largely devoid of agency, as they are rendered in social constructivism's idea of discourse, objects are recognized in their own right. 'The material', it is argued, has agency and makes demands. It has, in Bennett's (2010, p. 2) words, *thing-power*.

Thing-power. Paradoxically (given the problem of the dominance of discourse!) but inevitably, the current debates demand new language in order to produce or find that *something else* – the obscured materiality of objects and nature. The idea, according to Barad et al., is to bring subject and object into inseparable, equal (flattened), intra-connection or intra-action. In order to express a non-binary, or to collapse binaries, writers have had to invent awkward new terms such as *agential* and *intra-connection*. In English, new vocabularies have had to be invoked for theorists to encounter a material world quite different from that assumed in dominant Western epistemologies. So it is not uncommon now to find such phrases as nature-culture, matter-energy, the material-discursive, intra-action, assemblages, relata, thingly power, entanglements and flows. For instance: 'matter is substance in its intra-active becoming – not a thing, but a doing, a congealing of agency' (Barad, 2008, p. 139); 'An assemblage, in its multiplicity, necessarily acts on semiotic flows, material flows, and social flows simultaneously' (Deleuze and Guattari, 1987, p. 22); 'this particular mode of matter-energy resides in a world where the line between inert matter and vital energy, between animate and inanimate, is permeable' (Bennett, 2004, p. 352). Bennett (2010, p. 119) confesses that in order to write her book *Vibrant Matter* she needed to compose and recompose words and sentences as she tried to find appropriate verbs (*'intra-act'*) and nouns (*'actant'*, *'intra-action'*) for her argument.

Method: How to proceed?

How might we encounter thing-power? To make some progress in our experimental posthumanist engagement with Hongi Hika's tā moko, it seems we must reach towards *something* that exceeds language: an *attitude*, a sympathy, a feeling, an openness. The tā moko image provides particularly fecund data for such attitude and relationship work. It *is* so many things: an object, text, an image (reproduced on the pages of this book, in front of you, and also inhabiting an 1819 land deed), the mana (authority, presence) of a man and a tribal group, a signature, a face, an object of exquisite aesthetic beauty; it is intensities of ink, intra-actions of shape and body, assemblages of paper, hau and mana. The whole document is made of organic materials, paper and ink, with a wax seal. Being so viscerally material and textual, so material-discursive, it provokes us in a multitude of ways. And, along with the object 'itself' and its contexts of representation, there is the intra-active encounter between us and it (let's say the 'us' is you, the reader, and the 'it' the object we have to imagine, reproduced in a one-dimensional printed copy here).

How do we find our attitude? How do we make ourselves available to thing-power, and vice versa? What research methods are suggested by the methodologies – the concepts in action – of posthumanism or new materialism; how might object-subject intra-actions express their encounter (if they must)? It is all very well for Karen Barad to complain that discourse theory offers 'precious little guidance on how to proceed' in examining the material world (2008, p. 141) because it automatically guides our attention to the discursive and away from the material. But what about posthumanist guidance on how to proceed?

It is remarkably difficult to find suggestions for *method* in the new debates. This may be because 'method' is, in itself, always already a human-centred activity when we are being asked to centre the object-that-would-have-been-called-data (Maclure, 2013, p. 558). An invitation to engage in intra-action seems, scarily, as much about *experience* as 'method'. Some new materialist theorists in social sciences suggest that we proceed 'by giving special attention to matter' (Dolphijn and van der Tuin, 2012, p. 85) or that we 'move beyond discursive construction and grapple with materiality' (Alaimo and Hekman, 2008, p. 6). What we (Alison and Te Kawehau) find is that we, whether Western or Indigenous scholars, are always already caught in our human-centredness when we *grapple with* or *give special attention* to matter, and then express that engagement in writing (in this case) in English. As the grapple-ee, matter remains, necessarily dualistically, the *object* of *our* attention. We feel stuck, and uncertain about our procedural method.

Maybe this does not matter. Maybe the provocation is to encounter uncertainly the object-world. Maybe method is an ongoing struggle and constant connection-attempts rather than a set of rules for procedure. The resulting written accounts will have the (irritating or exhilarating) characteristics of fluidity, contingency, ambiguity – and obscurity. That is the territory we are working on/with; our research method opens to a range of new terms, impressions, languages, expressive forms and ways of seeing. This is what, it seems, is suggested about method by scholars such as Jane Bennett. In a typically lively way, Bennett famously indicates *her* method on encountering objects – in this case, a pile of trash on the street: 'Glove, pollen, rat, cap, stick. As I encountered these items, they shimmied back and forth between debris and thing – between... stuff to ignore... and stuff that commanded attention in its own right, as existents in excess of their association with human meanings' (2010, p. 4). Matter's potentiality and capability, she finds, require novel regimes of perception.

Bennett concludes her seminal book *Vibrant Matter* with a call to devise new ways of looking 'that enable us to consult nonhumans more closely' (p. 108). She suggests we researchers 'encounter' objects as they 'command attention' *from us*. That is, objects require/demand/engage/exist in a *relationship* (with us and with other objects). But instead of being 'merely' a product of that relationship – to be understood as interpretation, in this case, debris – objects simultaneously maintain their own singularity as 'thing', stoically *outside* our human encounter with them. Bennett seems to suggest that we turn to that thing outside and inquire of it, foregrounding the possibility that it might 'have something to say' to us in the process of our consultation.

But – we have to persevere with this line of questioning for the moment – the *manner* of such consultation remains far from obvious. How might that vitality of things such as Hongi Hika's signature, which 'exceeds comprehensive grasp' (Bennett, 2010, p. 122), be revealed, not to mention represented, or should we abandon even that desire? Bennett is persistent. She suggests: a 'cultivated, patient, sensory attentiveness to nonhuman forces' (p. xiv); an alertness to matter as 'vibrant, vital, energetic, lively, quivering, vibratory, evanescent, and effluescent' (p. 112), or, as Massumi (2002) suggests, a sensitivity to 'the scent of a thingly power' (p. xiii). These strange methodological suggestions remind us how radically difficult it is to speak *about* (this very phrasing makes the separation, again!) matter's vibrancy. Again, we have to add, parenthetically for the moment, in case we forget, we are all speaking here in a language that contains and determines what we can think and say.

As she struggles to talk about a method for engagement with matter, Bennett suggests researchers undertake 'a careful course of anthropomorphization' to allow for 'moments of methodological naiveté' (2010, pp. 17, 122). Quoting Mitchell, she asks: 'But how to develop this capacity for naiveté? One tactic might be to revisit and become temporarily infected by discredited philosophies of nature, risking "the taint of superstition, animism, vitalism, anthropomorphism, and other premodern attitudes" ' (p. 18). Interesting. This kind of statement can be too easily read, as Juanita Sundberg (2014) does, with understandable indignation, as an invitation to Western scholars to visit questionable primitive – including Indigenous – ontologies that are, surmises Sundberg, *'capable* of giving "things" their due as co-producers of daily life, but *incapable* of producing knowledge relevant to theorising materialism' (p. 38) – a kind of risky 'dash and grab' from magical non-modern Others that re-enacts the colonizing imperative. Bennett's suggestion, that in seeking new intra-active methods of connecting with our objects of attention, 'we' scholars (temporarily) embrace pre-modern attitudes, is certainly provocative.

Any idea of a 'temporary infection' with pre-modern (let's say Indigenous) attitudes, or what Latour (1993) calls non-modern cultures, as a research method for postmodern researchers is simply unhelpful. Quite aside from the politics of such a move, any good understanding of, say, mauri or hau – or thing-power, for that matter – requires immersion in the languages and cultures that produce them. Both sets of ideas spring from and produce quite different realities that have long cultural and political histories. As we mention above, Indigenous (Maori) ontologies always already assume a profound sameness, and therefore sense of recognition, between the abilities and sensibilities of objects and those of humans. For Indigenous scholars, the struggle is to find a way to enable these ontologies to be recognized and reproduced in their academic work. For Western researchers intrigued by new materialist arguments, the ontological struggle is different. Within/against Western ontologies, it becomes necessary to create a new vocabulary and to trouble the familiar language of empiricist or interpretivist social science in order to open up a space where objects can express their vitality and agency – or, at least, where humans can experience their (objects') vitality.

In our shared work, we do not attempt to ask whether mauri or hau are 'the same' as thing-power. We do not collapse materialist and Indigenous ontological ideas, or even compare them in any sustained way. Rather, coming as we (Te Kawehau and Alison) do, from different linguistic and cultural traditions (and this is an oversimplification), we try to find ways to allow these traditions to 'work' in our work. Indigenous and new materialist ontologies come face to face, recognizing the other, engaging maybe in an exchange of hau, breath. We recognize the politics of this situation: the power dynamic at work between Western and Indigenous thought systems. One set of ontological assumptions has been relegated to the 'outside' of scholarly thought; the other considers itself, in social theory today, 'cutting edge' scholarship. This fact infuses all our engagements as scholars. Nevertheless, our calm, interested, persistent, open, face-to-face encounter is possible. It is fluid, messy, contradictory, impossible, stimulating and never settled. Just like our engagement with Hongi Hika's mark on paper.

Back to the 'data'

Return to the tā moko on the land deed. We follow Bennett's instructions for a new materialist methodology. That is, we try to mobilize: a 'cultivated, patient, sensory attentiveness to nonhuman forces'; a sensitivity to 'the scent of a thingly power'; an alertness to matter as 'vibrant, vital, energetic, lively, quivering, vibratory, evanescent, and effluescent'. And we bring these posthumanist methods face to face with the immanent relationality of Indigenous ontologies as we consider the tā moko on paper that plays its part in two quite different but equally important New Zealand histories.

Hongi Hika, with his Ngāpuhi people, held the mana whenua or the 'authority of the land' that had been offered to the Pakeha (European settlers), and that those settlers wanted to purchase. On that land at Kerikeri, a small group of missionaries and some local Ngāpuhi chiefs and other observers would have sat down to discuss the dimensions of the agreed land area, and its landmarks, places of Ngāpuhi mana. The talk would have been extensive. Birds would have been flying across the land, maybe a light, mud-smelling, wind moved up the tidal river from the sea. The season was whiringa-ā-rangi, the warmth of the sun was beginning to be felt. Words naming the agreed land area were written on a document (Figure 5.2) by the Pakeha purchaser at the conclusion of

Figure 5.2 The Kerikeri land deed of 1819
Source: Hocken Library, University of Otago. Ref: S08-122 – MS-0070/A

the discussion about the boundaries, and about the quality of the gifts being offered. The sheet of paper, perhaps weighted down with stones or hands against the breeze, was laid on a flat surface. Nearby was placed a bottle of ink, a quill pen, a seal and a block of red sealing wax – these technologies becoming additional participants of engagement. Hongi Hika would have grasped the quill and dipped it in the ink to carefully draw his own tā moko, whose shapes, which traced his identity, he knew by heart. Hongi Hika was familiar with the quill-like implements of tuhi-making (marking the face prior to the tā moko being chiselled into the skin), and had previously held a quill to draw experimental alphabet letters on paper. In his experience of Europeans, he had noted the signature as the imprint of a person's authority and – because *his* chiefly authority was written on his face – invented the idea of the tā moko drawn on paper as a mark equivalent to the Pakeha signature. Hongi Hika could not write his name – but his name on a piece of paper, even penned by his hand, would not have conveyed his mana and authority in the way his tā moko could (see Henare, 2007, pp. 115–116; Ellis, 2014). The time required for Hongi Hika to execute his tohu (sign) in all the small detail he provides, dipping the quill several times into a pot of ink, would have extended the ritual of the exchange between the parties. The venerable rangatira (chief) Rewa added his own tā moko on the lower left. Red wax was dripped on to the paper, and a seal pressed down. Then, rather than only shaking hands with their Europeans, Hongi Hika and Rewa would have pressed their faces to those of the purchasers in a hongi, a solemn exchange of hau, breath, and a seal on enduring relational engagement and mutual loyalty.

Among Maori, chiefly authority or power traditionally resided intra-actively in the responsiveness of people to the chief's presence and his or her words. Here, in this object, for one of the first times in history, the mana (authority and identity) of a chief becomes embedded in paper; the tā moko signature announces the historical moment when Maori authority relations take a new form. By carefully placing his (written) face on a page of other important marks, Hongi Hika's authority enters the page, thereby bringing paper into flows of Maori power. This object – the deed with his imprint – expresses a relationship; it requires something of us; it speaks. This tā moko – with its lines of huge significance, beauty and individual identity – becomes a face against which we might press our own in a hongi, feeling the ridges carved in to the surface of the skin, and mingling our breath with his. Its invitation – 'come feel the warmth of my nose', as Maori say (Shortland, 1990) – does not push us, you ... the Kerikeri land, *away*: alienated forever. It pulls us *in*, in to a relationship with the flows of power represented here.

New materialist attention, with its ontological sensitivities, its positing of objects as actants, opens the researcher to this relationship demand. For many Maori, a line of engagement with the tā moko already exists. Indigenous ontologies already recognize the mauri and the mana – the thing-power and the actant quality – of the signed paper, as outlined above. For Ngāpuhi Maori, Hongi Hika's animate signature is an ongoing movement, an *act*: binding parties together, a covenant sealed by the gift axes. As Hugh Rihari, a descendent of Hongi Hika's people, said, discussing the question of the land sale: rather than a 'full and final payment', the gift exchange of axes for the land was 'to bind the parties together'. The axes, he said, signified 'the obligation of the ancestors to provide the newcomers with protection; to sow them into the land; to weave them into the local tribe – with all the privileges and responsibilities that entailed' (Rihari, 2010, p. 7; see also Salmond, 2012). European land purchasers in the 1830s, such as the explorer John Polack, reported these obligations. Polack said that after signing a land deed with Kamara, the chief declared that Polack 'had become incorporated in his tribe, as an actual possessor of territory in the same district as themselves' (see Jones and Jenkins, 2011, p. 112). Hongi Hika's tā moko, and the ritual gift exchange of axes in return, brings *his* (understood as a collective term here) Pakeha onto *his* land, into *his* territory, into a relationship with Ngāpuhi, and gives them authority to be there, and the authority to use the plants of the land and the forests indefinitely or until their displacement by war (Hohepa, 1999). Hongi Hika's power, including the guns he would gain from his Pakeha, would have meant that displacement was unlikely. The tā moko and the accompanying hongi actively provide that protection. Hongi Hika's willingness to place his tā moko on the paper was itself an act of generosity in his people's interests. He knew that the paper-and-ink language was the language that the Europeans understood: their co-operation – indeed, their purchase of the land and thereby his purchase of them (Hohepa, 1999) – could be assured by the shared engagement with paper.

Finally

Following Bennett's new materialist method, on encountering the inked tā moko on the parchment, we 'scent' its 'thingly power', its desire. Its mauri strikes an open viewer with force. This piece of matter is 'substance in its intra-active becoming – not a thing, but a doing, a congealing of agency' (Barad, 2008, p. 139). The agency of the paper, the ink, the quill, our interpretive gaze, the authority and desires of the mark-maker, and hundreds of thousands of elements came together in this mark: churning assemblages of dead trees and birds and plants (the paper, quill and ink), cotton sails, sea waves, wet wood, fantasies of power, warm bodies, rough ropes, landscapes, religious theories, sweat, pointing hands, axes stacked together, a sly container of gunpowder not mentioned on the deed, birdsong, entangled together to congeal in this text created within swirling, ongoing and incommensurable Indigenous and imperialist meaning systems. All we can do methodologically in the face of these complexities is to 'be', and to remain engaged, and quietly and openly to forestall interpretation.

In Western research contexts, such as this book chapter, we are compelled to reduce analysis to the logic of the sentence, written on the page – not to mention the very significant fact of writing in English, and reproducing the object via a disembodied photographic image. Yet the actant-nature of the tā moko (or any other object) in its self-expressive setting is necessarily in excess of what can be written. It demands to be encountered experientially, affectively, spiritually, in the complex swirling past and present acts of relationships and engagements. And, as an actant, it will not always express itself in the same way. Within a different ontological style, within te ao Maori (the Maori world) Hongi Hika's tā moko speaks differently, no doubt.

References

Alaimo, S. and S. J. Hekman (eds.) (2008) *Material Feminisms* (Bloomington, IN: Indiana University Press).
Barad, K. (2007) *Meeting the Universe Halfway: Quantum Physics and the Entanglement of Matter and Meaning* (Durham: Duke University Press).
Barad, K. (2008) 'Posthumanist Performativity: Toward an Understanding of How Matter Comes to Matter', in S. Alaimo and S. J. Hekman (eds.) *Material Feminisms* (Bloomington, IN: Indiana University Press).
Bennett, J. (2004) 'The Force of Things: Steps towards an Ecology of Matter', *Political Theory*, 32, 347–372.
Bennett, J. (2010) *Vibrant Matter: A Political Ecology of Things* (Durham: Duke University Press).
Clammer, J., S. Poirier and E. Schwimmer (eds.) (2004) *Figured Worlds: Ontological Obstacles in Intercultural Relations* (Toronto: University of Toronto Press).
Clough, P T. (2009) 'The New Empiricism: Affect and Sociological Method', *European Journal of Social Theory*, 12(1), 43–61.
Colebrook, C. (2010) *Deleuze and the Meaning of Life* (London, NY: Continuum).
Deleuze, G. and F. Guattari (1987) *A Thousand Plateaus: Capitalism and Schizophrenia* (London: Athlone Press).
Deloria, B., K. Foehner and S. Scinta (eds.) (1999) *Spirit and Reason: The Vine Deloria, Jr. Reader* (Colorado: Fulcrum Publishing).
Dolphijn, R. and I. van der Tuin (2012) *New Materialism: Interviews and Cartographies* (London: Open Humanities Press).
Durie, M. (2001) *Mauri Ora: The Dynamics of Maori Health* (Auckland, NZ: Oxford University Press).
Ellis, N. (2014) 'Ki tō ringa ki ngā rākau ā te Pakeha? Drawings and Signatures of Moko by Maori in the Early 19th Century', *Journal of the Polynesian Society*, 123(1), 29–66.
Henare, A., M. Holbraad, M., and S. Wastell (2006) *Thinking through things : theorising artefacts ethnographically* (New York: Routledge).
Henare, M. (2007) 'The Maori Leaders' Assembly, Kororipo Pā, 1831', in J. Binney (ed.) *Te Kerikeri 1770–1850* (Auckland, NZ: Auckland University Press).
Hohepa, P. (1999) 'My Musket, My Missionary, My Mana', in A. Calder, J. Lamb and B. Orr (eds.) *Voyages and Beaches: Pacific Encounters* (Honolulu: University of Hawai'i Press).
Horton, J. L. and J. C. Berlo (2013) 'Beyond the Mirror', *Third Text*, 27(1), 17–28.
Hoskins, T. K. (2012) 'A Fine Risk: Ethics in Kaupapa Maori Politics', *New Zealand Journal of Educational Studies*, 47(2), 85–99.
Hoskins, T. K. (2010) 'Responsibility as a Framework for Governance and Care of Water', in G. Williams and B. Martin (eds.) *Responsible Governance of Watersheds: Global Issues of Care for Watersheds with Views from Aotearoa-New Zealand and the Pacific* (Wellington, NZ: Waterscape and Response Trust).

Hoskins, T. K. and A. Jones (2012) 'He aha te kaupapa? Critical Conversations in Kaupapa Māori', Special Issue, *New Zealand Journal of Educational Studies*, 47(2).
Hoskins, T. K., B. Martin and M. Humphries (2011) 'The Power of Relational Responsibility', *Electronic Journal of Business Ethics and Organization Studies*, 16(2), 22–27.
Ingold, T. (2004) 'A Circumpolar Night's Dream', in J. Clammer, S. Poirier and E. Schwimmer (eds.) *Figured Worlds: Ontological Obstacles in Intercultural Relations* (Toronto: University of Toronto Press).
Jones, A. (1999) 'The Limits of Cross-Cultural Dialogue: Pedagogy, Desire and Absolution in the Classroom', *Educational Theory*, 49(3), 299–316.
Jones, A. (2012) 'Dangerous Liaisons: Pakeha, Kaupapa Maori, and Educational Research', *New Zealand Journal of Educational Studies*, 47(2), 101–113.
Jones, A. and K. Jenkins (2008) 'Indigenous Discourse and "the Material": A Post Interpretivist Argument', *International Review of Qualitative Research*, 1(2), 125–144.
Jones, A. and K. Jenkins (2011) *He Kōrero: Words between Us – First Maori-Pakeha Conversations on Paper* (Wellington, NZ: Huia Publishers).
Latour, B. (1993) *We Have Never Been Modern* (Cambridge, MA: Harvard University Press).
Maclure, M. (2013) 'Researching without Representation? Language and Materiality in Post-qualitative Methodology', *International Journal of Qualitative Studies in Education*, 26(6), 658–667.
Marsden, M. (2003) *The Woven Universe: Selected Writings* (Otaki, NZ: Estate of Rev. Māori Marsden).
Massumi, B. (2002) *Parables for the Virtual: Movement, Affect, Sensation* (Durham, NC: Duke University Press).
Pihama, L. (2010) 'Kaupapa Maori Theory: Transforming Theory in Aotearoa', *He Pukenga Kōrero*, 9(2), 5–14.
Rihari, H. (2010) 'Brief of Evidence by Hugh Te Kiri Rihari', 3 June 2010, Te Paparahi o Te Raki Tribunal Inquiry, Waitangi Tribunal, WAI 1040, B013(a).
Roberts, R. M. and P. R. Wills (1998) 'Understanding Maori Epistemology: A Scientific Perspective', in H. Wautischer (ed.) *Tribal Epistemologies: Essays in the Philosophy of Anthropology* (Burlington, VT: Ashgate).
Salmond, A. (2012) 'Ontological Quarrels: Indigeneity, Exclusion and Citizenship in a Relational World', *Anthropological Theory*, 12, 115–141.
Shortland, W. (1990) 'The Unseen World', *New Zealand Geographic*, 5, http://www.nzgeographic.co.nz/.
Smith, G. H., T. K Hoskins and A. Jones (2012) 'Kaupapa Maori: The Dangers of Domestication', *New Zealand Journal of Educational Studies*, 47(2), 10–20.
Smith, L. T. (2012) *Decolonizing Methodologies: Research and Indigenous Peoples* (2nd ed.) (London, NY: Zed Books).
Stengers, I. (2008) 'Experimenting with Refrains: Subjectivity and the Challenge of Escaping Modern Dualisms', *Subjectivity*, 22, 38–59.
Sundberg, J. (2014) 'Decolonising Posthumanist Geographies', *Cultural Geographies*, 21(1), 33–47.
Thomas, N. (1991) *Entangled Objects: Exchange, Material Culture, and Colonialism in the Pacific* (Cambridge, MA: Harvard University Press).

Viveiros de Castro, E. (2004) 'Exchanging Perspectives: The Transformation of Objects into Subjects in Amerindian Ontologies', *Common Knowledge*, 10(3), 463–484.

Wub-e-ke-niew (1995) *We Have the Right to Exist: A Translation of Aboriginal Indigenous Thought: The First Book Ever Published from an Ahnishinahbæóⁿjibway Perspective* (New York: Black Thistle Press).

6
Thinking with an Agentic Assemblage in Posthuman Inquiry

Alecia Youngblood Jackson and Lisa A. Mazzei

Introduction

During the autumn of 2014, a 50-pound standard-issue dormitory mattress made its way across various spaces on the campus of Columbia University in New York. At times, the dark blue foam mattress was carried by one woman, Emma Sulkowicz – a senior visual arts major at Columbia. At other times, Sulkowicz was joined by others on campus (friends and strangers) in a collective carry to share the burden of movement. These solitary and participatory carries were not merely acts of taking one ordinary object from one place to another. Rather, the thing – the mattress – is the focal point of a performance piece, *Carry That Weight*: the senior art thesis conceived by Sulkowicz as a protest against Columbia University's mishandling of her complaint of sexual assault. Sulkowicz has asserted that, two years earlier on the first day of her sophomore year, she had been anally raped in her dorm room by a fellow student with whom she had previously had consensual sex. A university hearing found the accused 'not responsible', a decision that she appealed, yet was upheld.

Sulkowicz turned her abysmal treatment by both the police and university officials into action by conceiving *Carry That Weight* at the intersection of art and political protest. In *New York Magazine*, Sulkowicz stated: 'I was raped in my own dorm bed, and since then that space has become fraught for me. And I feel like I've carried the weight of what happened there with me everywhere since then' (see Roy, 2014). For the protest and performance, she decided to focus on one extra-long twin mattress identical to the model in her dorm room, carrying it until she graduated that spring of 2015 or until the accused left campus. In a video published by the *Columbia Spectator* (see Frost et al.,

2014) Sulkowicz said, 'A mattress is the perfect size for me to just be able to carry it – enough for me to continue with my day but also heavy enough that I have to continue to really struggle with it.' The mattress goes with her wherever and whenever she is on university property. She does not seek help carrying the mattress, but others can carry it for her on their own accord – all part of the 'rules of engagement' for the performance-protest. In a show of support and solidarity, students across the world participated in an international day of action on 29 October 2014: *Carrying the Weight Together* occurred as faculty, staff and students carried mattresses on college and university campuses to support survivors of sexual assault and to raise awareness about sexual and domestic violence.

In this chapter, we think with Jane Bennett's concept of the agentic assemblage together with *Carry That Weight* in order to experiment with its methodological potential for qualitative analysis in the posthuman. We posit posthuman analysis in qualitative research as attending to what happens when things get knotted up with other things in an assemblage, which acts with an agential force. We do this by drawing attention to a heterogeneous assemblage of political protest and performance art and avoid attributing agency solely to people; instead, we take seriously the mobility and trajectory of the nonhuman and its efficacious vitality. We maintain that any agency is *not attributable* to any one thing, but rather *bound to* an assemblage. We conclude that human actions are only one force – and quite possibly the least vital component – in an agentic assemblage, and thus other things must be given their due in a posthuman analysis.

Spatializing posthuman research practices: Thinking with an agentic assemblage

Carry That Weight is a performance-protest event that not only symbolically but also materially compels support and action for victims of sexual violence on college campuses. For our purposes in this contribution to posthuman research methodologies, *Carry That Weight* serves as a site of a spatialized methodology that we use to disturb a conventional, interpretive, qualitative case study method and its boundedness to a specific place, time and event. That is, we are able to refuse a container model of space in case study research that is absolute and inherently bounded. In using a posthuman framework, we are able to map a dynamic, changing typology that is continually being re(con)figured by discursive-material intra-active practices of humans and nonhumans

(Barad, 2007). A spatial methodology in educational research, then, would contest the rigid tracking (i.e., predictable methods) of inquiry that fixes and fixates on that which is presumably within a specific context.

As we will detail through our analysis of *Carry That Weight*, the contours of the event have no specific, enabling background that can be predicted or traced; its context is not limited to Columbia University, or one single rape accusation, or Sulkowicz herself. Similar to Barad's (2007) reconfiguration of space in the posthuman, Bennett's (2010b) conception of context is neither a background that is passive and inert nor a structured constraint that humans use to make meaning. Bennett's perspective of context is important for a posthuman, material analysis. For Bennett, who maintains a 'dogged resistance to anthropocentrism' (p. xvi), context is something that forms a 'contingent tableau' (p. 5) for vibrant matter. Thinking with an agentic assemblage in a posthuman frame, then, challenges the imperative to consider context as a stable, referential and foundational site of meaning-making: *our analysis shifts from a human (i.e., contextual) experience of objects to the vibrant matter animating an agential assemblage.*

Matter, both human and nonhuman, becomes vibrant in an assemblage; objects take on 'thing-power' (Bennett, 2010b, p. xvi). That is, objects become things when they become energetic and make things happen. Agency, in this assemblage, is spatially distributed among vibrant matter, rather than traced to a single source or marked off by a particular boundary. Thus, we treat Sulkowicz's *Carry That Weight* as an 'agentic assemblage' (Bennett, 2010b, p. 111). We do so in order to capture a range of vibrant matter with its own trajectories that, if we pay attention to them, 'enable us to consult nonhumans more closely, or to listen and respond more carefully to their outbreaks, objections, testimonies, and propositions' (Bennett, 2010b, p. 108). Doing so, according to Bennett, is an eco-political imperative.

How does the agentic assemblage of *Carry That Weight* function as an eco-political imperative, while also potentially contributing to new ways of responding to the nonhuman in posthuman research methodologies? *Carry That Weight* is infused with political narratives around rape culture, social justice, activism, symbolic art, gendered violence and institutional policies. Yet the vital materialities of *Carry That Weight* matter too: the mattress, semen, blood, saliva, tears, hair, skin, and the physiology of muscle soreness and growth from carrying such weight. What might be the affective and agential qualities of this materiality? How does the *emergent* porosity of psychic pain, emotional trauma, discursive politics, bodies that carry weight, and the tiny ecosystem of a dorm mattress (even as a stand-in) assemble to produce agency? And how does accounting for these qualities contribute to a posthuman research methodology? These are analytic questions (Jackson and Mazzei, 2012) that we tangle with in this chapter.

To summarize, in our mapping of a spatial methodology for educational research, we use *Carry That Weight's* materiality for its efficacy in/as an assemblage: its 'emergent causality' that produces various intensities and effects that are not fully predictable (Bennett, 2010b, p. 42). We offer an experiment with analysing how matter is neither dull nor static, but can be thought instead as alive and vibrant (Bennett, 2010b). We think with Bennett's concepts of thing-power, the agentic assemblage and distributive agency to provide an account of how a vital materiality is activated in Sulkowicz's performance-protest art. In accounting for the vital materiality in Sulkowicz's performance art, we interrogate the affective and agential qualities of materiality, for example, the mattress, to ask what is made possible when we think the mattress not as a thing, but as having thing-power. Bennett's ontology of vibrant matter offers a style of analysis that 'stretches received concepts of agency, action, and freedom sometimes to the breaking point' (2010b, p. x). Such stretching prompts us to identify possible elements in the agentic assemblage (the mattress, Emma, her accused rapist, students, the media, campus common spaces, institutional administration) that together become an-other body or agent.

In what follows, we tune in to Bennett's movements from thing-power to assemblage to agency and bring to bear the force of her concepts onto our own analysis. Like Bennett, we hope to 'bear witness to the vital materialities that flow through and around us' (p. x) while at the same time according them their due as forceful agents. Such a stance requires that we give up on practices that attempt to sustain the fantasy that as humans we are the only ones in control, thus contributing to what we see as possible for posthuman research methodology.

Thing-power

Bennett (2010b) develops her theory of vital materiality by emphasizing the 'active role of *nonhuman* material in public life' (p. 2, emphasis in original). Bennett rejects the binary distinctions between subjects and objects, as well as the supremacy of human action over things. Her project is an ethical one. She writes that, for the vital materialist, ethics is the recognition of human participation in a shared, vital materiality. We *are* vital materiality and we are surrounded by it, though we do not always see it that way. The ethical task at hand here is to cultivate the ability to discern nonhuman vitality, to become perceptually open to it.

(2010b, p. 14, emphasis in original)

Developing a sense of shared materiality and broader definitions of what ontologically matters is 'good for humans' because these newfound perceptions can be extended to all bodies; 'in a knotted world of vibrant matter, to harm one section of the web may very well be to harm oneself' (2010b, p. 13). Bennett's ethics asks us to pause, linger and playfully delight in our fascination with objects, to creatively (and temporarily) anthropomorphize[1] them and experiment with our own naiveté. We do this by imagining the material vitality that we *incompletely* share with nonhumans so that we treat things more ecologically, ultimately offering that ethical treatment to humans.

To notice the subtle connections between and overlap of human and nonhuman, how we and it 'slip-slide into each other' (p. 4), Bennett proposes that we attend to the force of things. Things are not simply 'there', inert; neither are things merely symbols nor representations of human conditions. 'We' are not really in charge of those 'its', claims Bennett, and she positions nonhuman materialities as potentially forceful agents, as 'vivid entities not *entirely* reducible to the contexts in which (human) subjects set them' (p. 5, emphasis added). The force of a vital materiality is called 'thing-power'.

We can turn to Sulkowicz's protest-performance piece and the thing-power of the mattress to experiment with Bennett's vital materiality, 'to see how analyses of political events might change if we gave the force of things more due' (p. viii). For example, many reports in the media analyse the collective carries as symbolic; in a *New York Times* article, Smith (2014) wrote, '*Carry that Weight*... involves Ms. Sulkowicz carrying a 50-pound mattress wherever she goes on campus.... Analogies to the Stations of the Cross may come to mind, especially when friends or strangers spontaneously step forward and help her carry her burden, which is both actual and symbolic.' Certainly, we do not deny the culturally symbolic force of the performance-protest, but we want to analyse the political nature of *Carry That Weight* differently by positioning the mattress as vital materiality – not as an object, nor a mere metaphor, but as something that, in the assemblage, takes on thing-power.

As we have described, Sulkowicz created *Carry That Weight* as a political response to Columbia University's mishandling of her rape case. Sulkowicz has described her process of artistic creation as at first including a stationary range of elements, including recordings of her interviews with police, but then finally settling on using only the mattress in her mobile work of art-protest. Yet, we argue that the *composite* of *Carry That Weight* becomes an actant[2]; agency is not solely granted to a human. That is, Sulkowicz is only one actant in *Carry That Weight*, and perhaps not the most forceful one: the mattress as imbued with thing-power distributes agency differentially, 'across a wider range of ontological types' (Bennett, 2010b, p. 9). We will return to this idea of a composite actant in the next section on assemblages, but in the remainder of this section, we describe the thing-power of the mattress.

Thing-power, according to Bennett (2010b), is 'the curious ability of inanimate things to animate, to act, to produce effects dramatic and subtle' (p. 6). By positioning the mattress as having thing-power, we can perceive how it *acts* as a catalyst for protests and collective displays of solidarity as friends or strangers step in to help carry Sulkowicz's burden. The mattress, though it is not the actual mattress on which the rape occurred, produces effects and affects: the mattress compels action. Our point is that the collective carries result not simply from a plea on the part of Sulkowicz (we pick up ideas of causality in a later section). In a vital materialism, it becomes possible for others to participate in the protest because of the shared vitality between human and nonhuman, between people and mattresses – how people may be in and of their own relations, identifications and histories *not with another human but with the world of an object*. As we discussed earlier, because of the thing-power of the mattress, the 'context' of *Carry That Weight* is not reduced to Sulkowicz's case – the event spreads, and other mattresses are carried on other campuses across the world in solidarity. The mattress becomes vital to making these things happen, and not always in a figurative or representational sense. Everything in a collective carry is full of vibrant matter: the mattress itself gathers pieces of humans and nonhumans as it is picked up, carried, dragged, dropped – accumulating skin, dirt, dust and sweat, and perhaps taking on different shapes as it is handled and squeezed into tight spaces.

In the *New York Times* interview, Sulkowicz said that the performance is giving her new muscles and an inner strength she didn't know she had. Thus, the mattress sheds its own materiality onto humans, and its weight produces change in human bodies on physiological levels: lifting heavy things disrupts homeostasis in the body, which spurs muscle growth through chemical changes in cells, metabolic stress and hormone shifts. Becoming stronger via a protest, then, is not limited to spiritual or emotional growth but has its own material dimensions that are compelled by the thing-power of the mattress. This gestures towards the ethical dimensions of the event in Bennett's terms: that experimenting with how we share and *exchange* vital materiality with things in our world helps us to extend that perspective to all bodies, human and nonhuman. To carry a mattress in this event is to notice the vitalism of the thing, as well as caring for humans who have been traumatized – the mattress, as an intervener, holds all potential responses, exchanges and differences on a flat plane. These effects, 'dramatic and subtle', are animated by the thing-power of the mattress.

When things demand attention, when things provoke affect, when they make things happen – they become more than simply 'stuff' (or isolated, singular objects) but full of thing-power. Thing-power is entirely ontological, in that it acknowledges what things *do*: their capacities to affect, their interventions and their roles as active players. The mattress's thing-power 'brings to the fore the becoming of things' (Bennett, 2010b, p. 8). Humans and nonhumans in *Carry That Weight* are becoming-mattress, becoming-activist; the becomings are distributed across all ontological types. Everything is heightened and raised to be 'vibrant matter' in the way that Bennett (2010b) argues: 'If matter itself is lively, then not only is the difference between subjects and objects minimized... All bodies become more than mere objects' (p. 13).

As an actant in an assemblage, the mattress takes on liveliness with its own agential force. The mattress's vital materialism brings its agency 'into sharper relief' (Bennett, 2010b, p. 13). We have touched upon the assemblage and agency in our discussion of thing-power, and we move more specifically towards those concepts in the next sections.

Assemblage

Bennett's 'agentic assemblage' (2010b, p. 111) is a concept that flows from the vitalism of Deleuze and Guattari and does not reduce nonhuman agency to the purview of human action. What Bennett offers moves beyond Deleuze and Guattari's concept of the assemblage towards a grouping of 'things' both animate and inanimate. The mattress, the sexually assaulted student, the accused, outdated and ignored policies on sexual assault, campus landmarks and classrooms, staircases, elevators, politicians, bystanders, fellow victims, affects, sweat, muscles – 'proper to the grouping as such', all belong to the assemblage in a way that produces an 'agency *of* the assemblage' (p. 24).

> Deleuze and Guattari (1987) wrote that an assemblage comprises two segments: one of content, the other of expression. On the one hand it is a *machinic assemblage* of bodies, of actions and passions, an intermingling of bodies reacting to one another; on the other hand, it is a *collective assemblage* of enunciation, of acts and statements, of incorporeal transformations attributed to bodies.
>
> (p. 88, emphasis in original)

Deleuze and Guattari's assemblage includes multiple elements: discursive signs, utterances, bodies – all existing on different temporal and spatial scales that work collectively to produce a territory.

Bennett pushes further the materiality of the assemblage away from objects in a human domain: 'While [assemblages] include humans and their (social, legal, linguistic) constructions, [they] also include some very active and powerful nonhumans' (p. 24). Rather than attributing agency to the discrete objects and bodies that come together in the assemblage, in this reading we look at the 'grouping' as such that 'not only has a distinctive history of formation but a finite life span' (p. 24). In other words, it is an agency of the assemblage enunciated in this moment of spacetime re(con)figuring (Barad, 2007). As the persistence of rape culture on university campuses in the US is widely reported in the news media, and protests and forums are held on campuses nationwide to challenge the weight with which big-time college athletics and a system of university-sanctioned fraternities and sororities contributes to this rape culture, enter *Carry That Weight* and the vibrant materiality of Sulkowicz's mattress that gathers force more robustly than might occur in a different moment of spacetime re(con)figuration. While Bennett's thing-power draws attention to the vital materiality of objects, she is careful to emphasize that objects, such as the mattress, take on thing-power when they are *of* assemblages, in a 'complicated web of dissonant connections between bodies' (p. 4). She goes on to explain:

> Assemblages are ad hoc groupings of diverse elements, of vibrant materials of all sorts. Assemblages are living, throbbing confederations that are able to function despite the persistent presence of energies that confound them from within. They have uneven topographies, because some of the points at which the various affects

and bodies cross paths are more heavily trafficked than others, and so power is not distributed equally across its surface.

(Bennett, 2010b, pp. 23–24)

The mattress with its thing-power intervenes precisely because of its location (both spatially and temporally) in an assemblage: it 'makes things happen, becomes the decisive force catalyzing an event' (p. 9). By placing thing-power *as* an assemblage, Bennett gestures towards a distributed agency, rather than an agency 'being a capacity localized in a human body or in a collective produced (only) by human efforts' (p. 23). While the elements of the assemblage work together, their 'coordination does not rise to the level of an organism. Rather, its jelling endures alongside energies and factions that fly out from it and disturb it from within' (p. 24). This jelling, this distributed agency happens *as* an agentic assemblage.

Distributed agency as an agentic assemblage

In order to further explore materiality in Bennett's agentic assemblage and as an example of the 'swarm of vitalities' at play, we look again at *Carry That Weight*. Thinking agency as constituted as a swarm is to refuse the positing of *a* subject as 'the root cause of an effect' (Bennett, 2010b, p. 31). The task then, according to Bennett, is to identify the contours of the swarm and the kind of relations that are made and unmade between its bits (p. 32). Conceived at the intersection of art and political protest, *Carry That Weight* combines aspects of endurance, participatory relational aesthetics and a significant expenditure of time and energy. Because of the mattress's mobility into public common areas, hallways, classrooms, buses – into any space that is owned by Columbia University – it is no longer an inert object but a thing doing something. The mattress intervenes in spaces that are outside its ordinary place of human context and use. That is, things exhibit thing-power when material 'stuff' becomes recognizable, not for how it is associated with the human (i.e., a mattress 'belongs' in a private dorm room) but becomes a catalytic force. All these 'things' then contribute to the contour of the swarm, of the bodies in the swarm, and of this assemblage that pulsates with energy in this timespace. The thing-power of the mattress is to be understood in the network of the other affiliates of the assemblage and how they act in this particular spacetime configuration to produce a condition of possibility. We view agency as Bennett does, through the relatedness of the terms 'efficacy', 'trajectory' and 'causality', in order to loosen our hold on intentionality attributable to a rational, humanist subject and to provide an alternative to conventional, interpretive, qualitative case study method and its boundedness to a specific place, time and event.

Sulkowicz, who designed and is carrying out the protest-performance, acts with 'efficacy', explained by Bennett as the 'creativity of agency', or 'capacity to make something new appear or occur' (p. 31). In an interview, Sulkowicz spoke of her interest in art that elicits a powerful response, and it is this creativity that animates or propels the mattress in a way not previously conceived. The point is that the subject, in this case Sulkowicz, is not the single, root cause of an effect, as she could not predict the type of response that her performance or the mattress would evoke. Certainly, Sulkowicz might have a hoped-for response, but the particular assemblage is a product not just of her intervention, or the presence of the mattress, or the response by bystanders, but is made possible in the moment of distributed agency. If we consider agency in the way that Bennett does as a swarm of agents, then we 'loosen the connections between efficacy and the moral subject' (p. 32). The moral subject, Sulkowicz, does design the thesis project; however, the response by others to carry that weight with her is attributable to 'power possessed by nonhuman bodies *too*' (p. 32, emphasis added).

The actions by bystanders who step forward to help Sulkowicz carry her burden in the form of the 50-pound mattress speak to agency as bound to Bennett's idea of 'trajectory' in which intentionality or causality are not ways of thinking agency. Instead, actants 'produce a movement *away* from somewhere' (p. 32, emphasis in original). While *Carry That Weight* was conceived as a protest-performance piece with specific 'rules of engagement', it is not *only* Sulkowicz's or other student's experiences of sexual assault that 'causes' others to help in a collective carrying of the mattress. Nor is it her act of carrying the mattress in public spaces that has 'caused' protests on the campus to raise awareness of sexual assault, or the filing of a complaint against the university's handling of gender misconduct or sexual assault cases. The concept of trajectory helps us explain this as a condition of possibility, understood by Bennett via Derrida's messianic notion of that which is to come, a future that affirms the 'existence of a certain trajectory or drive to assemblages without insinuating intentionality or purposiveness' (p. 32). The condition of possibility in this instance is located in the sight of a slight woman burdened by the weight of a 50-pound mattress, spreading into heterogeneous spaces. This distribution creates the condition of possibility or movement of others to attach to the 'vibrant matter' (the mattress), thus becoming part of the assemblage.

The third element in Bennett's agentic swarm is that of causality, which she rightly cautions is the most vague. If agency is distributive, which she asserts and we agree, then pinning down instances of 'efficient causality' in which a chain of simple bodies acts as the sole impetus for an effect is exceedingly rare (p. 32). Bennett explains this as causality in an emergent, fractal sense rather than as linearly and directly causal. The mattress, the performance-protest piece, the alleged bungling of a sexual assault complaint, a victim's decision to resist, contracting muscles and other bodies who share the burden: all are agents in the agentic assemblage. Yes, the artist did design a thesis project to be carried out over a period of up to eight months, enacted in a very visible and public fashion that invites performers, and it is obvious that her design and actions may have 'caused' others to respond in a particular way, but we cannot 'know' why others take up burdens of protest – we cannot trace causality to a single source. The point is that, in an agentic swarm of fractal causality, other actants contribute to a distributive, emergent agency that spreads across a flattened plane. Everything in the assemblage works as an aggregate: the interminglings produce affects, potentialities and desires. The *assemblage* is that which creates a territory and the potential for re- and/or deterritorialization – not an individual, intentional subject. Bennett uses Deleuze and Guattari's assemblage and leverages its heterogeneity to argue that 'the locus of agency is always a human-nonhuman working group' (p. xvii) and produces her theory of a distributed agency in the 'agentic assemblage'.

Our aim in providing an analysis of *Carry That Weight* is to demonstrate what a posthuman methodology might look like. In addition to theorizing distributed agency, and advocating a spatialized methodology, we take our cue once again from Bennett, who urges that what is needed is a rewriting of the 'default grammar of agency, a grammar that assigns activity to people and passivity to things' (p. 119). Such rewriting might produce an anthropomorphizing that, while risky, works against an entrenched anthropocentrism 'bound up with a hubristic demand that only humans and God can bear any traces of creative agency' (p. 120). If researchers continue to rely on the accounts provided by humans to provide a basis for knowledge claims, then they remain stuck in an ontological divide that continues to 'insinuate a hierarchy of subjects over objects' and that obstructs thinking agency otherwise (p. 120).

> It is hard to fathom the effect 'Carry that Weight' will have as it proceeds – on Columbia, on Ms. Sulkowicz, on the consciousness of sexual assault on campus, or on the thinking of people who encounter her performance.
>
> (Smith, 2014, p. C5)

It is not *understanding* the effect that is important, but *noticing what is set in motion* – at Columbia, on university campuses in the US and abroad, or for those whose encounters are rewritten by the agency of the agentic assemblage. Furthermore, we believe that attending to a spatialized, flat distribution of agency is, as Bennett asserts, a political project. For qualitative research methodologies, this becomes important in, for example, educational research that is short-sighted in attributing all political problems (in schools) to the level of individuals, thus missing the vital materialities that come into play. A posthuman methodology would have us ask: what actants in an agentic assemblage set in motion educational issues and problems? We argue that refusing a container view of space that puts boundaries around human-centred case study research (via planned methods and definitions of 'the case') can help to activate political analyses of *emergent* agentic assemblages.

Conclusion: The agentic assemblage and posthuman inquiry

In this chapter, we have experimented with an analysis of an event using Bennett's posthuman concepts in order to illuminate their use for qualitative methodologies, in particular case study; we aimed to show not only the importance of attending to the agency of vital materialities in analysis but also the spatialized reconfiguration of method and analysis. We have attempted to show that bodies and actors in a network, or assemblage, can no longer be thought as subjects and objects. Nor can we any longer think of doers (agents) as a *single* force behind deeds or actions. The materiality of *Carry That Weight* in an agentic assemblage 'draws human attention sideways, away from an ontologically ranked Great Chain of Being and toward a greater appreciation of the complex entanglements of human and nonhuman' (Bennett, 2010b, p. 112). We agree with Bennett (2010a) that nonhuman materialities should be presented as themselves bonafide agents rather than as 'instrumentalities, techniques of power, recalcitrant objects, or social constructs' (p. 47). As we have described above via our analysis of *Carry That Weight,* these nonhuman materialities are bonafide agents with 'thing-power' (Bennett, 2010b, p. 2). In an agentic assemblage, these things act with a force. It is not just that separate things in the assemblage act with a force, but the assemblage itself produces intensities in a theory of distributed agency, which is both emergent and contingent. What might this contingent and emergent agency – not residing in one thing but continually made and unmade as an assemblage – offer qualitative inquiry (particularly analysis) in posthumanism?

With no subjectivity or centre, the agentic assemblage is a hub of emergence and possibility with various agents coming in and out of focus. Analysis, then, in this posthuman agentic assemblage is not bounded by space, place, or time. There are no agents that act qualitatively differently than others. Speaking of the agency of assemblages 'is likely to be a stronger counter to human exceptionalism' (Bennett, 2010b, p. 34), thus compelling researchers to be vigilant to the compulsion to link actions, motives and outcomes to specific subjects, be they human or nonhuman. Rather than identifying the discrete agents in the assemblage, we, as researchers attempting posthuman methodological practices, consider forces, vitalities, things, that act on and through vital materialities to produce the assemblage that we also become with/in. The implications for thinking what constitutes 'analysis', or what is given weight in the doing of analysis, is no longer a relevant question. The question becomes how to attend to emergent and contingent forces.

Bennett's agentic assemblage within a posthuman frame of 'vibrant matter' is a *political analysis*; the imperative is to attend to agentic capacity as 'differentially distributed across a wider range of ontological types' (2010b, p. 9). If agents are everywhere in the artefacts of our research, in the materiality of our field sites, in our analyses, and in our knowledge-producing practices, then what is to happen to our practices, our researcher selves and our thinking qualitative data and data analysis differently? To do *analysis in the posthuman* is to embrace an ethical responsibility of attending to vibrant matter in all aspects of our projects and mapping the forces (or actants) as an agentic assemblage. Rather than reducing qualitative analysis to rely on the so-called 'knowable' that appears via a 'conscious' human subject (including ourselves), a posthuman orientation seeks to notice, as much as possible, the workings and doings of *all* agents as an assemblage. These agential forces are not something to be mined in the textual artefacts of our research, nor is it to ascribe meaning by a focus on what our participants (or we) say about those forces, but it is to watch for – and more importantly, *attend to* – what happens when heterogeneous things intra-act with force and affect.

In such a posthuman ethical analysis, we give up on worn-out concepts of intentional human subjects and attend to an unpredictable movement of flows with an eye towards how particular entanglements pressure and produce reconfigurings. Doing so helps us to avoid traps of humanistic or interpretive analytic strategies that tend to take for granted what agency 'is' (what humans do and say) and that seek to fix meaning based on one's articulation of 'experience'. According to Bennett, 'A lot happens to the concept of agency once nonhuman things are figured less as social constructions and more as actors, and once humans themselves are assessed not as autonoms but as vital materialities' (p. 21). Being faithful to the 'distributive quality of "agency"' (p. 21) is noting that these things, these vital materialities, together as an agentic assemblage, possess agency: not in and of themselves, but in this agential assemblage they become an-other body or agent.

Ackowledgement

The authors wish to thank the reviewers of this chapter, and the book editors, for their insightful and provocative comments.

Notes

1. See pp. 119–120 of *Vibrant Matter* for Bennett's discussion.
2. Bennett (2010b) relies on Latour (1996, 2004) for her use of 'actant': 'a term for a source of social action; an actant can be human or not, or, most likely a combination of both...An actant is neither an object or subject but an "intervener" ' (p. 9).

References

Barad, K. (2007) *Meeting the Universe Halfway: Quantum Physics and the Entanglement of Matter and Meaning* (Durham: Duke University Press).
Bennett, J. (2010a) 'A Vitalist Stopover on the Way to New Materialism', in D. Coole and S. Frost (eds.) *New Materialisms: Ontology, Agency, and Politics* (Durham: Duke University Press), pp. 47–69.
Bennett, J. (2010b) *Vibrant Matter: A Political Economy of Things* (Durham: Duke University Press).
Deleuze, G. and F. Guattari (1987) *A Thousand Plateaus: Capitalism and Schizophrenia* (Minneapolis: University of Minnesota Press).
Frost, F., B. Guthrie and M. Cunnane (2014) 'Emma Sulkowicz, CC '15, to Mix Performance Art, Sexual Assault Protest', *Columbia Daily Spectator*, Retrieved from http://columbiaspectator.com/multimedia/2014/09/02/emma-sulkowicz-cc-15-mix-performance-art-protest. Accessed October 2014.
Jackson, A. Y. and L. A. Mazzei (2012) *Thinking with Theory in Qualitative Research: Viewing Data across Multiple Perspectives* (London: Routledge).

Roy, J. (2014) 'Columbia Student Will Carry a Mattress Everywhere Until Her Alleged Rapist Is Expelled', *New York Magazine*, Retrieved from http://nymag.com/daily/intelligencer/2014/09/columbia-student-art-project-protests-her-rapist.html. Accessed October 2014.

Smith, R. (2014) 'In a Mattress, a Lever for Art and Political Protest', *The New York Times*, Retrieved from http://www.nytimes.com/2014/09/22/arts/design/in-a-mattress-a-fulcrum-of-art-and-political-protest.html?_r=0. Accessed October 2014.

7
Flickering, Spilling and Diffusing Body/Knowledge in the Posthuman Early Years

Rachel Holmes and Liz Jones

Introduction

Following Deleuze and Whitehead, we begin with a movement from without, a process, never with a 'subject' of a process. This page merely opens onto what Manning and Massumi describe as 'a commotion of relational activity, each vying to be written down, to be the conduit of the field's summing up in a determinate expression' (2014, p. 12):

> Texts are traversed by a movement that comes from without, that does not begin on the page (nor the preceding pages), that is not bounded by the frame of the book; it is entirely different from the imaginary movement of representation or the abstract movement of concepts that habitually take place among words and within the mind of the reader.
>
> (Deleuze, cited in Blondel, 1985, p. 145)

Amid this commotion, the moment of beginning our chapter is defined by what our senses are compelled to attend to (Mukhopadhyay, 2008). Yet even before our pen and paper begin to seduce each other in virtual intimacy, relational activity is already at work across heterogeneous fields of experience: the echoes of an invitation to write; our calling to familiar systems of linguistic symbols; collaborating in the imaginary of the emerging book; awkward relations with deforestation; seductive ecologies of preceding chapters; the ebb and flow across French, Canadian, Italian and American theorists; the shifting terrain and traditions of philosophy; the politics of the printing press and technology; the nourishing workings of the dorsal aorta and a multiplicity of intensely vibrating senses. Caught among the pulsations of such commotion, we are compelled to attend to the most captivating of expressions and orient ourselves towards some text and an image, acknowledging that 'there is a politics to how we distribute our attention' (Ahmed, 2008, p. 30).

Mummy, do you like being human?

No, not really. Do you?

No. I'd like to be something useful, like a door handle.

(Alfred, 2015)

Figure 7.1 Francesca Woodman, untitled
Source: Providence, Rhode Island (1976).
Note: Vintage gelatin silver print, image size 5 15/16 x 5 13/16 in Estate ID / File Name P.057.

When Mukhopadhyay sees the door he does not immediately see a threshold for passage...He sees qualities in a texture of integral experience...As it becomes determinate, an object form separates out from the dynamic form, an affordance opens, and the tendency for describing makes itself felt, turning to language. The field has pressed on toward expressing itself in language.

(Manning and Massumi, 2014, p. 16)

Empirical materials, an image and a quotation – we are struck by their immanent relationality. As the text and image pass between us, a background movement of affordances somehow manoeuvres the image and text to the forefront of the aforementioned and ongoing commotion. Unfolding in/onto each other, as generative forces that participate in the production of new subjective possibilities, as 'one artwork catches another in its movement of thought' (Manning, 2015, cited in Grusin, 2015, p. xxiii), they produce ideas of doors, handles and wood; shadows and surfaces; fullness and flatness; voices and vibrations; human bodies, edges, flows and intensities. For Liz and me as researchers and following Guattari (1995), the movement of thought caught not in the presence of passively representative images, but in vectors of subjectivation, bridging the text, absorbs our attention into *'door handle'*, arising from, while remaining deeply entangled with the splintering fibres striating the flat surface of the door. The handle somehow modulates our collaborative, differentiated experiencing, busying our disintegrating bodies and creating a panoply of sense (Manning and Massumi, 2014): 'When the moment has [door handled] itself into a determinate emergence, consciousness begins to flicker...the singled-out object "[door handle]" bears all the weight of it' (Manning and Massumi, 2014, p. 15).

With consciousness flickering in the movements of the ideas passing between and across us both, we scavenge around the transgressive posthuman spaces evoked by the images and text, already preparing to write about Alfred's imagining of himself as a *door handle*, 'already tending toward expressions in use-value' (Manning and Massumi, 2014, p. 8) – an opening, into another space, an escape, solace, place to hide. In this use-value, the handle-ness almost disintegrates, instead figuring as already opening the door to pass through. It's use-full-ness is critically apparent to us. However, Mukhopadhyay (2008) has other stories to tell:

I would remember a wall not by its flatness but because of a nail that had cast its shadow under the overhead light. And because of that nail, I could imagine and grow my probable stories around it... The story behind the object is far more important to me than the object.

(2008, pp. 35, 54)

This opening paragraph allows us momentarily to 'out', but also to slow down our tendencies to foreground the for-ness and use-value of objects as carriers of sense and meaning-full expression in qualitative research. In slowing down our anthropocentric urgencies, we hope to 'find the force that gives a new sense to what... [we]... say, and hang the text upon it' (Deleuze, 1997, p. 145), where different stories around the door, the door handle (and other empirical materials) will grow. We can question whether the human subject (as researcher) alone is sufficient to account for any field's fuller relational activities. And if not, how can movements in a much richer event effect interruptions to our modulating experiences? How do fields of tensions resist our surrendering of them to recognizable, digestible structures? If, as Manning (2014) proposes, there is never a body, an object, an entity as such, then how do we experience the edgings and contourings, forces and intensities of the field itself, to 'perceive the relational quality of a welling environment that dynamically appears in a jointness of experience' (Manning and Massumi, 2014, pp. 7–8)? What of the shadow, the non/sense, the thing, figures, openings, temporality, abstraction, movements, intervals, immanence and curation that feature jointly in this commotion of a foreground-background embrace, co-actively producing door handle, nail, bodies and language in the images and empirical materials?

This chapter augments the idea of process ontology as we consider what it means to open ourselves as researchers to fuller relational activities in qualitative inquiry. We will consider what our open approach to post/ nonhuman theoretical ideas might offer us as researchers in the field of childhood studies and engage with extracts of empirical materials to examine how the idea of nomadic thought or process ontology produces a complexity that refuses straightforward stories, explanations and deconstructions that occupy anthropocentric resting places. The chapter is organized as three related sections: the first examines how the post- and nonhuman turn in qualitative research affords us moments of methodological improvisation and curation, where our senses might pay attention differently to the relational processes at work in empirical materials and in dismantling the human-form as researcher: 'In the wonder of improvisation, the "I" is effectively left behind' (Manning, 2014, p. 165). In the second section, we take a closer look at the idea and processes of the nomad in relation to our research writing practices.

Taking flight from the captivating expressions brought to our attention earlier by Woodman, Mukhopadhyay and Alfred, we spend time here interfering with cross-disciplinary fields. Carried by the impulses of art and philosophy as they course through the molecules of door handles, nails, full and flat worlds, across surfaces, into shadows and luminous air, we document our adventures (Whitehead, 1967) felting empirical materials. The third section continues working with nomadic possibilities for posthuman studies of early childhood in the hope of dismantling what Braidotti describes as 'hegemonic and exclusionary views of subjectivity' (Braidotti, 1994, p. 23). We augment the chapter's commotion of relational activity further, drawing in empirical materials from early years practice, literary and technoscientific studies to produce shadow stories as spectral figures that pollute the natural order of the 'proper' child in education.

The post- and nonhuman turn: Challenging that which we thought we had already rethought

> The middle is by no means an average. On the contrary it is where things pick up speed. Between things does not designate a localizable relation going from one thing to the other and back again, but a perpendicular direction, a transversal movement that sweeps one and the other away, a stream without beginning or end that undermines its banks and picks up speed in the middle.
>
> (Deleuze and Guattari, 1987, p. 28)

Given that much of our time is spent mingling in the terrain of early years education, we are entangled, inexplicably, with modernity and Enlightenment logic. Yet, we have also been swept up by theories that have sought to erode the very foundations upon which contemporary early childhood education is founded. Such foundations are secured by salient discourses including liberal humanism and rationality, which together mark the child out as a redemption figure, an emissary of and for salvation. Our past and continuing immersions in, for example, post-structuralism (Brown and Jones, 2001) postmodernism (MacLure et al., 2011), feminism (Jones et al., 2011), feminist post-structuralism (Holmes and Jones, 2012) and deconstruction (Holmes, 2010; Jones, 2010) butt against and seek to constantly erode the bastions of Enlightenment logic that MacLure (2011, p. 997) succinctly summarizes as a 'belief in reason and progress, unmediated access to truth and the agency of the centred, humanist self'.

As muddlers within the Deleuzeguattarian middle, the momentum that gathers within the ebbs and flows of posthumanism catches and snags transversally, moving us into ever more sceptic streams, where the (re)thought always already needs to be rethought. For us this is particularly imperative where neoliberalism, government policies and a particular notion of progress ensure, for example, that the decentring of the subject is an unfinished project. 'The child' within neoliberalism augments, underpins and sustains a confidence that 'human beings are exceptional, autonomous and set above the world that lies at their feet' (Badmington, 2011, p. 374; see also Cannella and Wolff, 2014). Such anthropocentrism is further sustained by the pervading and persuasive tenacity to cling to the 'reassuring familiarity of common sense' (Braidotti, 2013, p. 1) where narratives of rationality, normality, progress and mastery are secured. As other critical commentators have made clear, much of this common sense in early childhood education is predicated on and reproduced through developmental psychology that legitimizes certain truths (Burman, 1994/2007; Cannella, 1997; Walkerdine, 1988) and in so doing positively privileges some children while rendering others as 'other'; that is lacking intellectually, socially, emotionally, linguistically and so on. As a 'technology of the self' (Foucault, 1975), linear narratives of growth and development are directed towards organization and stratification of the body so what is produced is a generalized standard, a 'norm' that stands for 'normality, normalcy and normativity' (Braidotti, 2013, p. 26; MacLure et al., 2011). Deleuze and Guattari summarize:

> You will be organized, you will be an organism, you will articulate your body – otherwise you're just depraved. You will be signifier and signified, interpreter and interpreted – otherwise you're just a deviant. You will be a subject, nailed down as one, a subject of the enunciation recoiled into a subject of the statement–otherwise you're just a tramp.
>
> (1987, p. 159)

The world, as many have noted, is caught in a maelstrom of eruptions where the escalation of matter, including robotics, reproductive technologies, advanced prosthetics and so on, has blurred traditional dyads that have traditionally served to secure 'man' as the subject (Braidotti, 2013). Yet, as we have inferred, many of our academic endeavours are situated where children are constantly encouraged to practice forms of mastery couched in liberal humanist discourses, where caring for the class rabbit, the guinea pig, an African snail or tiny tiddlers becomes a practice in caring that has quasi-colonial connotations embedded within it. And while we recognize that learning to care is quite a reasonable expectation, have we not got to the position or a situation where the very notion of 'reasonableness' is readily understood as an 'outcome', an outcome moreover that can be quickly summarized, cross-checked and rendered into a 'fact'? And in so doing, have we not then subtracted care so that it is stripped of complexities and becomes a readily recognized, universal and over-generalized single entity: care = common sense?

Caught as we are in the tendrils of modernity where the legacy of the Enlightenment still persistently trails, we persist in finding pockets of air. Our own transversal movements with posthumanism molecularly garner and mingle with previous theoretical movements. Herbrechter and Callus (2013) propose that posthumanism could be understood as a theory of 'replenishment' compensating for post-structuralism's theoretical acute focus on language. And while this line chimes with Barad's statement that 'Language has been given too much power' (Barad, 2003, p. 801) we want to understand language as molecular, where our task is less to do with subtracting language and more to do with sensing its relational activity. This, as Massumi and Manning (2014) forewarn, takes time: 'It takes time for the field of experience to actively sort itself out towards its coming to a determinate expression' (Manning and Massumi, 2014, p. 16).

Picking up speed, taking our time

While we agree with Badminton that anthropocentrism – with its assured insistence that human exceptionalism is 'no longer an adequate or convincing account of the way of the world' (Badminton, 2011, p. 381) – such a situation does raise some tricky questions for us. Looking across at our own endeavours, while we have tried to remain faithful to the mantra of 'opening- up' so as not to code, box or tie data down (Holmes, 2014; Holmes and Jones, 2013; Jones, 2013) we have also played safe, lacking courage to move beyond the banal, where a 'bland dialect of mutual regard' worked at 'suppressing, idiom, diversity, affect, and conflict' (MacLure, 2011, p. 998). It is, we think, within the process of data analysis that this is exceptionally challenging, particularly when one wants to question the status quo but where endemic habits surrounding research predispose some forms of outputs while diminishing others. Nevertheless, as the UK settles down for another five years of Tory government there is an urgency to rethink so as to reconfigure ways of thinking, feeling and writing. How, for example, do we (re)address a concept such as 'quality'? In general, there is a universal discourse where the notion of 'quality early years education' is implicated in an agenda that is directed at raising educational standards both nationally and globally, engendering a stable society and securing economic stability. Yet what might be some of the repercussions if a concept such as 'quality' is examined within the epistemological and ontological theoretical shifts that are afforded by posthumanism? As researchers, how would we work with data in ways that avoid making judgements against a normalized standard of what does and does not constitute 'quality'? In what follows, while we will not be addressing the concept of 'quality' per se, we will nevertheless be attempting to articulate the methodological/ epistemological/ontological work that we are practising, where we try to pay acute attention to stuff that is immeasurable. Such an endeavour necessitates embracing a different logic, a different way of thinking where the mental habits of linearity and objectivity are resisted. As feminist researchers we need to (continue) to invent ways to live and write posthuman research, to reconceptualize what Braidotti (2006, p. 199) describes as 'a new politics on the basis of a more adequate understanding of how the contemporary subject functions'.

This contemporary posthuman subject is a fascinatingly controversial figure conceptualized as co-constituted of matter, symbolic, sociological, material, biological and political forces; she makes cuts, is intra-active, entangled and always becoming. The feminist politics are claimed; the body in 'its very materiality plays an *active* role in the workings of power' (Barad, 2003, p. 809). As Frost proposes, our job is to closely examine 'how the forces of matter and the processes of organic life contribute to the play of power or provide elements or modes of resistance to it' (2011, p. 70). In this endeavour, Braidotti stresses the need for thinking as 'a nomadic activity, which takes place in the transitions between potentially contradictory positions' (2006, p. 199). Treading warily and (re)presenting nomadically at the transversal movements of modernity/postmodernity /posthumanism, we want to eschew the straight, the automatic, the banal and the harmoniously polite. In so doing, we will (re)set our sights and pursue the desire to 'acknowledge nature, the body and materiality in the fullness of their becoming'. Goaded by Barad, can we resist 'resorting to the optics of transparency or opacity, the geometries of absolute exteriority or interiority?' Can we refuse 'the theorization of the human as either pure cause or pure effect?'

(Barad, 2003, p. 812). Can we, as Manning suggests, leave the 'I' behind? And in so doing can we practice and pursue nomadic inquiry, process ontology or what Braidotti refers to as 'as-if' – a 'technique of strategic re-location in order to rescue what we need of the past in order to trace paths of transformation of our lives here and now' (1994, p. 6)?

Nomadic (writing) movements: Door, handle, shadows and alchemy

This second section of the chapter develops our interest in research as nomadic and trans-situational, an interest that situates the research process as aggressively creative, in continuous flux but always demanding disruption to that flux. Deleuze, while refusing to pin the concept of nomad down, does forewarn that 'It's not enough simply to say concepts possess movement: you also have to construct intellectually mobile concepts' (1995, p. 122). In our previous work we have taken up Deleuze's challenge in that we have tried to mobilize the concept of 'problematic behaviour' within the context of early years education. Under the direction of Rachel a film was developed which presents a collection of visual, sound and text images drawn from a range of sources and an array of disciplines, including art, dance, philosophy, education, psychology, special education, UK policy documents, film and popular media. The film gets straight to the gut. It incites affect. It gnaws at comfort zones in relation to children and childhood. It is deliberately molecular where music + image + movement + culture + politics and so on work at polluting habitual and sedimented ways of thinking. (To view the film please see http://www.esri.mmu.ac.uk/resprojects/project_outline.php?project_id=127.)

In furthering our ambitions for nomadic movements we move to make trans-situational links which Massumi argues involves 'a reconstellation of concepts' (cited in Walter, 2014, p. 258), where ideas are extracted from their home systems and encounter others from another system. Braidotti (1994) suggests that becoming nomadic entails dissolution of imaginary sites of authentic disciplinary identities. More recently she has argued that a nomadic subject should never be taken as a new metaphor for the human condition, but rather as a cartographic tool that helps us compose materialistic mappings of situated, that is, embedded and embodied, social positions (Braidotti, 2014). She goes on to suggest that cartography should be a theoretically based and politically informed reading of the present which fulfils the function of providing both analytic and exegetical tools for critical thought and also creative theoretical alternatives. She proposes 'a politics of location, or situated knowledges, rests on process ontology to posit the primacy of relations over substances' (2006, p. 199). Writing in a constant state of 'in-process' necessitates movements including stirring up our own ontological and epistemological (un)certainties.

Taking up the space afforded by Woodman's image and Alfred's words allows us to distribute our selves among a fulcrum of writing possibilites, becoming a 'streaming, spiralling, zigzagging, sneaking, feverish line' (Deleuze and Guattari, 1987, p. 550). This line, space and movement assemble the critical and the political in our inquiries, challenging the corrosive effects of habit. As Colebrook (2002, p. 6) reminds us, there is always more than this actual world; 'there are also all the potential worlds we might see'. In our own feverish desires to see other worlds, other possibilities, we begin with ordinary things – a door and a door handle. Yet, when they are caught in Alfred's mouth and in Woodman's image something happens to these ordinary things. Both Alfred and Woodman set us off zigzagging along a stream strewn with speculations. Deleuze (re)reminds us that 'there is an extraordinarily fine topology that relies not on points or objects, but rather on haecceities, on sets of relations...' (Deleuze and Guattari, 1987, p. 382). Attending to haecceities means that door and door handle are not understood as a determinable, known object. Rather we are encouraged to contemplate 'doorness' and 'door-handleness'; that is, their discrete qualities or what Manning and Massumi describe as 'qualities in a texture of integral experience' (2014, p. 16), complex sets of relations or a commotion of relational activity. Manning and Massumi go on to note 'that experience does not preclude the efficacy of use; it includes it differently' (ibid., p. 16).

While doors might typically and habitually be understood as a threshold allowing passage, Woodman's image encourages us to defy habit. For us, Woodman's image is an intensive space of affects. It is open-ended, nonlinear, haptic, a nomadic space. It is full of latency, of hidden, implicit, reserved things. It communicates yet 'with no immediate need for language' (Manning and Massumi, 2014, p. 10). It works on our bodies and minds, as we in turn work on it. Stuff resonates, evades and precludes us. The image brings us towards 'singularities... turning points and points of inflection... points of... condensation ...part of what constitute the virtual proper being of things, their unique being, their haecceity or thisness' (Deleuze, 1990, p. 63). The wood, the metal hinge, the forces, reflective light, contours and edges constitute fullness, haecceities and shadows that Barthes paradoxically describes as 'luminous' (1993, p. 110), where the stilling of the door as 'a door' casts ghostly movements, hints at other narratives, where dead air breathes uncanny forms of life, making 'individuation and relation possible' (Irigaray, 1999, p. 136). No longer functional, seemingly forgotten, this door escapes 'being a door', yet tilts at other possibilities. Its door-ness is provocatively suggestive of becoming attentive to a field of immediacy rather than being with habit. Woodman's image is excessive. As a commotion of relational activities, it cast doubts on our typical, habitual, logical and reasonable ways of making sense, including making sense of [a] door.

Manning and Massumi (2014, p. 11) note that 'a mode of existence never preexists an event'. Aptly, they continue, 'the mode of existence has to do with the emergent quality of the experience, not with the factually cross-checked identity of the objects featuring in it'. In turning back to Alfred's conversation with his mother we find ourselves caught again in the thick of it. Just as the door, walls, masonry, bricks, shadows, dust, light and air were in a field of experience, so too is Alfred. It is a field that, like Woodman's image, confounds us because it refuses to shake down into patterns of predictability. Door handle is put into (com)motion with human. Alfred, while momentarily claiming 'I', squashes any sort of primacy within the field of experience/relations. He does not set his sights on and/or assume his Cartesian birthright of mastery. Instead, he offers an alternative relational way of thinking about (him) self where he would *like to be something useful, like a door handle*. Alfred, together with his mother, becomes an event where a virtual door handle together with actual questions triggers something that borders on shock. Alfred has titled the world, where our perceptions of the normal state of things have been skewed.

Nomadic possibilities: Dismantling hegemonic and exclusionary views of subjectivity

Deleuze proposes: 'Once you start writing, shadows are more substantial than bodies' (1995, p. 134). As nomadic meddlers caught in the middle of things we find shadows irritatingly troublesome, yet it's an irritation that serves as an incitement to see. We want to turn now to data that stems from ethnographic work undertaken in the very earliest stages of schooling. Our suggestion is that by considering the data as shadows we can begin to contemplate who or what is being shadowed.

When collecting data we began to notice certain phrases that peppered adults' accounts of young children and their behaviour. Words

Figure 7.2 Caterina Silenza, untitled
Source: Untitled, © Caterina Silenza, private.

such as 'feral' and 'running wild' were used. On another occasion a girl was described thus: 'She's just like sap, so slow, dreary.' While we must stress that these terms and descriptions were not regularly used, they did nevertheless happen. For us, they resonate with Deleuze and Guattari's 'you're just a tramp' (1987, p. 159), where the child and the system and its organizations are out of kilter. They also interestingly recall Deleuze's shadow as a 'zone of indiscernibility or undecidabilty', opening up an interval, interstices between child and animal, when, for example, the shadow in Francis Bacon's Triptych (1973) 'escapes from the body like an animal we had been sheltering' (Deleuze, 2013, p. 16).

These extracts of data have become a series of striating moments when particular language-forms somehow began bearing all the weight of our consciousness as we encountered the children, the adults and the early years settings. In juxtaposition with one another, the terms create a panoply of (non)sense (Manning and Massumi, 2014). Working in much the same way as Alfred's door handle, terms such as 'feral', 'running wild' and 'sap' stand out as elements that modulate our experiencing of the surface of events, interfering with our rush to document the use-fullness of the 'proper' (tame/d) child (MacLure et al., 2011). We also recognize how terms such as these are overwhelmed by tendencies-to-form. That is, they become solidified among anthropocentric theoretical work around young children's development, including for example Piagetian animistic thinking (Piaget, 1929, p. 201) and Freudian animality theorizing of the dark forces within the human character (1930). Derrida's deconstructive thinking (2002) reduces animality to a figuration of alterity, outside every horizon, the space-between, in which no one is anything, neither human nor nonhuman but *a*human. We are also mindful of post-anthropocentric animal movements 'away from being and towards becoming, away from objectifications and towards process... the Deleuzean goal seems to be directed to this increase of force, of life' (Kubiak, 2012, p. 53). Similarly, Haraway's figurations of interrelationality (1996) evoke a philosophy of multiple becomings of the nomadic subject, simultaneously materialist and political, interestingly caught up in the idea that 'our... aggressive passions do not in fact "bubble up" from our animal bodies but "trickle down" from our uniquely human minds' (Carveth, 2012, p. 156).

Seduced yet again by the luminous workings of the shadows cast by these terms as we look across these very different, yet related theoretical fields, we are reminded of Ahmed's (2008) caution to resist clearing the ground of what has come before us. We sense, as early years educators, how we remain entangled with Piagetian and Freudian modernity as well as Derridean (ir)rationality, while being swept up into Haraway's and Deleuze's more-than-human worlds. So, although we accept that the concepts evoked by these terms do often become fixed over time, alluding to a child's *in*adequacy, *in*ability, *un*readiness, *im*properness in these early years settings, crucial work requires us to find new ways to escape the contours of the fixed forms they always already seem to inhabit. To do this, we return to the promise and possibilities of the shadow, a glimpse of the threshold between form and formlessness, between knowing and unknowing (Phelan, 2004).

In turning we encounter a tormented shadow, the *onco*, from the Greek word for 'tumour' – the shadow within/out. According to Shorett (2002), a transgenic mammal called the OncoMouse was named for its possession of an inserted gene sequence conferring susceptibility to cancer. This animal came to be seen as an ideal test subject for toxicology studies and therapeutic developments in cancer research. In 1988, the OncoMouse became the first animal ever given patent protection for its animal technologies. Haraway works with the OncoMouse™ as a composite image, a manipulated creature. For her it embodies questions about the artificiality of dualisms between humans and animals, culture and nature, and science and technology. Weisberg refers to Haraway's analysis of OncoMouse™ as nothing much beyond 'frivolous excursions into the limits of discourse' (2009, p. 60) and Crist suggests OncoMouse™ is 'ontologically indeterminate... white noise... an elusive trickster amenable to indefinite registrations, totally reliant on humans to assign it meaning' (Crist, 2004, p. 8). However, our interest in Haraway's use of OncoMouse™ is as composite image, breaking 'the purity of lineage... a spectral figure: the never-dead that pollutes the natural order simply by being manufactured and not born' (Braidotti, 2006, p. 202).

The accumulation of the limits of discourse, elusive tricksters, white noise, deconstructing boundaries and being 'witness' to, are all importantly captivating thoughts for us as researchers, who have registered discomfort with those animalistic language-forms such as 'feral' and yet not known what to do with our sensations in those instances. What Braidotti might describe as nomadic devices, the language-forms unsettle traditional codes and destabilize the subject as they, like the door handle and door, cast dark and tantalizing shadows across the 'proper' child, becoming spectral figures, tramps who pollute the natural order. Staying with the idea of pollution, we are carried into the darkened, noisy space of Kafka's burrow as well as 'The Castle'.

The burrow (Kafka, 1971) is a human polluted, diseased body; the various creatures within it are micro-organisms of one sort or another. Deleuze and Guattari, musing on Kafka's work, write: 'It is a rhizome, a burrow'; 'The Castle' [for example] has many entrances ...' They continue: 'Among these entrances, none seems privileged; no sign over the entrance announces that this is the way in. The reader of Kafka's work will choose an opening and map the passage he [sic] finds himself following. The map will change if a different entrance is chosen' (Brinkley, 1983, cited in Deleuze et al., 1983, p. 13).

The idea of multiple doors draws our interest towards the many ways we might 'interpret work which does not offer itself to anything but experimentation' (Brinkley, 1983, cited in Deleuze et al., 1983, p. 13). There are many ways into thinking about 'feral' and 'sap'. They cast interesting shadows over flat(ened) surfaces, upsetting the 'natural order' of the proper child. We want to explore how they become increasingly polluted, noisy words and move into the burrow, where Kafkaesque tormenting sounds of whistling and hissing become too much to bear. In Kafka's work, the narrator tries to locate their point of origin, to speculate on their possible causes and on possible means of eliminating them. In our writing here, the smooth entangled, felted fibres of disciplines, ideas and empirical materials that are incessantly whispering, humming, gnawing at and chattering in our ears, ensures our work is becoming increasingly busier, noisier, a maelstrom, a cacophony, 'beyond the immediate range of "sound", a kind of tumult or chaos' (Stevenson, 2004, p. 11).

From the commotion at the outset of the chapter, our violent agitation of ideas continues and is intensifying as we try to stay open to the chaotic, throbbing more-than-human-worlds we find ourselves scrambling around. With moments that modulate our experiencing of the world coming in and out of focus, we are deliberately resisting the urge to clear ground, dispel commotion, find causes, origins and eliminate our tormentors. 'Feral', like 'sap' and 'wild', behaves as a conduit of the tumultuous field's 'summing up in a determinate expression' (Manning and Massumi, 2014, p. 12). Yet, these language-forms are helping us to pay closer attention to what Deleuze suggests is the out-of-field, that which 'refers to what is neither seen nor understood, but is nevertheless perfectly present... the thicker the thread which links the seen set to other unseen sets the better the out-of-field fulfils its function, the adding of space to space' (1986, p. 17).

Spilling/stilling: Concluding thoughts

We wrote earlier about our commitment to finding pockets of air within theoretical movements and across the accumulation of empirical materials. The movements of 'feral' and 'sap' behave like a 'tenuous umbilical cord' (Barthes, 1993, p. 110), pulling us back while also compelling us forwards. As researchers we are trying to rethink data as words but also as images, movements, politics, molecules, affect, noise, haecceity and pollution. We wonder whether, if our attention was located on just a door or a handle or indeed a child, our thinking might remain without shadows? If so, would the for-ness and use-value of the subject remain forever visible and fixed, rather than in movement, becoming-imperceptible (Bertelsen, 2013)? The importance of researchers attending to the shadows cast by children marked out as 'feral', 'like sap' and 'running wild' is that they always render the subject persistent but in ways which are 'about reconstituting the nature of the perceptual field and changing the "threshold" of the perceivable world' (Deleuze and Guattari, 1987, p. 281).

The threshold of the flat perceivable world of the proper child becomes fuller, noisier and more tumultuous with 'feral' and 'sap', as they 'feature as tonal differences in a field modulating the whole experience at all levels, composing an overall mode of existence that is in a different key' (Manning and Massumi, 2014, p. 8). They exist here as written representations of what once were spoken words; they gesture towards images of a wild, animal-like child and an oozing thick substance; they conjure wounds, insult, fear, denigration; but they also gesture to movement – energetic, unpredictable and excruciatingly slow. Or as Massumi suggests, 'a veritable laboratory of forms of live action' (2014, pp. 12–13). Following Manning (2014), we propose that words such as 'feral' and 'sap' and the schooled concepts that lie behind them such as 'not disciplined' and 'without motivation' never pre-exist their movement, but are always edging into themselves as 'object', shading into themselves as 'figure' (Manning, 2014, p. 164). Perhaps, like the spectral body, they are 'the other at the edge of life' (Derrida, 1994, p. 26); as words and concepts, they are merely a brief instantiation or constellation of what those movements have become. However, if we think of 'She's just like sap' as movement, experiencing it as durational performance, it refuses to be tethered to its for-ness or use-value, but continues to work across the flat surfaces of the 'proper' child, of the adult, the early years setting, as singularity inferred in and through engagement, lingering to make contact, exchange sensations, pollute, find resonance of hidden things one with another. It produces worlds of pace, noise and radiations, time, vibrations and sensation as it wonders the more-than-human-world in movement (Manning, 2014, p. 165). As sap gradually oozes out from the flat surfaces and pursues its slow descent, we are taken to *Marina Abramović Presents* at the Whitworth Art Gallery (2009), and in particular Kira O'Reilly's three hour stair falling reinterpretation of Duchamp's *Nude Descending a Staircase, No. 2* (1912).

Reflecting on her falling, O'Reilly writes of how it 'allows metric, linear time to collapse into an unexpected topography of proximities and distances where other connections are made and events pulled backwards and forwards in the same time at the same place' (2008, p. 100). The idea of slowly flowing sap forces O'Reilly to reconsider linear time, something that ruthlessly striates the early years setting and the lives of the children who inhabit that space.

In the classroom, the movement evoked by 'She's just like sap' modulates the adult's acute pull of gravity to insist on space-time conformity, while simultaneously gesturing at many tensions. The complex and entangled vectors of time, space and intensities flow among the early years classroom and are suddenly forced into stark relief. It is 'as if' components of heterogeneous series are colliding, flickers, clashes and vibrations of different speeds erupt into language that, in this chapter, has bolted through sharp turns and crooked paths, drawing its trajectory

 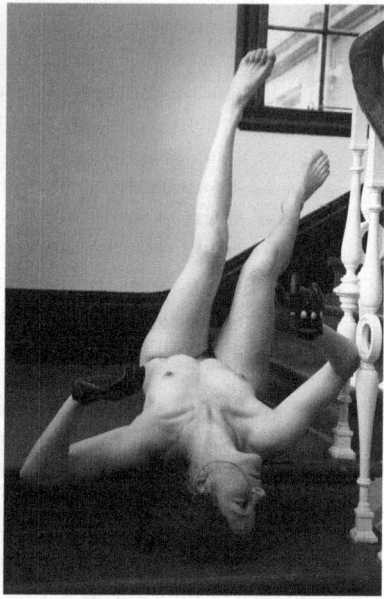

Figure 7.3 Kira O'Reilly, stair falling
Source: Kira O'Reilly Stair Falling, Photographs by Marco Anelli © 2009.

as it goes. The adult's imaginary of a 'proper' classroom speed is drawn and as striated apparatus of the state, is marking out how particular functions secure the child's contribution to the success of the collective. Sap only finds its flow from the tree when a wound gives way to internal pressure. O'Reilly goes on: 'the caress of stone and skin, the effect of gravity and gaze burdened and unburdened my body. It was as much a dancing of becomings and molecular shifts as anything' (cited in Snæbjörnsdóttir and Wilson, 2010, p. 47).

Among these classroom, art gallery and forest forces, abrasions and skirmishes, it is the call to pay attention to movements in the process of creating the human body. The movements of this language-form cast shadows that refuse to find, and resist the consolations of form, perhaps offering up greater stories of no-thing-ness as they co-compose with movement's inflexions to stir something in excess of themselves. We come to rest momentarily where we (re)consider what further possibilities might be encountered if we continue to move within the forces of process philosophy. For us, we find degrees of shadowy optimism in the nomadic movements that are materialized in fields for experience that does not begin and end with the human subject.

References

Ahmed, S. (2008) 'Open Forum, Imaginary Prohibitions: Some Preliminary Remarks on the Founding Gestures of New Materialisms', *European Journal of Women's Studies*, 15(1), 23–39.

Badminton, N. (2011) 'Posthumanism', in B. Clarke and M. Rossini (eds.) *Routledge Companion to Science and Literature* (New York: Routledge).

Barad, K. (2003) 'Posthumanist Performativity: Toward an Understanding of How Matter Comes to Matter', *Signs: Journal of Women in Culture and Society*, 28(3), 801–831.

Barthes, R. (1993) *Camera Lucida: Reflections on Photography* (London: Vintage Classics).

Bertelsen, L. (2013) 'Francesca Woodman: Becoming-woman, becoming-imperceptible, becoming-a-subject-in-wonder', *Performance Paradigm*, 9, http://www.performanceparadigm.net/index.php/journal/article/view/132, accessed 6 May 2015.

Blondel, E. (1985) 'Gilles Deleuze: Nomad Thought', in D. B. Allison (ed.) *The New Nietzsche* (Cambridge, MA: MIT Press), pp. 142–149.

Braidotti, R. (1994) *Nomadic Subjects: Embodiment and Sexual Difference in Contemporary Feminist Theory* (New York: Columbia University Press).

Braidotti, R. (2006) 'Posthuman, All Too Human: Towards a New Process Ontology', *Theory, Culture & Society*, 23, 197–208.

Braidotti, R. (2013) *The Posthuman* (Cambridge, MA: Polity Press).

Braidotti, R. (2014) '*Rosi Braidotti: Thinking as a Nomadic Subject*', https://www.ici-berlin.org/event/620/, accessed 6 June 2015.

Brinkley, R. (1983) 'Mississippi Review: What Is Minor Literature?' *Essays Literary Criticism* 11(3) (Winter/Spring), pp. 13–33, http://www.jstor.org/stable/20133921, accessed 23 October 2015.

Brown, T. and L. Jones (2001) *Action Research and Postmodernism: Congruence and Critique* (Buckingham: Open University Press).

Burman, E. (1994) *Deconstructing Developmental Psychology* (London: Routledge).

Burman, E. (2007) *Deconstructing Developmental Psychology* (2nd ed.) (London: Routledge).

Cannella, G. S. (1997) *Deconstructing Early Childhood Education: Social Justice and Revolution* (New York: Peter Lang).

Cannella, G. S. and K. Wolff (2014) 'Conceptualizing Critical Qualitative Research In/Against Global Neoliberalisms', *International Review of Qualitative Research*, 7(1), 1–14.

Carveth, D. L. (2012) 'Freud's and Our Paranoid Myth of "the Beast"', *Canadian Journal of Psychoanalysis*, 20(1), 153–157.

Colebrook, C. (2002) *Gilles Deleuze* (London: Routledge).

Crist, E. (2004) 'Against the Social Construction of Nature and Wilderness', *Environmental Ethics*, 26, 5–24.

Deleuze, G. (1986) *Cinema I* (London: Continuum).

Deleuze, G. (1990) *The Logic of Sense* (hereafter, *LS*), trans. Mark Lester with Charles Stivale, ed. Constantin Boundas (New York: Columbia University Press).

Deleuze, G. (1995) *Negotiations, 1972–1990* (New York: Columbia University Press).

Deleuze, G. (1997) *Essays Critical and Clinical* (D. W. Smith and M. S. Greco, Trans.) (Minneapolis: University of Minnesota Press).
Deleuze, G. (2013) *Francis Bacon: The Logic of Sensation* (London: Bloomsbury Academic).
Deleuze, G. and F. Guattari (1987) *A Thousand Plateaus: Capitalism and Schizophrenia* (B. Massumi, Trans.) (London: Continuum).
Deleuze, G., F. Guattari and R. Brinkley (1983) 'What Is a Minor Literature?', *Mississippi Review*, 11(3), 13–33.
Derrida, J. (1994) *Specters of Marx* (P. Kamuf, Trans.) (New York: Routledge).
Derrida, J. (2002) 'The Animal That Therefore I Am (More to Follow)', *Critical Inquiry*, 28(2), 369–418.
Figueira, D. M. (2008) *Otherwise Occupied: Pedagogies of Alterity and the Brahminization of Theory* (New York: State University of New York Press).
Freud, S. (1930) 'Civilization and Its Discontents', *S.E.*, 21, 57–146.
Foucault, M. (1975) *Discipline and Punish: The Birth of the Prison* (New York: Random House).
Frost, S. (2011) 'The Implications of the New Materialisms for Feminist Epistemology', in H. E. Grasswick (ed.) *Feminist Epistemology and Philosophy of Science: Power in Knowledge* (Dordrecht: Springer), pp. 69–83.
Guattari, F. (1995) *Chaosmosis: An Ethico-aesthetic Paradigm* (P. Bains and J. Pefanis Trans.) (Sydney: Power Publications).
Grusin, R. (ed.) (2015) *The Nonhuman Turn* (Minneapolis: University of Minnesota Press).
Haraway, D. J. (1996) *Modest_Witness@Second_Millennium.FemaleMan©_Meets_OncoMouse™. Feminism and Technoscience* (London: Routledge).
Herbrechter, S. and I. Callus (2013) *Critical Posthumanism, Critical Posthumanisms 1* (Amsterdam: Rodopi).
Holmes, R. (2010) 'Risky Pleasures: Using the Work of Graffiti Writers to Theorise the Act of Ethnography', *Qualitative Inquiry*, 16(10), 871–882.
Holmes, R. (2014) 'Fresh Kills: The Spectacle of (De)Composing Data', *Qualitative Inquiry*, 20(6), 781–789.
Holmes, R. and L. Jones (2012) 'Limit-less Provocations of the "Safe", "Secure" and "Healthy" Child', *International Journal of Qualitative Studies in Education*, 26(1), 75–99.
Holmes, R. and L. Jones (2013) 'Flesh, Wax, Horse Skin and Hair: The Many Intensities of Data', *Cultural Studies <=> Critical Methodologies*, 13(4), 357–372.
Irigaray, L. (1999) *The Forgetting of Air in Martin Heidegger* (London: Athlon Press).
Jones, L. (2010) 'Reflexivity as a Ground-Clearing Activity within the Context of Early Years Pedagogy', *Qualitative Inquiry*, 16(5), 342–348.
Jones, L. (2013) 'Becoming Child/Becoming Dress', *Global Studies of Childhood*, 3(3), 289–296.
Jones, L., M. MacLure, R. Holmes and C. MacRae (2011) Children and Objects: Affection and Infection', *International Journal of Early Years*, 32(1), 49–60.
Kafka, F. (1971) 'The Burrow', *In The Great Wall of China and Other Short Works* (M. Pasley Trans.) (London: Penguin Books), p. 185.
Kubiak, A. (2012) 'Animism: Becoming-Performance, or Does This Text Speak to You?', *Performance Research: A Journal of the Performing Arts*, 17(4), 52–60.
MacLure, M. (2011) 'Qualitative Inquiry: Where Are the Ruins?' *Qualitative Inquiry*, 17(10), 997–1005.

MacLure, M., L. Jones, R. Holmes, and C. MacRae (2011) 'Becoming a Problem: Behaviour and Reputation in the Early Years Classroom', *British Educational Research Journal*, 38(3), 447–471.

Manning, E. (2014) 'Wondering the World Directly – or, How Movement Outruns the Subject', *Body & Society*, 20, 162–188.

Manning, E. (2015) 'Artfulness', in R. Grusin (ed.) *The Nonhuman Turn* (Minneapolis: University of Minnesota Press), pp. 45–80.

Manning, E. and B. Massumi (2014) *Thought in the Act: Passages in the Ecology of Experience* (Minneapolis: University of Minnesota Press).

Massumi, B. (2014) *What Animals Teach Us about Politics* (Durham: Duke University Press).

Mukhopadhyay, T. (2008) *How Can I Talk If My Lips Don't Move?: Inside My Autistic Mind* (New York: Arcade Publishing).

O'Reilly, K. (2008) 'Marsyas – Beside Myself', in J. Hauser (ed.) *Sk-interfaces: Exploding Borders – Creating Membranes in Art, Technology and Society* (Liverpool: Liverpool University Press), pp. 96–101.

Phelan, P. (2004) 'Marina Abramović: Witnessing Shadows', *Theatre Journal*, 56(4), 569–577.

Piaget, J. (1929) *The Child's Conception of the World* (New York: Harcourt Brace).

Shorett, P. (2002) 'Of Transgenic Mice and Men', *GeneWatch*, 15(5), https://itp.nyu.edu/classes/germline-spring2013/files/2013/01/CRG-Of-Transgenic-Mice-Men.pdf, accessed 11 May 2015.

Snæbjörnsdóttir, B. and M. Wilson (2010) 'Falling Asleep with a Pig', interview with Kira O'Reilly, Antennae: *The Journal of Nature in Visual Culture*, 13, 38–48.

Stevenson, F. W. (2004) 'Becoming Mole(cular), Becoming Noise: Serres and Deleuze in Kafka's "Burrow"', *Concentric: Literary and Cultural Studies*, 30(1) (January), 3–36.

Walkerdine, V. (1988). *The Mastery of Reason: Cognitive Development and the. Production of Rationality* (London: Routledge).

Walter, C. (2014) *Optical Impersonality: Science, Images, and Literary Modernism* (Baltimore, MD: John Hopkins University Press).

Weisberg, Z. (2009) 'The Broken Promises of Monsters: Haraway, Animals and the Humanist Legacy', *Journal for Critical Animal Studies*, VII(II), 22–62.

Whitehead, A. N. (1933/1967). *Adventures of Ideas* (New York: The Free Press).

8
'Local Girl Befriends Vicious Bear': Unleashing Educational Aspiration through a Pedagogy of Material-Semiotic Entanglement

Susanne Gannon

Introduction

In education, posthumanist approaches require us to pay attention to the more-than-human contexts within which young people come to take themselves up in the world, and to the affordances and capacities of worldly things and affective flows to shape young people's desires and ways of being in the world. While there has been considerable work in early childhood contexts (e.g., Blaise, 2013; Davies, 2014; Hultman and Lenz Taguchi, 2010; Pacini-Ketchabaw and Taylor, 2015; Taylor, 2013), in secondary schools the more-than-human requires researchers to look beyond taken-for-granted rational, cognitive, curriculum contexts to attend to surprising configurations where bodies, things, affect, desire, matter, imagination and pedagogy collide to form new assemblages and possibilities. The material-semiotic entanglements of pedagogy are complex, multiple, uneven, unstable, emergent, and contingent on the specificities of particular times and places. In school education, pedagogy tends to be a taken-for-granted concept, shorthand for all manner of practices around teaching and learning, and in its most common usage it foregrounds the humanist master narrative that positions careful teacher planning for student learning as the most significant aspect of the classroom experience.[1] Deviations and surprises, lessons that veer away from intended outcomes, unexpected 'pedagogical encounters' provoked by things other than people are elided rather than understood as part of complex assemblages where pedagogy is emergent, relational and ethical, opening towards intensities and difference (Davies, 2014; Davies and Gannon, 2009). The pedagogical encounter glimpsed in this chapter was a career planning day in a secondary school. However, its pedagogical trajectories and intensities extended beyond that time and place to incorporate researchers and research apparatus.

In this chapter I experiment with some of the (im)possibilities of posthumanism in thinking through conventional empirical research in education. I do not intend to present a definitive demonstration of posthuman research at work in a replicable way, or to provide a comprehensive review of scholarship in this burgeoning arena. Rather, by returning to a fragment of data from a completed research project, I aim to provoke questions and incite problems that cannot be resolved here, but that I hope will continue to resonate with readers into their own work, as they do in mine. The key strategy that I take up here is that of following the object, attempting to look awry or aslant by privileging a nonhuman, non-animate object – a bear suit in this case – in the data story, and tracing the fleeting assemblages it forms with other objects (including people) that are temporarily drawn to and away from it. Apart from the difficulty of doing this, in thinking against the grain of educational research when human intentionality (teacher, student, curriculum) is so central a focus, further tensions arise in the delineation of objects. Where and how do they begin and end? How might their motion in assembling and disassembling, rather than their edges and separations, be the focus? How might we attend to the transient affective vectors that they form? To what extent can (or should) objects/ assemblages be fixed for the analytical researchly gaze? What if they come (as 'data') already fixed, delineated, labelled, quarantined from interference and demanding particular (conventional) modes of analysis? And why is visuality – the 'analytical gaze' – the default mode through which analysis usually proceeds? Another imperative of 'post' approaches, including the so-called posthuman, is the unravelling and constant articulation and disarticulation of research apparatus and researcher-data assemblages and the need to pay attention to their implications and pretensions, and to search for ways to slide between the habits and patterns of research-as-usual. This chapter is a tentative beginning in this direction.

Trajectories, aspirations and slippages

The data that I discuss in this chapter is an extract of two slides from a longer PowerPoint presentation created by year 9 and 10 girls in 2012, whose school was one of five included in the STAR (Student Trajectories Aspirations Research) project (Somerville et al., 2013). These two slides formed an artefact, or rather an assemblage of artefacts – still and moving images, audio file, text box, scanned handwritten document, which are organized and fixed into a particular sequence and layout – that purported to represent the aspirations of a girl who I call SH through this chapter. Bodies of other girls – in bear suits and as offscreen voices – are arranged to intensify the representation of SH's desire to be a zoologist. However, across the components of the PowerPoint slides, this declared aspiration alters and slips around, and various invented and imagined personas are deployed by the wilful subject of SH, who orders her future for us and for herself in the PowerPoint slides. While it is possible to track discursive slippages and inconsistencies, this approach keeps analysis locked into an all-too-human reading where it is what people say and do (or fail to say and do) that takes precedence. Approaching data as 'fragment' – rather than as 'set' – suggests instability, singularity and an inclination to fall apart rather than to hold together, and the capacity to come together in different formations with other fragments.

The STAR project was conventionally designed and externally funded. Five researchers worked with two primary and three secondary government schools in a high-poverty area of western Sydney, Australia. The process included collaborative planning with teachers and the data set from each school comprised focus group interviews with teachers and parents, and the collection of artefacts representing aspiration created by the children. There were more than 200 student participants from kindergarten to year 11 overall, and around 50 adults participated in teacher and parent focus groups.[2] Artefacts ranged from drawings in coloured pencil through to edited films. Given the volume of data, my decision to work with just one of these artefacts in this chapter, and to do so in such an unconventional way, might seem perverse from the perspective of research-as-usual.

The STAR project aimed to answer three questions: *What are the aspiration trajectories of children? What are the enablers and barriers to their participation in further education? What factors can facilitate the development and support for aspirations to participate in further education?* While these questions are important to the researchers, the schools, families and children we worked with, and to our own university and the funding body, and we have endeavoured to answer aspects of them elsewhere (Gannon et al., 2015; Somerville, 2013; Somerville et al., 2013), it requires agility, flexibility and the capacity to forget or to un-know the ways I have already come to know the data and the problem. I hope to articulate some of the complexities and (im)possibilities of this struggle to (un)know and to (un)see in this chapter.

The teachers at each school created the conditions for students to create artefacts representing their aspirations. Students were explicitly told that they were contributing to university research on young people's aspirations. Two of the secondary schools positioned students as researchers of themselves and others as they conducted and edited interviews using a predetermined interview schedule. The student artefacts were organized by teachers and students as data and when they were ready were either collected in hard copy, scanned, put on USB sticks or uploaded and shared through a DropBox folder. Thus the slides that I discuss in this chapter were delivered to the university researchers already labelled as 'data'. They also produce me (a researcher) as an expert viewer with the capacity to ascribe meaning to the artefact within a network of data, academic desire, obligations, theories and potentialities. None of this is neutral. Furthermore, the research site is striated by policies and practices that are not apparent in the data, nor in the school sites where data was created. These include the *Higher Education Participation Program*, a national funding scheme introduced in 2010 by the previous Australian Labour government to support the recommendations of the Bradley *Review of Higher Education* to increase enrolments of under-represented groups of young people in universities including those from economically disadvantaged contexts (Bradley et al., 2008).

As I have noted, this provocation for thinking through a posthumanist approach begins from the data fragment of two PowerPoint slides compiled by a year 9 girl to represent her career aspirations. This is – on the one hand – unremarkable data, as was the intention of the research design, which invited teachers to create opportunities for students to create artefacts representing their aspirations in any way that would fit everyday practices within their school. Part of my aim in this chapter is to attend to the 'wonder' of data, that emerges in the 'entangled relation of data-and-researcher' (MacLure, 2013a, p. 228). This requires a researchly disposition that assumes that '[w]e, and the data, do not prexist one another' and, as MacLure demonstrates, is particularly incited by the materiality of objects and the ways they move, assemble and disassemble (2013a, p. 229).

At this single-sex school, the creation of the artefact was embedded in a career planning day for 50 year 9 and 10 girls during which they completed a range of tasks at different activity stations through the day, working individually and with peers. They wrote newspaper articles, poems and letters at a creative writing station, took stylized digital photographs of themselves and arranged these into digital montages at another activity station, and video-recorded interviews with peers at a further activity station. Twenty-seven girls compiled their materials into PowerPoint slides, and these were given to the researchers as part of the data set. While the creation of the artefacts was embedded within everyday practices, where students do what they normally do by producing work samples as evidence of their learning, and using technologies that they have used before, as 'data' it is very complex.

The multimodal approach meant that the slides included multiple photographs, written text and a video-recorded interview, arranged in particular ways by the students, the teachers and the software itself. The staging of aspiration was overt and deliberate as props, costumes, symbolic items and imagined personas (zoologist 10 years into the future, media interviewer, media celebrity) were deployed, enacted and arranged. Assemblages of bodies, things, voices and technologies were drawn together in a particular moment in space and time, 'captured' through software, packaged and delivered as data for research. Already, my chapter seems doomed and analysis impossible. As I have noted, there is an inherent tension in the notion of capture of an assemblage, which, in a Deleuzian sense, is oriented towards movement rather than stasis, requiring cartographies of bodies, things and ideas as they assemble, disassemble and reassemble in fragmented and creative ways. They resist interpretation. Failure is part of the story of research if the arrogance of interpretation and the confidence of coding are abandoned. Despite the ambition to put on a posthuman 'lens' to read empirical data that may be inferred through this chapter, posthuman approaches present more radical challenges to the conventions of qualitative research. Lenses are superficial, instrumental, optical and optional, whereas posthumanism, as St. Pierre (2013) points out, marks a more radical ontological break to the representational logic that purports to see. Everything, including meaning, is on the move. Potential subjects – figures, voices, the very idea of 'aspiration' – emerge momentarily within the slides and beyond them as the desires and practices of teachers, researchers and families continue to circulate, connect and disconnect with one another and with other things in the world. Borrowing from MacLure, and despite my post-hoc approach, within a 'materially informed post-qualitative research', it might be better to consider this 'a fragment of what would have been called data' (2013b, p. 658).

Nevertheless, I have chosen to begin with these two slides as though they are data, though to some extent they seem to have chosen me, as each time I viewed the slides, the images of girls and bear suit stood out from all the other elaborately costumed and staged imaginings of future lives as nurses, models, cosmetic dermatologists and veterinarians. They are the most complete and elaborate, and the most explicit in 'more-than-human' terms because the figure in the bear suit appears in both images and in the written text. It's the bear – the bear suit in particular, the hint of girl-becoming-bear-becoming zoologist in this assemblage of two girls and a bear suit, and the digital technologies that suture them together – that throws me this cue to posthuman thinking. I also want to consider the more radical impacts on research-as-usual of the posthuman challenge in the all-too-human context of qualitative educational research. The following short section is a brief visit with some of the posthuman theory that has provoked my directions in this chapter.

Posthumanist educational research

As is explored elsewhere in this book, posthumanist researchers adopt various descriptions for their approaches – including 'relational materialism', 'feminist materialism', 'new empiricism' – and they move beyond the anthropocentric focus of earlier poststructural paradigms in educational research. Their interpretive apparatuses are variously informed by the theoretical work of Deleuze and Guattari (1987), Braidotti (2013), Bennett (2010a, 2010b) and Barad (2007) among others. What they have in common is recognition of the co-constitutive effects of material and affective flows of bodies, spaces and things in educational research; a willingness to invent method anew in each research instance; a move beyond the deconstruction of binaries, and – to varying degrees – the supposed linguisticism of educational poststructuralism; and a commitment to a 'flat' ontology that foregrounds the nonhuman elements of an educational assemblage, while recognizing that assemblages are simultaneously constituted by 'semiotic flows, material flows, and social flows' (Deleuze and Guattari, 1987, p. 25).

The 'matter' of the material is differently positioned in posthuman work, as is the agency of matter. In her work on the vibrancy of matter, Bennett challenges researchers to consider nonhuman materialities as 'bona fide agents rather than instrumentalities, techniques of power, recalcitrant objects, or social constructs' (2010a, p. 47). However, agency arises not in the fixed or stable bounded things or beings but within 'a human-nonhuman working group' (2010b, p. xvii). Objects gather together with each other and with other matter and bodies that become new things together in their movements. What Bennett calls 'thing-power' signals 'the strange ability of ordinary, man-made items to exceed their status as objects and to manifest traces of independence or aliveness' (2010b, p. xvi). But this agency of things is 'congregational' or 'distributive'; that is, it 'always depends on the collaboration, cooperation, or interactive interference of many bodies and forces', rather than on any single 'thing' no matter what it is or its apparent will to agency (2010b, p. 21). Bennett draws on Deleuze to envisage assemblages as 'ad hoc groupings of diverse elements... living throbbing confederations... with uneven topographies' and unequal distributions of power (2010b, p. 23).

In her reworking of quantum physics for feminist theory, Barad is also insistent on the dynamism of matter. Barad views matter in the most minute way, where even 'the smallest parts of matter [are capable] of exploding deeply entrenched ideas and large cities' (2007, p. 3). She suggests that researchers should be distrustful of ascribing agency to particular discrete things or bodies; rather we must recognize that *all* phenomena are formed of inseparable and intra-acting agencies (2007, p. 333), and given shape through material-discursive practices, including our own methodological practices. Analysis must therefore focus on entanglements, relationalities and 'intra-actions' of all sorts of matters and agencies, including the singular entanglements of data-researcher-method. The concept of 'intra-action' means that 'distinct agencies' – including the assumed agencies of researcher, research subject and research apparatus – 'do not precede but rather *emerge* through their intra-action' (2007, p. 33, italics added). The anthropocentrism of humanist qualitative research is challenged in what she calls a '*posthumanist performative* approach' that turns its analytical attention to 'practices, doings and actions' (2007, p. 135) and introduces new analytical provocations such as 'diffraction' to draw attention to methodology. As Davies describes it, diffraction is useful both as a metaphor and as a practice, as it 'makes for a significant interference in thinking as usual' (2014, p. 2). Insights are 'read through one another in ways that help illuminate differences as they emerge: how different differences get made, what gets excluded and how these exclusions matter' (Barad, 2007, p. 30). Research becomes a series of encounters or movements as analysis 'interferes with the research problem and the questions being asked, and the questions interfere with the analysis... emergent and unpredictable, a series of encounters' (Davies, 2014, p. 5). How might analysis inclined towards interference – diffractive analysis – trouble the girl-bear dyad in the PowerPoint slides?

Exploring how a posthumanist orientation might enable new readings of a data fragment from an empirical study is an immensely difficult endeavour as humanist practices and ways of researching and reading the world are omnipresent and insistent. The posthuman – or more-than-human – is not just a tokenistic addition of nonhuman or non-animate detail to descriptions of research settings or data. It doesn't mean merely that we start to notice the 'scenery against which the humanist adventures of culture are played out' (MacLure, 2013b, p. 659). A gulf exists in my endeavour in that conventional qualitative methodology – such as this inquiry into how children speak and write about, imagine and represent their futures – ought to be placed under erasure if we take on the ontological challenge of 'the posts' in order to 'reimagine being' itself (St. Pierre, 2013, p. 646). These new approaches recognize that '[u]tterances do not come from "inside" an already constituted speaking subject' (MacLure, 2013b, p. 660), but they are instituted through and by the event of research, and in this case, a pedagogical event where the girls took up, and were taken up by, the bear suit and its potentialities. Curiosity about young people's aspirations, within a research project designed to invite young people to articulate their aspirations, and to 'capture' these in student work samples, that then purports to be able to describe, understand and use them as evidence of some truths, is deeply mired in a representational logic. A post-hoc analytical strategy that endeavours to trouble this is a limited albeit necessary strategy. How to think differently through the genesis and design of a research project is another step altogether.

Finding the bear

The two PowerPoint slides that are my data fragment produce a 14-year-old girl, SH, as a subject of aspiration. They ascribe and attach demographic details – name, age, gender, career aspiration – 'Zoologist or optometrist' – and socio-economic status (SES) to this figure in a text box. Part of the problem with this fragment is that it is such a tightly bounded artefact. Every component seems to insist on being acknowledged and accorded attention, and the subject of Susan Hughes and her wilful intent to shape her future in a particular direction are preeminent. How can the data be pressed to find points of rupture, or dislocation, that might help with thinking otherwise? Old habits are hard to break. As we begin to work with the data, my research colleague privileges 'voice' by transcribing, extracting and collating excerpts from the interview into a table under thematic headings, and disregarding everything that is not spoken. I work in the opposite direction, attending to everything, excessively. I write detailed descriptions of every component, and transcribe the full text of the newspaper article on slide 2 into one of my versions of this chapter, before erasing it again as I move between drafts. Looking for the bear, when everything else is screaming for attention, reminds me of the viral video of the bear moonwalking across the basketball court, supposedly a version of an experiment in perceptual inattention.[3] This is my goal. Looking for the bear in this data fragment means learning not to look at those elements that draw my initial attention. It means, as research always does, making decisions about what not to notice as well as what to notice. 'Noticing' in this instance includes feeling, thinking, seeing, listening, not only to the data but to the random loops and lines the data throws out to elsewhere and other texts, moments and events. This time it is the bear that I am noticing. How is the bear suit implicated in forming a 'human-nonhuman working group' in these slides? How does it acquire thing-power, in Bennett's terms, not as a property of a bounded object, such as the bear suit per se, but as it is mobilized in relation with other bodies, affects and technologies, entangling and assembling in particular pedagogical moments?

There are three digital photographs of the girl and the bear. If we 'read' the slides following the conventional directionality of English – left to write, top to bottom – it is possible to privilege a sequence of images across the slides. In Figure 8.1, the girl in the bear suit stands upright in two photographs, not yet quite bear. The first small photograph at the top of the page shows the girl-bear running away from the girl zoologist, who has caught her by the shoulders. In the second photograph she grimaces, in a bear-like way, as the zoologist embraces her, and wears a conspicuously human beige neck-tie. In the final large photo on the second slide, the concluding item in the sequence, the girl-bear is on all fours, human trappings abandoned, mouth open and roaring, but held firmly on a leash by the girl zoologist. What does this assemblage of girls and bears mean in this data fragment? Does the bear call the zoologist into being? Does the bear costume, with its shiny acrylic softness, call the zoologist into being with a loving affect, as she strokes the skin, embraces and, in the written narrative, 'befriends' the bear? Does the girl-bear become more bear-like as the photographs proceed – getting down low to the ground and growling in the third image, but not quite bear in the previous ones?

The written text in Figure 8.2 – an imaginary front page news article from *The Daily Star*, a newspaper of the future – situates the zoologist in a zoo, and constructs an elaborate narrative of a future where they achieve global fame respectively as the most successful zoologist and

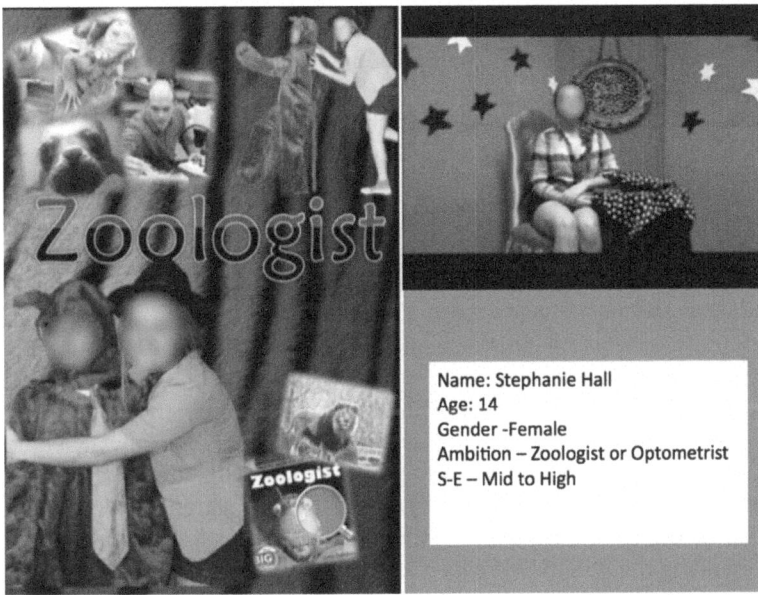

Figure 8.1 Slide 1, Zoologist

Figure 8.2 Slide 2, *The Daily Star*: 'Local girl befriends vicious bear'

the most vicious bear in the world. The ironically named 'Cuddles' – an abandoned Sun Bear from Thailand – has an inherently 'violent nature' but the wild beast is gradually tamed through 'techniques including bribes with food, toys, talking to the bear and even [ˆtryingˆ]⁴ hug Cuddles'. Its realization happens 'when Cuddles finally accepted a hug'. The American President, the Guinness World Records Medal, Thailand, television and Sydney's Taronga Zoo are all deployed to materialize aspiration and desire along a nonlinear temporal axis that links 8 November 2022 with two 14-year-old girls and a bear suit in the present. So much detail, so much language – written, spoken, image and audio – demanding analysis (whatever that is) makes it difficult to do what I want to do, which is to follow the bear.

The bear hug in the second photograph flows into the news story written at the creative writing activity station, and becomes a pivot point for an imagined future bringing international fame to both zoologist and bear. The addition of the word 'trying' signifies the difficult circumstances of the hug, reinforcing the wildness of the bear and enhancing the remarkable achievement of the zoologist who tames the bear. The article closes with the altruistic desire to 'help all animals live the life they deserve' and to 'save the environment for them to live in'. This suggests an ethical stance of responsibility and mutual entanglement of human and earth others – environment, animals, humans – albeit within a paradigm of human exceptionalism. And does the happy accident of the bear costume in the dress-up box mean that zoologist triumphs over optometrist in the representation of aspirations for careers and university courses? The text box on the first slide declares 'zoologist or optometrist'. The video interview, embedded in the first slide, is more circumspect. An offscreen girl's voice asks a series of predetermined interview questions, including *What are your plans when you leave school? What would you like to be happening in your life in ten years? What would be required for you to achieve this?* To the question, *What did you dream of being when you were in primary school?*, the girl answers 'Rapunzel...or an optometrist like my parents.' While the news story inscribes a singular future for a renowned zoologist and articulates a desire to 'strive to help all animals live like they deserve', the video-recorded interview asserts that the girl will study 'either optometry, zoology, or dietician because I have this thing where I really want to be helping people'. Even zoology is included as among the string of professions that help people. There is no bear, no animal of any sort in the video interview. Helping animals and saving the environment, which are elaborated in the feature article on the second slide, are not evident in the interview that is embedded in the first slide. In the interview, optometry is ascendant, or other careers that are about helping people. The bear has disappeared from the scene. It's easy to imagine the dress-up box with the costume discarded, the bear-girl who was positioned as Cuddles in the narrative text disappeared, and the acrylic fur lying limp and thin in the bottom of a basket or hanging in a wardrobe, in the back of the drama room. Other researchers have written about the affordances of the dress-up box for young children in acting out other ways of being (human) in the world (Davies, 2003; Pacini-Ketchabaw and Taylor, 2015; Taylor, 2008). Davies (2003) traces how gendered play with items from the dress-up box creates possibilities for both experimenting with and policing gendered identities and performances. Taylor notes 'young children's predilection for wild fantasy and eccentricity' (2008, p. 197). She recounts the story of Policeman Thelma, demonstrating how 'kids who dress in drag' simultaneously draw upon and disrupt normative gendered practices and expectations (2008, p. 210). In recent ethnographies on the entanglements of children and animals in common worlds (Pacini-Ketchabaw and Taylor, 2015), Taylor considers the affective and material impacts of a kangaroo suit on a child during a regular expedition into a kangaroo habitat by a Canberra preschool, wondering whether the child who has brought a kangaroo suit to school and who confidently 'breaks with the human group and hops towards the mob' is being drawn into a 'transspecies mode of intersubjectivity' (2015, p. 59). In contrast, in secondary schools – outside drama classes, prom nights and studies of school uniforms and their variations – the materiality and affective capacities of the costume have not been the focus of research. Furthermore the materiality of these objects is, at best, an afterthought. Nor is it, yet, part of the story of girl and bear. The matter of the body – the body enclosed and encased in fur – is missing.

The body and the bear: An interruption

This brief section aims to interfere with the data by looping into another text from another research project. This is a modest enactment of researcher-data entanglement well away from the site of the aspirations research, a brief exercise in peripheral vision, an experiment in interference. During a creative writing camp that I ran several years earlier with secondary schools from southwest Sydney, writer-in-residence Margo Lanagan had us write our way, bone by bone, muscle by muscle, through a transformation from human into animal body in precise and meticulously imagined detail. This mirrored human-bear transformations in her novel *Tender Morsels* (2009) as young men are laced into bear suits in an annual ritual where boy-bears chase the girls and women through the town. In several instances during the complex narrative, the boy-bear assemblages become so merged that a character becomes more bear than boy. Here is Thomas Ramstrong, on the day he is selected as a bear:

> Uncle tied my skin shirt at the back. Except for the bonnet, I couldn't take these clothes off myself... [Uncle] clapped my furry arm and his touch was a dead thump, thick with feeling... like a hint of brawn-liquor it came alive in my stomach: Bear Day. It was ours and no one else's ... I was not myself anymore. I was one of the four Bears. I cannot tell you the relief. Up the tower steps we ran, out into the sunshine and across to the wall. As soon as they saw us, men shouted below, and women screamed, and the rest of the crowd turned up their faces. It were the women screaming gave us our power: the sound hit my ears painful as knife-edges, but in my stomach it was like fat meat and clean ale, filling me for my day's wild work.
>
> We roared and clawed the air and ran back and forth along the battlement. We all but threw ourselves off the top, leaning out fierce and threatening ... we were the real bears that children wanted to be, to terrify the world and bring spring... The girls that cringed and shrieked and ran, I pursued. I brought them down, gave them a good dose of my hand's soot and grease, messed them right up... I uttered no word to anyone. I could feel it in me the force of spring.
>
> I was all slime inside my skins; sweat was drabbling from under my bonnet. How long had we run? And we must run, and kiss and paw and roar and smash, until we were stopped... A Bear moved fast so as not to be recognised, so as not to be himself, to stay a stranger and a bear.
>
> (Lanagan, 2009, pp. 132–135)

And here is Ramstrong again, after he has inadvertently leapt through a portal into a parallel world where he stumbles through the snow to a cottage:

> My hands surprised me, they felt so clawed and furred, so lumpish with the cold... 'I will not hurt you', I said but my voice came out growls into the room though it were words in my head and on my lips, wherever they were... My costume had changed and thickened; my bonnet had extended as a mask down my face... my eyes had

changed too, and the mind that translated what they saw... [t]he bird distracted me. I was not hungry, yet when I saw it there I could not stand the sight of the plush breast intact when I knew what goodness lay inside; I tore it in half and crunched it in my teeth and, feathers and splintered bones and all, both halves went down and were delicious. I licked the blood from every crease of my hands... [Later, as the girls in the cottage brush his matted fur] The feeling of being a man inside a bear inside their brushing had my whole skin and brain busy. They were brushing a bear into existence from my matter – I began to sense and then to see that I had claws, that I had paws, as they did their delicate work upon them.

(Lanagan, 2009, pp. 140–141)

What point is there in this brief looping into fiction and back to the girl in the bear costume? I have resisted outlining the full novel, or detailing the many other scenes where what is at stake in the configuration of human body and bear, particularly in terms of sexuality, desire and the intricacies of gendered violence, is much greater. Nor will I give a close reading of these excerpts – except to note the relationality within which bearness emerges – hands 'brushing a bear into existence' and the 'men shouting and women screaming' and the whole apparatus of custom in a particular place and time. What these excerpts from the novel alert me to is that the costume of the bear is a potentiality that can enclose and change the human body into something else, something strange and not quite in the world of the present. It can give rise to new desires and can intensify nascent desires. It draws attention to the materiality of the costume, its weight and the ways that its inside layer touches the skin, contains the sweat and provokes transformations that are unpredictable and perhaps beyond intention. This appears in a much more subtle way in the slides. By looking through the boys in bear suits at the girl in the bear suit, I want to interrupt my initial interpretation by suggesting that there may be a relative flattening of affect in the staged images in the photographs. This pertains to the bodies of girls, bears, researcher/audience, and perhaps to the very technology of capture that is the camera. That is, in the digital photographs, the body itself – sweaty, desiring, reaching out – can only be perceived from the outside and from a distance by the viewer who sees the images but can never be part of the scene. The embedded interview in the PowerPoint slide might have more potential but it too is staged and tight, with the girl SH contained in a set – with chair, table, backdrop carefully arranged – and her gestures tight and contained. Her legs appear to be pressed together, her hands are tightly clasped. She looks at the camera but her gaze is stiff and formal. The vigour of movement that is at least implied in the still images of girls and bear suit is lost in the formality of the television interview genre and its apparatus.

Posthuman pedagogy?

This chapter opens with a gesture towards pedagogy, and holds out the promise of a 'pedagogy of material and semiotic entanglement'. So far I have talked about the affordances of imagination that the bear suit brings to the assemblage of girls and imagined futures. What is pedagogical about this, and how might this be thought in terms of posthumanism? Elsewhere I have written about pedagogy as ethical encounter, unpredictable and enacted as particular people come together in particular places and times, dependent on what they bring with them and on what comes to hand. Pedagogical assemblages are co-created among teachers, students, objects and practices that conventionally include 'planning and preparation, resources, texts generated in class, languages, modes of organizing furniture, funneling movement, "managing" space, time and behaviour... each particular to a classroom, a school, a group of students, a specific historical and "geo-ontological moment" ' (Gannon, 2009, p. 86). If I push this sense of pedagogical encounter further towards the posthuman, this requires me to take more seriously the material objects, spaces and places of pedagogical becoming.

Two recent publications offer some ways to begin to think posthumanism pedagogically. An issue of *The Journal of Curriculum and Pedagogy* features a 'Perspectives' section offering insights into how potentialities might be pressed and thinking extended beyond the human. These include the possibilities of sound 'dis-organ-izing the subject' and disrupting the usual 'desire to interpret, decode and thus understand', as an artwork emits acoustic signs 'that are fleeing, escaping and leaking'; that is, they are inclined to affect and sensations rather than representation (Beier, 2013, p. 23). The forces of becoming are prioritized in this pedagogy rather than representational logic. Jagodzinski turns to avant-garde art as a public pedagogy that resists capture by capital as the 'art "disappears" as an event' – rather than a commodity, and 'where interactive attention is drawn to the borders of public-private space, human-inhuman and nonhuman symbiosis, and the duration of time' (2013, p. 33). Radomska turns to the ephemeral affects of 'semi-living bioart' which '[does] away with the central position of the human subject while simultaneously focusing on the relations between human and nonhuman (both organic and non organic)' (2013, p. 30). Posthuman pedagogy entails a relational ethics that arises from the mutual entanglement of human and nonhuman worlds. Finally, making animal-human entanglements explicit through the relationship of Timothy Treadwell – or 'Grizzly Man' – with bears in Alaska, and his own experience volunteering in an animal shelter, Goebel talks of an 'enfleshed pedagogy' that is 'attentive to the bodies of (what we call) humans and animals as sites of messy relations and indeterminate openings to affectivity' (2013, p. 21).

Adding to these principles are further insights from *Posthumanism and Educational Research* (Snaza and Weaver, 2015). They ask: 'What if the human doesn't have to be the measure?' – the measure of superiority, of dominance, of what matters in the world, and in schools and school-based research, curriculum design and disciplinary divisions (2015, p. 3). They argue for an 'open definition of posthumanism' and refuse to provide 'specific answers', given that we are mired in humanism, irretrievably trapped within the discourses and practices that we need to deconstruct so that 'it is not even remotely possible at the present moment to...outline the contours of a posthuman pedagogy' (2015, p. 3). Rather they suggest we should seek to deterritorialize what seemed 'solid' and knowable, so that 'things blur together; everything gets mixed up and moved around' (Snaza and Weaver, 2015, p. 3). In the context of aspiration, and the imaginings or plans of young people for specific futures that was our interest in the STAR project, the suggestion of Snaza and Weaver that letting go of planning in education is a necessary posthumanist gesture directly challenges the logic underpinning the research. Their concern that the production of the neoliberal economic subject – worker and consumer – is the central goal of conventional education also disturbs the assumptions of our research that it is the work, education and training that a person will take up that is the most important aspect of their futures. Nevertheless, returning to the data fragment, though at first glance it does seem to 'capture' plans for the future, the play between girl and girl-bear, costumes, props and technologies also serves to loosen the logic and linearity of any such plans.

Though the career day was – no doubt – carefully 'planned' by teachers, and this would have contributed to its success as an opportunity for students to rehearse, explore and articulate their aspirations, it was simultaneously a pedagogical event, or rather a series of less predictable events and encounters, inclined towards difference. At each moment this could be inclined towards repetition, or to the reification of the wilful neoliberal subject – 'an optometrist like my parents' – but it was also, and at the same time, unpredictable, messy and affectively generative. Entanglements of bodies, beings and things incited lines of flight and imagination, things blurred together and became mixed up and moved around, on the career planning day as well as in my approach to the data in this chapter. Research requires attention to the indeterminate openings that data offers, prising them open, mapping movements, and turning to them again and again in the expectation that each time something else will shimmer and catch the eye.

If I turn again to the PowerPoint slides that produce mobile assemblages of girls' bodies, props, costumes, voices, images, expressions, gestures, visual and software compositions, configurations of time and place that exceed the present, what is evident is the pleasure that the play evokes. The warm timbre of the voice in the video, the sound of laughter, the smiles and grimaces in the photographs suggest that this was an affectively potent experience. There are many ambiguities in the performance of SH as a subject of aspiration – will she be zoologist or optometrist? Help humans or animals? Hug a bear or hold it on a leash? – and these positions are held simultaneously as who knows what the future can bring? Pedagogy is emergent, as Springgay (2008) describes. It does 'not exist prior to these sites [the teachers, the students, the career planning day, the photography and videorecording] rather pedagogy [is] created, materialised, and mobilised' (2008, p. 123). Rather than the intentions and prior planning of the teacher dominating what can happen in the spacetime of learning, pedagogy 'seeps into the cracks' between bodies of students and teachers, bodies of knowledge and classroom practice, and material spaces, objects and technologies (2008, p. 123). Thinking through posthuman pedagogy requires seeing the career planning day as an event where objects and bodies are thrown together to produce outcomes that may be unexpected and ambiguous, where what emerges is different from what would have been the case if the girls had worked without the accoutrements of costumes, cameras and each other to articulate possible futures.

The research assemblage

Finally, I turn to the research site itself and consider how this is put under erasure by posthuman thinking. Posthuman research practices demand attention to materialities and affects, and they prompt experiments and interferences with data. The materiality of the field in

Susanne Gannon 145

research in secondary schools, as Childers suggests, includes 'human bodies, buildings, desks, books, spaces, policies, theories, practices, and other animate and inanimate objects' which have affective force as they form the 'matter' of fieldwork (2013, p. 599). It redirects attention from the substantive focus of the study – for example, aspiration for higher education – towards the 'ontological practices of knowledge production' (2013, p. 602). I have experimented a little with these by returning to the data and following the figure of the bear suit through several texts, reading one through the other in an attempt to trouble my initial reading of the bear-girl. I must also attend to the researcher assemblage – which gave rise to the particular idiosyncracy of this reading. The figures and voices, props and costumes in these two slides repeatedly drew my attention, called me into relation with them, created a 'frisson' of interest through the incongruity of a girl and a bear in a project on education desire (MacLure, 2013b, p. 661). However, unlike Childers, I did not visit this school site and was not a participant in the pedagogical event from which the data fragment emerged – the career planning day. Nor was I yet a member of the research team at that moment when the data was collected or delivered to the university researchers. Another series of affective and material allegiances, emails and shuffling arrangements brought me into the project towards the end of a period of study leave. Data was reallocated to allow for an additional team member and I was given the data set from a different school. Research protocols required permissions, acknowledgements and territorial respect, which I have already perhaps contravened by putting my paws all over the data from a school where I was not the designated researcher.

In the first paper from this project, written by Margaret Somerville, theories of materiality via the concept of 'placetimemattering' inspired by Barad's 'spacetimemattering' are evoked (2013). The first published 'pass' through the data, therefore, focuses on two primary schools in the project – generalizing emerging storylines across the drawings produced by kindergarten and year 5 children and parent focus groups, and it begins to construct a theoretical apparatus. A book chapter (Gannon et al., 2016) works across two secondary schools, using focus group data from parents and teachers and student artefacts to construct patterns of aspiration and consider these through the different theoretical apparatus of superdiversity and globalization. Looking, as I do in this chapter, in a different corner of the data set – one artefact produced in a secondary school – could be considered as just another pass (of the multiple possible passes) through the data set, or perhaps evoking fragments of posthuman theory with bear-human data fragments is a mode of 'plugging in' theory and data, recognizing their machinic 'potential to interrupt and transform other machines, other data, and other knowledge projects' (Jackson and Mazzei, 2012, p. 137). A posthuman perspective requires me to keep the data (and myself) moving rather than fixing meaning or pinning down sense. However this is not enough, and this is not only a requirement of post-qualitative research that aspires to be posthuman. Nevertheless, it is a necessary start to make what seemed solid begin to blur and move about. In this chapter I've focused on a data fragment rather than a data set, I've disrupted this by following the lines of an object – a bear suit – through components of the data fragment and assemblages of girls, things, futures and pedagogies, and I've interfered by plugging in a peripheral text that casts new doubts on any analysis that might have begun to congeal. In Jackson and Mazzei's terms, data has not been 'centered or stabilized but used as brief stopping points and continually transformed' (Jackson and Mazzei, 2013, p. 265). I've worked as lightly as I can theoretically and empirically, keeping the 'posthuman' in my peripheral vision but resisting clarity or certainty about how it might be secured, asking questions rather than providing answers, and drawing attention to generative failures – that is, to the (im)possibilities of both method and pedagogy.

Notes

1. For example, see the definition in the online Aims and Scope of the journal *Pedagogies: An International Journal:* 'classroom teaching and learning in response to new communities and student bodies, curriculum and responses to new knowledge and changing disciplinarity, blends of traditional and new communications media in classrooms, and most importantly, how we might improve and renew the everyday work that teachers and students do in classrooms' (2014, np).
2. The STAR project was led by Margaret Somerville, with Carol Reid, Loshini Naidoo, Tonia Gray and Susanne Gannon as co-researchers. The data fragment that is discussed in this chapter was collected as part of the case study conducted by Loshini Naidoo, and I'm grateful to her for allowing me to work with this fragment of data.
3. Versions of the video can be found at https://www.youtube.com/watch?v=Ahg6qcgoay4.
4. Word 'trying' inserted into the sentence with arrows.

References

Barad, K. (2007) *Meeting the Universe Halfway: Quantum Physics and the Entanglement of Matter and Meaning* (Durham: Duke University Press).

Beier, J. L. (2013) 'Dis-organ-izing the Subject: Thinking with Sound', *Journal of Curriculum and Pedagogy*, 10(1), 23–25.
Bennett, J. (2010a) 'A Vitalist Stopover on the Way to New Materialism', in D. Coole and S. Frost (eds.) *New Materialisms: Ontology, Agency, and Politics* (Durham: Duke University Press), pp. 47–69.
Bennett, J. (2010b) *Vibrant Matter: A Political Ecology of Things* (Durham: Duke University Press).
Blaise, M. (2013) 'Activating Micropolitical Practices in the Early Years; (Re)assembling Bodies and Participant Observations', in R. Coleman and J. Ringrose (eds.) *Deleuze and Research Methodologies* (Edinburgh: Edinburgh University Press), pp. 184–200.
Bradley, D., P. Noonan, H. Nugent and B. Scales (2008) *Review of Australian Higher Education. Final Report*, Commonwealth of Australia: Canberra, www.deewr.gov.au/he_review_finalreport.
Braidotti, R. (2013) *The Posthuman* (Cambridge and New York: Polity).
Childers, S. M. (2013) 'The Materiality of Fieldwork: An Ontology of Feminist becoming', *International Journal of Qualitative Studies in Education*, 26(5), 599–609.
Davies, B. (2003) *Frogs and Snails and Feminist Tales: Preschool Children and Gender* (New York: Hampton Press).
Davies, B. (2014) 'Reading Anger in Early Childhood Intra-Actions a Diffractive Analysis', *Qualitative Inquiry*, 20(6), 734–741.
Davies, B. and S. Gannon (2009) *Pedagogical Encounters* (Rotterdam: Sense Publishers).
Deleuze, G. and P. F. Guattari (1987) *A Thousand Plateaus: Capitalism and Schizophrenia* (Vol. 2) (Minneapolis: University of Minnesota Press).
Gannon, S. (2009) 'Difference as Ethical Encounter', in B. Davies and S. Gannon (eds.) *Pedagogical Encounters* (New York: Peter Lang), pp. 69–88.
Gannon, S., L. Naidoo and T. Gray (2016) 'Educational Aspirations, Ethnicity and Mobility in Western Sydney High Schools', in D. Cole and C. Woodrow (eds.) *Superdimensions in Globalization and Education* (Dordrecht: Springer).
Hultman, K. and H. Lenz Taguchi (2010) 'Challenging Anthropocentric Analysis of Visual Data: A Relational Materialist Methodological Approach to Educational Research', *International Journal of Qualitative Studies in Education*, 23(5), 525–542.
Jackson, A. and L. Mazzei (2012) *Thinking with Theory in Qualitative Research* (New York and London: Routledge).
Jackson, A. and L. Mazzei (2013) 'Plugging One Text into Another: Thinking with Theory in Qualitative Research', *Qualitative Inquiry*, 19(4), 261–271.
Jagodzinski, J. (2013) 'Art and Its Education in the Anthropocene: The Need for an Avant-Garde Without Authority', *Journal of Curriculum and Pedagogy*, 10(1), 31–34.
Lanagan, M. (2009) *Tender Morsels* (Crows Nest: Allen and Unwin Publishers).
MacLure, M. (2013a) 'The Wonder of Data', *Cultural Studies ↔ Critical Methodologies*, 13(4), 228–232.
MacLure, M. (2013b) 'Researching without Representation? Language and Materiality in Post-qualitative Methodology', *International Journal of Qualitative Studies in Education*, 26(6), 658–667.

Pacini-Ketchabaw, V. and A. Taylor (2015) 'Unsettling Pedagogies through Common World Encounters: Grappling with (Post)colonial Legacies in Canadian Forests and Australian Bushlands', in V. Pacini-Ketchabaw and A. Taylor (eds.) *Unsettling the Colonialist Places and Spaces of Early Childhood Education* (New York and London: Routledge), pp. 43–62.

Radomska, M. (2013) 'Posthumanist Pedagogies: Toward an Ethics of the Non/Living', *Journal of Curriculum and Pedagogy*, 10(1), 28–31.

Snaza, N. and J. Weaver (2015) 'Education and the Posthumanist Turn', in N. Snaza and J. Weaver (eds.) *Posthumanism and Educational Research* (New York and London: Routledge), pp. 1–16.

Somerville, M. (2013) 'The "Placetimemattering" of Aspiration in the Blacktown Learning Community', *Critical Studies in Education*, 54(3), 231–244.

Somerville, M., T. Gray C. Reid, L. Naidoo, S. Gannon and L. Brown (2013) *Student Trajectory Aspiration Research (STAR): A Study of Aspirations, Enablers and Barriers to Further Education in the Blacktown Learning Community*, University of Western Sydney, May 2013, http://www.uws.edu.au/__data/assets/pdf_file/0011/504992/STAR_Report,_2013_v2.pdf, accessed 21 April 2015.

Springgay, S. (2008) *Body Knowledge and Curriculum: Pedagogies of Touch in Youth and Visual Culture* (New York: Peter Lang).

St. Pierre, E. (2013) 'The Appearance of Data', *Cultural Studies <=> Critical Methodologies*, 13(4), 223–227.

Taylor, A. (2008) '"Taking Account of Childhood Excess": Bringing the Elsewhere Home', in B. Davies (ed.) *Judith Butler in Conversation: Analysing the Texts and Talk of Everyday Life* (New York and London: Routledge), pp. 195–216.

Taylor, A. (2013) *Reconfiguring the Natures and Cultures of Childhood* (London: Taylor & Francis).

9
Decentring the Human in Multispecies Ethnographies

Veronica Pacini-Ketchabaw, Affrica Taylor and Mindy Blaise

Bridging the divide

Much has been written about the need to bridge the theory/practice divide by bringing them together in the 'praxis' of teaching. For researchers inspired by posthumanist theorizations, the task of bridging the theory/practice divide is particularly challenging because it is accompanied by the additional need to resist the nature/culture divide that keeps our human species 'hyper-separated' from all 'earth others' in the name of 'human exceptionalism' (Plumwood, 2002). The foundational nature/culture divide of Western humanism provides the structuring logic for our human-centric practices, and the challenge of decentring the human within the decidedly humanist practice of social science research cannot be underestimated. The challenge is compounded when this research is 'applied' in 'the field' – or, to put it another way, when it is enacted in the world beyond the academy. It seems much easier to theorize about decentring the human than to walk the talkand find congruent, innovative ways to 'put new concepts to the test' (Lorimer, 2010, p. 238).

Within a social science discipline like education, where it is axiomatic that our core business is to investigate human learning or the discursive practices and/or materials that guide and enable this learning, more-than-human research practice seems like an anathema. Nevertheless, one of our central research goals is to explore the possibilities of learning with other species in a more-than-human world. In this chapter, we first discuss the conceptual and methodological frameworks within which we work, namely common world and multispecies ethnography. Second, we illustrate and reflect on our attempts to shift focus away from the researcher and child as the central becoming-knowable subjects about animals and refocus on complex, entangled, mutually affecting and co-shaping child-animal relations.

This shift is easier said than done. Since embarking on our multispecies ethnographies in Hong Kong, Australia and Canada, we have experienced a disjuncture between articulating the need for research that decentres the human in theoretically coherent and compelling ways and fully realizing it in practice. While posthumanist conceptualizations are now firmly established, the doings of them are fraught with impasses. Resisting the tendency to default back to observing children in their interactions with animals feels more like an 'ontological struggle' than an epistemological one (Hinchliffe et al., 2005, p. 649) because moving beyond anthropocentric descriptions of animal behaviours requires continually reorienting from individual human to collective more-than-human subjectivities and agencies. In short, such a move entails relearning how to do research 'without the tools of human exceptionalism' (Haraway, cited in van Dooren, 2014, back cover).

While the practice of multispecies research has required us to push beyond our limits, the research itself pushes at the limits of intelligibility within the field of early childhood education, where we are situated. This is because of early childhood education's deeply sedimented commitment to pursuing child-centred pedagogies and addressing the developmental needs of the (becoming autonomous) individual child within the child's (exclusively human) sociocultural context. Discussions about our seemingly offbeat multispecies research inevitably lead back to human-centric questions such as: What are your findings about these children's relations with animals? What do the children in your research learn from their relations with animals? How does following the animal help us to better understand the child?

Common worlding

Our way of resisting the force field of child-centredness is to refocus on the 'common worlds' that we (children, teachers, educators and researchers) co-inhabit with multitudes of other species (Common World Childhoods Research Collective, 2014). 'Common worlds' is a term we borrow from Latour (2005), who speaks about the necessity to reassemble all of the constituents of our worlds – including nonhuman life forms, forces and entities – within a radically expanded conceptualization of the social. The insistence that we live in not just exclusively human societies but in common worlds with other species runs counter to the human-centric impulse to divide ourselves off from the rest of the world and re-enact the self-perpetuating nature/culture divide (Latour, 2004).

Moving away from research practices that separate the human off from the rest, we work hard at putting the notion of common worlds to work in an active, reconnecting and generative sense. In our multispecies research, we do this by tracing how our lives, children's lives and the lives of other animals in our common worlds are entangled, interconnected, mutually dependent, and therefore mutually 'response-able' (Haraway, 2008) for the commons (Pacini-Ketchabaw and Taylor, 2015; Taylor et al., 2013; Taylor and Pacini-Ketchabaw, 2015). We approach our research practice, then, as a political act of 'common worlding' (Taylor, 2013), as a collective and compositional practice that not only accounts for the other species with whom we live but acknowledges that these dynamic, entangled multispecies relations gestate our common worlds and bring them into being (Taylor and Blaise, 2014).

Multispecies ethnography

In line with our common worlds framework, multispecies ethnography is characterized by an attempt to move beyond research practices that confine themselves to exclusively human (or social) concerns and interests. It is a relatively new experimental and hybrid methodology associated with the 'animal turn' in the social sciences (Buller, 2014; Hodgetts and Lorimer, 2014; Weil, 2010); and assumes that human being and becoming and even sociality itself (Tsing, 2013) are entangled in complex, often asymmetrical, ways with the being and becoming of other species (Hamilton and Taylor, 2012; Kirksey and Helmreich, 2010; Lorimer, 2014; Rose et al., 2012; Whatmore, 2006). It is the lively connections among species (often, but not always, including humans), their collective effects and their ethical implications that provide the research focus.

Much has been written about the difficulties of resisting an anthropocentric frame of reference when conducting multispecies ethnographies and about the potential limits of human perception and communication (Hamilton and Taylor, 2012; Hinchliffe et al., 2005; Hodgetts and Lorimer, 2014; Kirksey and Helmreich, 2010; Lorimer, 2010; Moore and Kosut, 2013). To counter these difficulties, more-than-human scholars from anthropology and human geography speak of the need for taking risks (and being allowed to take risks) to experiment with new methods that stay open to multispecies interdeterminacies and resist human control (Tsing, 2011, p. 19), extend 'the company and modality of what constitutes a research subject' (Whatmore, 2006, p. 605) and rethink 'what forms of intelligence, truth and expertise count' (Lorimer, 2010, p. 239). Tsing (2013) puts a particularly positive spin on the inescapable fact of simply being human in a more-than-human research project. She recasts our humanness, not as a limiting factor, but as the starting point for entering into more-than-human relations. She reminds us that it is important to be present in our work, to be part of the interconnected multispecies worlds we are seeking to explore. As she puts it, 'we are participants as well as observers; we recreate interspecies sensibilities in what we do ... [We learn other species] and ourselves *in action*, through common activities' (p. 24).

Shifting focus in our Hong Kong, Canadian and Australian multispecies projects

In what follows, we outline how we are putting our more-than-human common worlds' conceptual framework to work *on the grounds* of these worlds. This has required us to try out the slow and attentive kind of applied research that Stengers (2005a, p. 1002) refers to as 'collective thinking in the presence of [nonhuman] others'. To do this we have had to immerse ourselves in multispecies worlds and to pay attention to what they tell us. We have been tested not to foreclose on thinking as an exclusively human activity, and to remain open to how our thoughts might be reshaped through our encounters with nonhuman life forms.

As a way of engaging with the challenges posed by conducting multispecies research, we describe sets of experimental shifts that we have been using to decentre the human in our work. Each description is followed by a reflection, in italics, which addresses the challenges and possibilities that the shift enables. Through these shifts we attempt to reorient our research from strongly held early childhood research practices (following the child, representing others as the objects of study, making meaning, focusing on innocent encounters, safety of thinking as an individual researcher) towards research practices within common worlds of human and nonhuman constituents, all exercising agency (following multispecies relations, engaging with more-than-human others as active research subjects, learning to being affected as researcher, attending to awkward encounters, risking thinking collectively). We draw from our multispecies ethnographic field notes to illustrate the shifts.

Veronica's project has unfolded in university childcare centres located in wet temperate urban forests on Canada's west coast. Participants include two groups of up to 16 children, eight early childhood educators, three graduate students, deer, earthworms, raccoons, stick bugs, lichen, fungi, mosses, chickadees, brown bears, crows, ravens, owls, ferns, douglas fir, arbutus, maples, blackberry, holly, English ivy and a myriad of other species. Affrica's research takes place in a dry urban bushland setting on a university campus in the Australian Capital Territory. Participants include groups of up to 15 children and two early childhood educators from the university early childhood education centre, occasional parents and teacher education students, innumerable ants, mosquito larvae, a large mob of eastern grey kangaroos, groves of eucalyptus and casurina trees, cicadas, mushrooms, grasslands and wild brambles. Mindy's three-and-one-half-year-long multispecies ethnography of dog and human entanglements took place across Hong Kong dog parks, *dai pai dongs* (outdoor restaurants), shopping malls and outdoor markets. Participants include individual dogs, their apparel and their human companions, significant material objects and her own body.

Shifting from following the child to following multispecies relations

Child-earthworm relations in Victoria

It rains a lot in Victoria, British Columbia, and with the rain, unexpected kinds of interspecies encounters take place in the course of everyday life. Earthworms, humans and other animals co-navigate the surface of their wet common routes of travel in this urban Pacific Northwest place. After every rain, the sidewalks are full of surfacing earthworms. The worms slither across the paths seeking puddles, taking advantage of the wet surfaces because they can travel more easily across them than they can through soil. Surfacing, however, brings risks – the earthworms are in constant danger of being squashed by passersby or being eaten by birds. We (a group of children, educators and researchers) often encounter these slithering sidewalk earthworms on our regular rainy-day walks. Their presence draws our attention to where we place our feet and heightens our awareness of the life and death responsibilities entailed in our relations with other small and vulnerable species. Attracted by the same puddles as the earthworms, but also encumbered by slippery and unwieldy muddy rubber boots, the children often come perilously close to squashing their wet sidewalk companions. They have to concentrate hard on what their feet are doing to avert potentially lethal encounters. Most of the time however, children's bodily encounters with worms are quite gentle and convivial, as curious small hands reach out to touch slimy earthworm bodies. The worms wiggle; the hands gently hold. Every embodied encounter changes both.

'Child-centredness' is axiomatic to most early childhood pedagogies and research projects. Attempting to do anything else feels very counter-intuitive. As this descriptive vignette shows, although we start off with the best intentions to follow the relations that emerge when children and earthworms meet on slippery pathways, we are only partially successful. By the end of the story we have relapsed into following what the children are doing to the worms, and of affirming their care for these small vulnerable beings. For educators and researchers alike, it is much easier to slip back into the familiar territory of casting these child-worm encounters as 'teacheable moments' in which 'naturally curious' children can learn about other creatures.

To stay with the relations themselves means becoming differently attuned to exactly what is emerging anew or being 'remade' in every 'dance of relating' that occurs 'when species meet' (Haraway, 2008, p. 25). We are only just beginning to cultivate the new modes of attention we need in order to be able to stay focused on all the moves of all the dancers, and to prevent ourselves from defaulting to observations that would limit the significance of the nonhuman partners to the pedagogical opportunities they afford the children. We have to keep reminding ourselves that the children are not the only ones choreographing this dance and we (the educators and researchers) are not the only ones fostering their curiosity. The worms are on their own travels, regardless of us (Abrahamsson and Bertoni, 2014). Through their very presence on the surface they are acting on the children and moving them to touch and be curious.

Tsing's insistence that we 'are made in entangling relations with significant others' (2013, p. 27) and her encouragement for multispecies ethnographers to pay attention to 'how humans and other species come into ways of life through webs of social relations' (Tsing, 2013, p. 28) reminds us that our task is to remember that there are innumerable threads that knit our common worlds together, including these small chance encounters of children and worms on the slippery pathways of everyday life.

Shifting from representing other animals as objects of study to engaging with other animals as active research subjects

Sensing dog worlds in Sheung Wan

It is a typical hot and humid afternoon in Sheung Wan, Hong Kong and I (Mindy) am sitting on a bench at a dog park with my eyes closed. I smell urine. It is impossible to ignore. Instead of dissipating, the smell only seems to become stronger and more intense. I have learned that urine marking is a method of communication among dogs, but I wonder if these dogs might be telling me something? The urine-infused air is sticky and hot. It touches and sticks to my skin, rising up from the concrete and co-mingling with my researching human body. While I can hear dogs barking and voices speaking Cantonese in the background, something strange and weird is happening to me. I am not sure that I belong here or what today's visit might entail. I have never noticed the urine before and I wonder, 'Whose territory have I entered?' Although I am tempted to open my eyes and see what kinds of dogs are barking, I keep them closed and wait.

Something brushes against my leg. Startled, I open my eyes and look down towards the ground. A small, brown poodle is looking up at me. She has dark brown eyes and she moves her tiny head slightly to the left and then the right. We have met before. She jumps up and puts her two front paws on my legs. Today her toenails are painted bright pink. For a moment, I am distracted and vaguely pleased by this queer vision, and I let out a soft laugh. I hesitate and look around for the dog's minder. The poodle moves her paws against my legs and then drops to the ground. She bends her head down towards the floor, with her bottom sticking up in the air, with her tail raised. Moving her body up, she is standing on all four legs, and bends her head down and sniffs my feet. While sniffing, she licks my toes and then my ankle. Her nose is slightly wet and the licking tickles my skin. Her tail wags quickly as she looks up at me. I smile at her, bend down and ask: 'Are you Cola? Haven't we met on Ladder Street?' I gently scratch her neck and pat her small, fluffy head. She moves her nose towards my hand and licks the back of it. She now moves under the bench and I am unsure where she is or what she is doing. I scoot back and bend my body down to look under the bench. Cola is now sitting with her head down on top of her pink-painted front paws.

Making the shift from representing animals as objects of study to engaging with animals as active research subjects requires a different set of habits, skills and dispositions. Shifting my research practices involves relearning traditional ethnographic observational methods in ways that do not rely exclusively on visual and textual representations (Blaise, 2013). I make this shift by leaving my pen, paper and camera behind. This practice might seem insignificant, but it challenges me to engage differently with the dogs as research subjects. Sensory ethnographic principles, such as emplacement, the interconnection of senses, and knowing in practice (Pink, 2009) have been instructive. They remind me that mind-body-place practices are relational and that separating out these practices, as well as the senses, is impossible. I am figuring out ways that challenge me to go beyond watching, listening and writing. Closing my eyes helps me privilege smelling, listening and feeling within a multisensory encounter. I am hoping that this multilayered and interconnected sensorial way of experiencing the dog and even being moved by the dog might help me to engage with dogs as subjects of their own worlds rather than as objects of my study. As I focus on sensing the dog, I am also waiting to be invited into a relationship. These practices are not about producing better representations and more accurate understandings of Hong Kong dogs. Rather, they are ways of shifting standard forms of research subject/object relationships, or doing what Hinchliffe and his colleagues (2005, p. 651) refer to as deliberately changing engagements. I am changing how my researching body engages with dogs as I smell, listen and feel while waiting to be approached. I am learning how not to be in charge (Tsing, 2013) of these research moments and more-than-human research relationships. Through sensory engagements on doggy terms, I am figuring out new ways that allow 'nonhuman knowledgeabilities to emerge' (Hinchliffe et al., 2005, p. 653). I have no idea what dog knowledgeabilities might be or how they will emerge because I am not a dog, but I do know that they involve experimenting with methods, taking a risk that I won't always be approached by a dog, and suspending my pull towards meaning making for long enough to sense dog worlds and dog agencies on dog terms.

Appropriating Sarah Pink's (2009) sensory apprentice methods, I am tuning into the dog's world of smell. For Pink, a sensory apprenticeship requires an emplaced engagement with the activities, practices and environments that one is exploring. For me, this involves a reflexivity about the learning process for Cola and myself, how I am establishing connections between Cola's and my own sensory practices, and how I am understanding the power relations within the dog park between Cola and other dogs and humans. I find out that unlike humans, who have a weak olfactory sense and mostly see the world, dogs interpret the world predominantly by smell. Depending on the breed, a dog's sense of smell is about 1,000 to 10,000 times more sensitive than a human's. Researchers using specialized photographic methods that detect how air flows when a dog sniffs are able to show that dog sniffing is neither a single nor a simple inhalation (Horowitz, 2009). As a sensory apprentice, I am learning that when Cola smells and licks me, she is taking in layers of complex odours and investigating me. This multisensory event between my human researching body and the pet dog researching body is significant because it is here where a new kind of researcher relationship emerges. I am no longer 'studying' and 'representing' the dog as my object of study: I am following Cola as my smelling mentor and research subject.

Shifting from meaning making about to learning to be affected by the world

Mindy's restrained experimental research practices, which saw her holding back, sensing and following Hong Kong dog worlds rather than rushing in to interpret and represent them, is in line with the broader more-than-human methodological shift that Sarah Whatmore (2006, p. 604) describes as moving 'from an onus on *meaning* to an onus on *affect*'. By affect, Whatmore is referring to the ways in which sentient beings, despite and often because of their incommensurable differences, are affected and moved by each other within the very fabrication of '"livingness" in a more-than-world' (p. 604). Affect is an embodied and relational exchange that alerts us to being alive and mutually vulnerable to other living creatures. It occurs at the threshold of encounters. Being open to being affected and moved by other species is a risky business. For our species, it entails risking the temporary suspension of a sense of sovereignty and rationality (Latimer and Miele, 2013).

Child-stick-ant dances in Canberra

It's striking just how much children, plants and animals affect and move each other during our weekly walks through Canberra's dry sclerophyll eucalyptus forests. Crunching through brittle forest litter and tripping over the carpet of fallen sticks and strips of bark, the children literally kick and trample their stumbling ways through the bush. They are marking trails with their bodies, even as the bush reciprocally scratches their legs and arms and marks them. There are large, gravelly ant nests in almost every clearing. The children find them endlessly fascinating. At least one child always has a stick in hand, collected on the walk. The sticks make great poking implements and also offer children a safe distance from their curious troublemaking. Tapping the nests with the sticks, the children provocatively goad the ants, triggering a pheromone of hyperactive response. Myriads of ants suddenly rush out of their tiny holes and swarm in all directions. They are biting angry. Beating a hasty retreat, the children scream and scatter. Some of the children slap at their legs to squash the invading ants that are now secreted in their clothing. It's an escalating dance of mutual affect. Abetted by sticks, the enlivened ants' and children's bodies are rapidly inciting, exciting, reacting to and moving each other while stimulating heightened 'new modes of body attention and awareness' in both species (Moore and Kosut, 2013, p. 5). Affected by the plights of ants and children alike, the alerted adults watch with anxious apprehension.

Witnessing this scene unfold affects us, as the 'responsible' teachers and researchers. We feel compelled to warn the children of the risks they take by upsetting the ants and getting too close to the nests. We don't want them to get bitten and we don't want them to disturb and hurt the ants. We want to support their curiosities about these teeming micro-worlds, and we also feel ourselves drawn by the ants to see exactly what these amazing, tiny animals are doing. We experience the pull of rational and affective forces within this contact zone of energizing multispecies encounters, experimental research practices, and competing human and more-than-human interests and concerns. 'Learning to be affected' (Latour, 2004) is one of our primary goals in this multispecies research project. To do this, we must risk sensing the world differently, as the children are doing, through attuning to our own and other bodies (Lorimer, 2010), not just studying the world through the safety of detached mental processes. Discomfiting as it can sometimes be, 'learning to be affected' requires us to viscerally experience the 'response-ability' (Haraway, 2008) of these other bodies – such as sticks and ants – to feel their capacities to act on and affect us, even as we act on and affect them. We cannot decentre the human without learning to be affected by the world that we also affect.

Shifting from innocent encounters to awkward encounters of mixed affect

Raccoon-child cohabitations on Burnaby Mountain

Not all multispecies events in early childhood spaces and places are innocent or unproblematic. Encounters are often awkward and marked by inconvenience, risk, confrontation and strange curiosities (Instone, 2014; Lorimer, 2014). Consider, for example, the cohabitations of raccoons and children in a childcare playground on Burnaby Mountain in Vancouver. Widely regarded as pests, a resident family of raccoons transgresses all manner of human boundaries at the childcare centre. They not only evoke the abject through dropping their infectious faeces in the playground, but they transgress notions of domestic/wild by knocking on windows to be let inside the building. Allow me to elaborate.

The resident raccoons spend more time in this playground than the children do. The children have become attentive to these unruly inhabitants and are beginning to know the place differently through the raccoons' movements. The sand in the sandbox is not just sand to play in, for example. It's where raccoons leave their signature paw prints. The tree in the playground has also been marked by the raccoons' 'handprints' and the children notice them. Accessing the toys in the outside shed is no simple matter. Raccoons may have their den there, so the children are not allowed to go into the shed. And it's not just the children who relate to the playground differently. So too do the educators who dutifully remove the raccoons' faeces from the playground every day. Raccoons are the primary host of *Baylisascaris procyonis*, a roundworm that exists in their faeces. The roundworm eggs stay in the soil and contaminate objects that, when put in human mouths, can cause infection. Putting objects into their mouths is something children do a lot, so the educators take seriously the task of picking up and removing raccoon droppings. Other forces are at play that intensify these risky encounters: the roundworm eggs become infectious only after two to four weeks. Thus, adult humans diligently remove raccoon dung daily before the children go outside. The raccoons watch curiously from high in a tree, while the cautious educators watch the raccoons' movements from below – a truly awkward zone of multispecies engagement (Tsing, cited in Lorimer, 2014, p. 203).

Awkwardness also emerges through the oblique connections between the raccoons and humans. Every day the raccoon family comes a bit closer to the childcare centre building. The raccoons might be observing us, getting to know us, trying to enter the building, looking for food, or perhaps even offering their 'charms'. They may be curious or trying to get our attention. It is certain, though, that their behaviours stimulate a range of negative and positive attachments for us humans. We are continually undone and redone, alternately at ease, uncomfortable, disconcerted, and surprised by the raccoons' charms. Is it the disarming tension between their 'nonhuman charisma' (Lorimer, 2007), on the one hand, that attracts us to affectionately recognize our own kind in their playful antics, and their well-held reputation as a risky 'infectious pest', on the other hand, which 'drives and configures [our] "ethical sensibilities"' (Lorimer, 2007, p. 928) through mixed affect? As the increasingly unruly raccoons knock on the building's glass windows, our carefully constructed binaries of human/nonhuman, domesticated/wild and nature/culture, among many others, are unsettled, confounded and threatened. These awkward moments that threaten human boundary making and control have been generative in prompting 'thought, practice and politics' among the children and educators (Lorimer, 2014, p. 196). They have moved us to discuss *how we are going to respond* to the simultaneously charming, infectious and cheeky raccoons in ways that allow cohabitation in which all can flourish (Haraway, 2008). Our encounters with this raccoon family have produced both pleasure (especially for the children, who find them very entertaining, but also for us adults, who are amused by the raccoons' insistence on staying in this place) and huge disconcertment, raising the question of how we might coexist in this urban mountain forest environment. The raccoons in the childcare playground unsettle normalized understandings of the innocence of children's spaces. Moreover, the mixed affects engendered by these provocative animals intensify our reflections upon the ethics and politics of multispecies coexistence, particularly in such a proximal zone of awkward engagement.

These awkward multispecies encounters pose ethical dilemmas for the educators in the childcare centre, but they also pose dilemmas for the research. We aim to create openings in highly contested spaces. In other words, we hint at what might be possible in, or what might emerge from these encounters, without necessarily seeking a final truth or a 'research finding' (Haraway, 2008; Tsing, 2013). We pay close attention to how we might undo, reposition and make strange the taken-for-granted notion of humans within these unconventional encounters. Ultimately, it is in these awkward relations that we are moved to care differently, to see our entanglements with other species, and to acknowledge our vulnerabilities. The ethics of how to respond to the raccoons as both infectious and charming animals is complicated. How do we care for them? How do we respond to them? Could we love these raccoons? Might distaste be easier than love? Or even fear? Is a generalizable response the most appropriate?

Embodied child and kangaroo encounters in the Australian bush

Large mobs of eastern grey kangaroos graze on open grasslands around the Canberra early childhood centre where we conduct our multispecies research. They are 'environmental refugees' who moved into the city precincts during the recent drought and are now permanent residents on this tract of land, which is ringed by major motorways. A recent geo-tagging study of Canberra's urban kangaroos showed that the vast majority of these canny animals avoid crossing major roads, indicating they are quite aware of the threat that speeding motor vehicles pose to them (Westh, 2011). Children and kangaroos, on the other hand, have a much more convivial relationship. They also have a keen awareness of each other, in a benignly curious and yet respectfully wary kind of way. From the children's side, at least, this is a relationship of affection and attachment. They care for the kangaroos. In particular, they care for the joeys, whom they love to spot in their mothers' pouches and often draw and name as their close friends. The children are learning from the kangaroos how to pay close attention to where they are and who and what is there with them. They have learned this by paying close attention to the kangaroos' bodies. For instance, the children have noticed how the kangaroos often stand bolt upright on their haunches, balancing on their enormous tails while attentively looking around. Kangaroos are hypervigilant of anything and anyone that approaches them. The children have seen how the kangaroos use their rotating ears to monitor the sounds of these approaches, and how quickly they can turn and hop away when their proximity zones are breached. They spend lots of time imagining and enacting what it would be like to live in a kangaroo's body – hopping with a big, heavy tail, listening carefully with swivelling ears, scratching furry chests and feeling tucked up in a furry pouch. The children are clearly stimulated and corporeally affected by their relations with these large animals.

The ways in which we are all affected, humans and kangaroos alike, are never entirely predictable, however, nor are they necessarily innocent. On a recent walk, we had an unexpected and disturbing encounter with a dead kangaroo. It had been killed on the adjacent highway and its body thrown back into the paddock to rot. The children were speechless and transfixed. The body they had affectionately come to know so well was now reduced to a lifeless, stinking, decomposing form. The fur was coming off the pelt and crows had pecked open the stomach cavity. Blowflies buzzed around the corpse and the stench of death was overpowering. The children screwed up their faces in disgust and held their noses, but they kept edging forward to get an even closer look. The kangaroo's neck was broken and its head thrown back. They could see its large teeth and exposed skull, the maggoty remains of its intestines coming out of an enlarged hole that was once its anus. Shock, fear, repulsion, morbid fascination, sadness, grief, curiosity – the mixed affects of an awkwardly compelling encounter were all present in that disconcerting and extended moment. Not long afterwards, the children returned to their own imaginary and embodied kangaroo play. With much laughter and release, this time they were listening for and fleeing cars, being knocked over and lying dead on the grass.

One of the decentring aspects of learning to be affected through paying close attention to our embodied multispecies relations is that we cannot presume to control the myriad ways in which we are and will be affected by these worldly relations. Once affected, however, we stand a better chance of appreciating the precariousness of life and recognizing the vulnerabilities we share with other living beings with whom our lives are entangled. This is particularly so when we are affected in difficult ways that are not of our choosing. After this first encounter with the dead kangaroo, the children asked to revisit its body three more times. At each of these rewitnessing events, they came away reflecting on their own stories of losing family pets and of nearly running over kangaroos on Canberra's roads. It seemed the children were registering a much deeper, amplified and sober sense of their own entanglement in the living and dying relations that make up their common worlds. Perhaps these various ways of sensing their own implication in common world relations of living and dying – smelling it, witnessing it, reflecting on it – indicate that they were beginning to grapple with the likelihood of ongoing awkward human-animal relations (Ginn et al., 2014). As disconcerting as these awkward relations might be, they nevertheless have the potential to prompt a new kind of multispecies 'affective and thus ethical logics' (Lorimer, 2014, p. 196). The acceptance of awkward relations is akin to the relational multispecies ethics that Haraway (2010) often refers to as 'staying with the trouble', not for the promise of an ultimate solution or a final peace, but because cohabiting in our common worlds in ways that allow all to flourish requires us to grapple with the difficulties of living with incommensurable differences – and to respond (2008, pp. 141, 41).

Shifting from exclusively human thinking to risking thinking collectively with other species

Thinking with an urban forest in Victoria

A group of children, educators and researchers comes together weekly in an art studio to think with the urban forest located next to the childcare centre. The studio is located in the middle of a forest of tall spruce and cedar trees choked by English ivy. A creek runs through it. In this studio, we are inspired by Tsing's (2011) invitation to slow down: 'Next time you walk through a forest, look down. A city lies under your feet. If you were somehow to descend into the earth, you would find yourself surrounded by the city's architecture of webs and filaments' (para. 1). As in any studio, I suppose, there is potential here for new constraints, requirements and possibilities. But unlike other early childhood art studios, here the forest is alive, the forest thinks (Kohn, 2013).[1] All species (including us humans) generate their own systems of values, constraints and obligations, and we are in the midst of these multiple relatings of the webs and filaments of ground, trees, water, plants, animals, insects, deer, cougars, clay and one another. As we think with the forest, we notice care-fully the deer watching us, the distinctly shaped trees that surround us, the sticks that the children pick up, the spider that lives in the hollow tree, the water that runs through the creek bed, the leaves that fall on the forest floor, the decomposing fallen trees, the thousands of pine needles that lie on the ground, the woodpecker eating bugs on a cedar tree high above our heads. New kinds of noticing emerge as the children become yet another forest species. The ways in which we relate to the forest and to one another – our actions, movements, words and the forest's own actions and movements – shift our ways of knowing and being. At some point, we stopped being observers in this forest. We are part of it. We converge in the act of accompanying and intra-acting with the many species that flourish and fail in these woods.

This studio is not just any studio. It is intimately known for its specificities. The children can remember every stump and hollow through the species they once encountered there and the clay they left behind. They return to the same tree over and over. This tree kept all of the pieces of clay that the children once stuck on its trunk. The wind, of course, helped dried the clay, changed its colour and its form. Everyone and everything participates in the studio. Clay helps us see connections to pine needles, sticks, rocks, soil, leaves, small branches and bits of garbage as all of these things and our fingers stick to it. These objects and the clay continually transform themselves as they come into friction. Clay never stays the same and nor do the objects it collects. The clay is transformed and transforms us. We never stay the same. The children notice this as they ask for more 'clean' clay. With us in it, the forest is creating new histories, just as we create new histories when we are in the forest.

How do we intersect with the histories this forest already knows? For example, violent movements of colonialism and commercialism forever altered the forests' architectures and ecological patterns of multispecies cohabitation when European settlers arrived on Canada's west coast. How do these histories and stories matter in our forest studio? Whose stories are visible here, and whose become invisible? How can we pay attention to what is already here? How do we see ourselves in relation to what's here? What do our ongoing visits do to the forest? How do our visits forever change the forest? These questions of what the forest knows and how the forest emerges are tangled up with our forest studio presences and our movements through the forest. The forest is in the midst of complicated relationships, in economic, cultural and ecological terms. Artist Gina Badger (2009) assists us in trying to acknowledge the multifaceted disruptions that have occurred and continue to occur through colonization. She believes we need to think about 'an ecology of colonisation that considers colonisation as a holistic process, one whose violence can be complicated and subtle, messed up somewhere between cultural and environmental' lines (p. 2).

Frictions like these are part of our collective thinking and doing in the forest studio. It is friction, Tsing (2005) says, that produces movement, action and effect. When we pay attention to friction, she observes, we see relationships as transformative and are 'not sure of the outcome' (2012, p. 510). Attending to friction opens our eyes to 'historical contingency, unexpected conjuncture, and the ways that contact across difference can produce new agendas' (p. 510). Friction encompasses problems, dangers and risks. Yet, friction also opens up to transformation. Being, thinking and doing through friction helps us avoid our tendency to separate, to know, to generalize. With friction, everything moves. Everything and everyone becomes something else all the time. Friction gives us a way to consider, for instance, how the forest might respond and object to colonialism and loss. Species such as raccoons, bears and cougars that once lived exclusively in these forests are responding and objecting to the loss of their habitat by adapting and learning to live – quite successfully – in urban environments. Their objections may threaten and inconvenience us, but perhaps if we learn to think collectively we might see these encounters differently.

Through our multispecies ethnographies, we practice 'slow science' – opening ourselves up to thinking collectively (with humans and more-than-humans), to attending to 'others' preoccupations, to their knowledge, to their objections' (Stengers, in Métral, para. 16). We constantly ask the question, how might we cultivate new relations? There are always risks in this process of fostering collective thought. The risks for us have been to not know where we are going, to open our thoughts and bodies too much or too little, to not pay close enough attention, to be bewildered. Yet, Stengers (2005a, 2005b) reminds us that if we don't open ourselves to risk, research will never become more than we are. The trick is not to represent a unified world but to risk creating new worlds – not perfect worlds, but worlds that might change what the world might become. We are risking common worlding with this multispecies forest rather than trying to control it by 'knowing' it.

Conclusion

Attempting to de-centre the human in research is disconcerting as it literally displaces the certitudes of humanist intellectual work. The shifts we have illustrated in this chapter gesture not only towards the conscious moves we have been making to decentre the human, but towards the myriad challenges we continue to face in this experimental research. Not only are we continually challenged by the ingrained 'tendency to view human subjects as the appropriate focus of (social) research'; but also by the risk of anthropomorphizing the more-than-human when seeking to account for their agency (Buller, 2014; Hodgetts and Lorimer, 2014, p. 291). Conducting multispecies ethnographies with children and the species we/they meet in their common worlds remains a radically open methodological experiment. By that we mean the engagement in open-ended and speculative 'practices likely to generate surprising results' (Lorimer, 2015, p. 10). These practices require us to persevere with risk taking, with trying to notice differently, with the potential of curiosity, with 'learning how to be affected' (Latour, 2004) even when this means feeling anxious and uncomfortable.

There are no grandiose research findings from our multispecies experimentations, nothing to prescribe, nothing to apply universally. Our situated studies are small, local, relational and decidedly non-heroic research events. There is, however, much to learn in the doing of such grounded relational research, in entering into these productively unsettling, everyday common world spaces. Within these spaces we learn how to work in an active, reconnecting, generative way *in* and *with* the world we research. We learn how to be present in a world that is not just about us and to recognize that there is much about this world that we never understand. We learn how to inhabit the disconcerting space of more-than-human research 'without the luxury of any perfect solutions or easy fixes' (van Dooren, 2014, p. 116). As Haraway (2010) reminds us, perhaps our greatest lessons are to be learned by 'staying with the trouble' in the contact zone of more-than-human relations. This is how we can become more 'worldly', more attuned to our place in the world.

Doing multispecies research has allowed us to notice that the world is far more curious than we first assumed, and that curiosity can draw us into new kinds of relationships and new obligations and responsibilities (Tsing, 2013). We hope these obligations and responsibilities are not just new ethical forms of research practices. We hope they 'might provide an avenue to more sustaining possibilities of life' (van Dooren, 2014, p. 85) in our common worlds – regardless of whether the lives are those of children, kangaroos, forests, dogs, ants, earthworms or racoons.

Notes

1. In his book *How Forests Think*, Kohn (2013) challenges us to open our understanding of representation beyond human linguistic and symbolic practices and to recognise that all life forms live with and through signs. He claims that it is the semiosis of multispecies relations that 'permeates and constitutes the living world' (p. 9).

References

Abrahamsson, S. and F. Bertoni (2014) 'Compost Politics: Experimenting with Togetherness in Vermicomposting', *Environmental Humanities*, 4, 125–148.
Badger, G. (2009) 'Plants Don't Have Legs – An Interview', *INFLeXions*, 3, http://www.senselab.ca/inflexions/volume_3/node_i3/PDF/Badger%20Plants%20Don%20t%20Have%20Legs.pdf, accessed 5 November 2014.
Blaise, M. (2013) 'Situating Hong Kong Pet-Dog-Child Figures within Colonialist Flows and Disjunctures', *Global Studies of Childhood*, 3(4), 380–394.
Buller, H. (2014) 'Animal Geographies II: Methods', *Progress in Human Geography*, first published on 31 March 2014, doi:10.1177/0309132514527401.
Common World Childhoods Research Collective (2014) Common Worlds, https//www.commonworlds.net, accessed 5 November 2014.
Ginn, F., U. Beisel and M. Barua (2014) 'Flourishing with Awkward Creatures: Togetherness, Vulnerability, Killing', *Environmental Humanities*, 4, 113–123.
Hamilton, L. and N. Taylor (2012) 'Ethnography in Evolution: Adapting to the Animal "Other" in Organizations', *Journal of Organizational Ethnography*, 1(1), 43–51.
Haraway, D. (2008) *When Species Meet* (Minneapolis, MN: University of Minnesota Press).
Haraway, D. (2010) 'When Species Meet: Staying with the Trouble', *Environment and Planning D: Society and Space*, 28(1), 53–56.
Hinchliffe, S., M. Kearnes, M. Degen and S. Whatmore (2005) 'Urban Wild Things: A Cosmopolitical Experiment', *Environment and Planning D: Society and Space*, 23, 643–658.
Hodgetts, T. and J. Lorimer (2014) 'Methodologies for Animals' Geographies: Culture, Communication and Genomics', *Cultural Geographies*, 1–11, doi: 10.1177/1474474014525114.
Horowitz, A. (2009) *Inside of a Dog: What Dogs See, Smell and Know* (New York: Scribner).
Instone, L. (2014) 'Unruly Grasses: Affective Attunements in the Ecological Restoration of Urban Native Grasslands in Australia', *Emotion, Space, and Society*, 10, 79–86.
Kohn, E. (2013) *How Forests Think: Toward an Anthropology Beyond the Human* (Berkeley, CA: University of California Press).
Kirksey, S. E. and S. Helmreich (2010) 'The Emergence of Multispecies Ethnography', *Cultural Anthropology*, 24(5), 545–576.
Latimer, J. and M. Miele (2013) 'Naturecultures: Science, Affect and the Non-human', *Theory, Culture, & Society*, 30(7/8), 5–31.
Latour, B. (2004) *The Politics of Nature: How to Bring the Sciences into Democracy* (C. Porter Trans.) (Cambridge, MA: Harvard University Press).
Latour, B. (2005) *Reassembling the Social: An Introduction to Actor Network Theory* (Oxford: Oxford University Press).
Lorimer, J. (2007) 'Nonhuman Charisma', *Environment and Planning D: Society and Space*, 25(5), 911–932.
Lorimer, J. (2010) 'Moving Image Methodologies for More-Than-Human Geographies', *Cultural Geography*, 17(2), 237–258.
Lorimer, J. (2014) 'On Auks and Awkwardness', *Environmental Humanities*, 4, 195–205.

Lorimer, J. (2015). *Wildlife in the Anthropocene: Conservation after Nature* (Minneapolis: University of Minnesota Press).
Moore, L. J. and M. Kosut (2013) 'Among the Colony: Ethnographic Fieldwork, Urban Bees and Intra-Species Mindfulness', *Ethnography*, 1–24, doi: 10.1177/1466138113505022.
Pacini-Ketchabaw, V. and A. Taylor (2015) 'Unsettling Pedagogies through Common World Encounters: Grappling with (Post)Colonial Legacies in Canadian Forests and Australian Bushlands', in V. Pacini-Ketchabaw and A. Taylor (eds.) *Unsettling the Colonialist Places and Spaces of Early Childhood Education* (New York: Routledge), pp. 63–91.
Pink, S. (2009) *Doing Sensory Ethnography* (London: SAGE).
Plumwood, V. (2002) *Environmental Culture: The Ecological Crisis of Reason* (London: Routledge).
Rose, D. B., T. van Dooren, M. Chrulew, S. Cooke, M. Kearnes and E. O'Gorman (2012) 'Thinking through the Environment, Unsettling the Humanities', *Environmental Humanities*, 1(1), 1–5.
Stengers, I. (2005a) 'The Cosmopolitical Proposal', in B. Latour and P. Weibel (eds.) *Making Things: Public Atmospheres of Democracy* (Cambridge, MA: MIT Press), pp. 994–1003.
Stengers, I. (2005b) 'Introductory Notes on an Ecology of Practices', *Cultural Studies Review*, 11(1), 183–196.
Taylor, A. (2013) *Reconfiguring the Natures of Childhood* (New York: Routledge).
Taylor, A. and M. Blaise (2014) Queer Worlding Childhood, *Discourse: Studies in the Cultural Politics of Education*, 35(3) [special issue], doi: 10.1080/01596306.2014.888842.
Taylor, A., M. Blaise and M. Giugni (2013) 'Haraway's "Bag Lady Story-Telling": Relocating Childhood and Learning within a Post-Human Landscape', *Discourse: Studies in the Cultural Politics of Education*, 34(1), 108–120.
Taylor, A. and V. Pacini-Ketchabaw (2015) Learning with Children, Ants, and Worms in the Anthropocene: Towards a Common World Pedagogy of Multispecies Vulnerability', *Pedagogy, Culture, Society*, http://dx.doi.org/10.1080/14681366.2015.1039050.
Tsing, A. (2005) *Friction: An Ethnography of Global Connection* (Princeton, NJ: Princeton University Press).
Tsing, A. (2011) 'Arts of Inclusion, or, How to Love a Mushroom', *Australian Humanities Review*, 50, 5–21.
Tsing, A. (2012) 'On Nonscalability: The Living World Is Not Amenable to Precision-Nested Scales', *Common Knowledge*, 18(3), 505–524.
Tsing, A. (2013) 'More-Than-Human Sociality: A Call for Critical Description', in K. Hastrup (ed.) *Anthropology and Nature* (New York: Routledge), pp. 27–42.
van Dooren, T. (2014) *Flight Ways: Life and Loss at the Edge of Extinction* (New York: Columbia University Press).
Weil, K. (2010) 'A Report on the Animal Turn', *Differences*, 21(2), 1–23.
Westh, S. (2011) *Kangaroo Mob*, DVD documentary (Producer S. Ingelton, Melbourne, Australia: 360 Degree Films), http://360degreefilms.com.au/productions/kangaroo-mob/, accessed 5 November 2014.
Whatmore, S. (2006) 'Materialist Returns: Practising Cultural Geography in and for a More-Than-Human World', *Cultural Geographies*, 13(4), 600–609.

10
Girls, Camera, (Intra)Action: Mapping Posthuman Possibilities in a Diffractive Analysis of Camera-Girl Assemblages in Research on Gender, Corporeality and Place

Gabrielle Ivinson and Emma Renold

Introduction

The short film 'Still Running', which is the focus of this chapter, came about as part of a project entitled 'Young People and Place' in which we explored young people's experiences of growing up in a post-industrial locale. Cwm Dyffryn is a fictional name for a former coal-mining valley town in south Wales with a proud tradition of masculine working class labour. Methodologically we focus on the process of creating the short film. This process is presented through the lens of the emergence of dynamic assemblages (Deleuze and Guattari, 1987) when seven teen girls (aged 14–15 years old) and three adults, including the film-maker, set off from the girls' secondary school with a boom, audio recorders, a professional camera and some basic running gear to make a film in a park on the edges of a major ex-mining town, just before the summer recess.

Across one day of filming, an affective intensity grew which we attribute to a series of intra-active elements (Barad, 2007) such as the camera, the location, landscape, the anatomy of female body and the history of the place, that gradually came to fuse together into emergent assemblages that carried an increasingly intense affective charge. In this chapter we suggest that these human and more-than-human elements diffracted girls' personal trajectories and created affective resonances with the greater story of the trauma of post-industrialization experienced in Valleys towns across south Wales. Drawing on our engagement in the film-making process, our field notes made during and after the day of filming, and our ongoing reflections as we have continued to work with girls in ex-mining towns, we make a bold claim that the camera as a posthuman participant in our filmic assemblages helped to interrupt dominant flows that objectify and constrain girls' movement in the ex-mining locale where they were growing up.

We decided to write about the film-making process because during the one day of intensive filming in Cyfarthfa Park, on the outskirts of a post-industrial town, we became entangled with each other and experienced intensities that we all felt as visceral, tangible (e)motion. The experience stayed with us as an affect that would not let us go (MacLure, 2013). This noticeable, affective quality grew as we worked together and we felt that the role of movement, the way we worked as a group and the anonymous eye of the camera were significant. As Couze Venn suggests, 'affect is process that links human and nonhuman actors; it requires mediation and "is a potentiality in living beings" ' (Venn, cited in Blackman, 2013, p. 174). Affect emerged through assemblages during the film-making. Even years later the affects still haunt and enthral us, the researchers. We ask if ghosts from the past might have infused our film-making process that provide tentative links to women and movement during industrialization? The reader can make what she likes of the tentative connections we bring to light in this chapter and we make no claims to know what the actual experiences of the girls were or where the affective intensities might have led them after the film-making day. All we can be sure of is that they led to our desire to write this chapter.

The need for creative methods in post-industrial research

The way the coalmines and steel and iron works were eventually closed for good in the 1980s, after a long struggle in which miners went on strike for the final time in these regions, has left its mark on many valley communities. Even after 30 years the long reach of trauma, exacerbated by cuts to the welfare system and policies of austerity, leave a lasting legacy of life as precarious (Walkerdine and Jimenez, 2012). Generations of mass unemployment have given rise to poverty, social marginalization and lower levels of educational achievement than in other parts of the UK. Our fieldwork has led us to explore how gendered legacies inherited from the industrial past such as the associations between masculinity, corporeal strength and movement remain active in everyday life (Ivinson, 2014). We have noted that girls around the age of 11 years give up many of the physical activities and hobbies that they may have practised up to that age (Ivinson and Renold, 2013a, 2013b; Renold and Ivinson, 2013, 2014). We suspect that girls come to develop docile bodies (Young, 2005) not only due to the hypersensitivity and self-consciousness experienced in general by many teen girls in relation to their changing adolescent bodies, but that the history of place, and in this case an ex-industrial place with a legacy of valuing the labouring male body, lends a further dimension that we shall explore further.

Film-making has become part of the multimodal, multi-phase, longitudinal ethnography that we have developed across a number of studies investigating the importance of place to young people living and growing up in ex-mining communities in south Wales. Our methods have arisen organically across a series of funded and non-funded research projects to deal with a persistent problem, namely that some girls in these ex-mining communities have been very reluctant to talk to us in one-to-one seated interviews. Our creative methods involve putting groups of people together who have different backgrounds and expertise in order to facilitate emergent, open-ended ways of working which aim to be sensitive to 'vulnerable' young people's expressed and nascent desires. To date we have worked with visual artists, sound engineers, musicians, choreographers and film-makers and each time we learn a little more.

We have been developing a range of creative ethnographic methods including collaborative film-making activities and walking tours in 'the wild' to get at the 'qualitative multiplicity' (Braidotti, 2013) and micro-intensities entangled in everyday life – intensities that are difficult if not impossible to articulate in 'traditional' seated qualitative interviews, particularly with the girls in our research. Using these methods, occasionally we were able to put ourselves in the midst of things and could pay attention, drawing on Bollas (2006), to the ways places call us into being, drawing on Foucault's notion of the 'haunting fantasies' of 'emplacement', how these callings carry different meanings and affects across time that fuse and infuse persons with landscapes.

Our posthuman approach then draws attention to 'the crucial recognition that nonhumans play an important role in naturalcultural practices, including everyday practices' (Barad, 2007, p. 32). Working with Deleuzo-Guatarrian (1987) concepts of 'assemblage' and 'becoming', we explore the methodological gains that accrued from using methods that reach beyond discursive data and that can be generated from multisensory ethnographic approaches. Specifically, our approach recognizes the more-than-human and pays attention to material, embodied and affective elements of lived experience. The creative method we present in this chapter was one of our earlier forays into film-making and was initially designed as a way to 'pay back' the young people who had undertaken one-to-one seated interviews with us during the Young People and Place project. We, the authors, are not film-makers. We describe our film-making method as collaborative and emergent. While our films are to some extent co-produced with young people, each time we work, different artefacts, artists and environments come together forming assemblages through which things emerge, sometimes in unexpected ways.

We describe the film-making through a 'diffractive methodology' (Barad, 2007; Haraway, 1992). Diffraction calls attention to patterns of difference whereby small processes can have consequential effects. Barad encourages us to shift our representations from seeing, observing and knowing from afar to entanglements and relationalities, focusing instead on making and marking differences from within as part of an entangled state. This is a way of doing research in which knowledge is always in process, always becoming and where transformation emerges in intra-action. Methodologically, a diffractive approach has much in common with participatory research practices where ethics, ontology and epistemology are often inseparable. We can also think about diffraction in terms of how visual-material-discursive entanglements (such as bodies and cameras) open up and close down possibilities and transformations for being and becoming in the world.

In this chapter we diffract the film-making process though provocations inspired by Iris Marion Young, Gilles Deleuze, Luce Irigaray and Chistopher Bollas as we reflect on the day when girls, cameras, movement and landscape came together in Cyfarthfa Park. We consider how the materiality of the camera, and specifically the features of the anonymous eye of the camera (Deleuze, 1985/1989), our collective rituals and the micro-dynamics of the film-making process allowed us to glimpse the emancipatory potential of this kind of film-making as we diffract elements of the process through other stories about movement and place.

We go on to read the film-making process through a range of lenses that highlight at times female bodies, histories of the place and patriarchy, and the significance of movement and fluidity. By placing ourselves in the midst of things as well as reflecting from afar, as it were, we glimpse the transformative potential of the film-making process. We suggest that the camera as specific kind of apparatus became a player in the process and that the emergent posthuman assemblages enabled transformations which allowed the girls to become more than they could otherwise be.

Making 'Still Running'

In 2011 we returned to two schools where we had interviewed 35 boys and 30 girls about the place where they were growing up in 2009. We offered them the opportunity to work with us and a film-maker, Pete Moles, to make a short film about any topic relating to place including hobbies mentioned in the interviews, but they were not confined to those topics. Fourteen young people (seven girls and seven boys) aged 14–15 years chose to work with Pete and us. We worked separately with boys and then with girls over two consecutive weeks for the pragmatic reason that they came from two single-sex schools. Those who took part were involved in three distinct phases: first, planning and imagining the film; second, acting in scenes and using film-making equipment to capture footage; and third, viewing the footage after it had been edited and created by the film-maker into six short films (between 6 and 12 minutes long).

The rest of the chapter focuses on making the film called 'Still Running' featuring Caitlin and Molly, aged 14 years. We cut our cloth according to our financial resources. Accordingly, we only had one day to capture enough shots to allow Pete, along with the other five girls aged 14–15 years as the film crew, to create a visual montage that would become the film 'Still Running'. At a first glance the description of what we did on the film-making day seems banal. For the best part of one day Caitlin and Molly ran on an a stretch of terrain within their chosen location, Cyfarthfa Park while the rest of us filmed them. The other five girls came to the Park and took it in turns to undertake the other roles of 'director', 'camerawoman', 'sound engineer' and 'look out', and to carry and look after the equipment, as described above. Thus apart from Pete, the film-maker, we were an all-girls' group and each girl had a specific job to do. In the following sections we pay attention to the details of the filming process and diffract descriptions of movement, artefacts, location and persons through stories and academic literatures in order to grasp something of the intensities that we experienced across one day of filming. We start by paying attention to the location of the film.

Exploring posthuman assemblage(s)

When Caitlin and Molly volunteered to make a film with us, their teachers were mystified. We were told that both girls were almost silent in school and that Caitlin had been in a special needs class for a long period of time because her literacy and mathematical skills were below her peer group average. Despite our gentle coaxing and considerable efforts, during the preparation stages Caitlin and Molly could not voice what they wanted to make a film about. Eventually we suggested they bring an object from home to the next meeting with the hope that we could use this as a starting point. The next day they both appeared with, and proudly presented, certificates that they had gained in a running competition. The certificates were our starting point and we decided to make a film about running. When Gabrielle asked, for example, if they would like the film to say something about girls and running, they were not particularly forthcoming. However, at one point they communicated to her that it was harder for girls to run as a regular hobby because it clashed with the requirement to wear make-up and dress in a feminine and fashionable manner. Collectively we coined the phrase 'girls have to leave a little bit of themselves behind to go running', a refrain that ended up running through the film. Working with these clues, we set out to re-enact Caitlin and Molly's pre-adolescent pleasure in running – a pursuit which as teenagers, they no longer engaged in. As we talked with these girls in the preparation stage, we sensed echoes of the kind of closed down, docile and silenced comportment that we had encountered so often in interview phases of our research with teen girls in Valleys communities.

Caitlin and Molly chose Cyfarthfa Park as the location for the film because they had in the past come here with their family and friends and sometimes to jog. Cyfarthfa Park is situated on the outskirts of a town close to where the girls lived that had been at the epicentre of the industrial revolution. We have deliberately not fictionalized the name of the Park because its history is central to our story.

Cyfarthfa Park was the site of the Crawshay family home, built in 1824. The Crawshays were owners of Cyfarthfa Ironworks in Merthyr Tydfil, Wales. The family house is often referred to as a castle, which stood in 158 acres (0.64 km^2) of parkland, now called Cyfarthfa Park and owned by the local council (http://en.wikipedia.org/wiki/Cyfarthfa_Castle, accessed 30 November 2014).

The imposing castle building overlooks an ornamental lake surrounded by a manicured lawn and a visitor's car park. In the interviews that we had previously conducted with young people they often referred to this part of the Park as welcoming and safe. Behind the castle the once well-kept parklands are now partly wild and overgrown. Although there are discernible pathways many trails disappear into dark wooded areas off the beaten track. These are the places that young people described as unsafe. Stories of rape and abduction circulate around Valleys communities and are often reported in the local press and on social media. Thus, even one story of a woman being attacked in Cyfarthfa Park is enough to anchor an image of the place as 'dangerous', especially for women and teen girls who fear being pursued by predatory men in the wild. For many girls, their fears are great enough to curtail where they go and how far they roam across their local landscape.

Traversing the landscape

During the day we gradually wandered from one place to another in the Park until we felt we had a good place for Caitlin and Molly to run and for the film crew to achieve a good vantage point for which to view them. We decided together that Caitlin and Molly would each take it in turn to run the same stretch of terrain consecutively. As we entered the Park, the lake at the front seemed to call out (Bollas, 2006) as a suitable place for our initial shoots. Our second location was a wild part of the Park behind the castle in a shadowy, wooded trail that had a dark and eerie atmosphere. The third place was a trail by the side of one of a series of terraced lily ponds that were partially hidden by overgrown plants and weeds and surrounded by trees and bushes, creating a kind of magical atmosphere. As we worked the sun shone through the trees, allowing us to film the lilies reflected in the water as a backdrop to the girls' moving bodies. We took the final shots on a tarmac path beside an open meadow with plenty of sky above and finished off by the lake again.

The phallocentric gaze

Initially, it was almost painful to view the obvious self-consciousness that accompanied Caitlin and Molly's running. They ran with their arms protecting their chests, preventing the upper torso from moving in synchronicity with the pelvis and striding legs. For the first few takes they ran quite slowly and we worried that we should have found a way to get the girls some running gear, especially a sports bra, before attempting to make such a film.

We found that like many girls, these girls were particularly conscious of the way boys and men openly stared at and commented on their breasts as they walked down school corridors full of boys and down streets populated by unemployed men. Girls have to work to deal with the objectifying gaze that renders parts of their anatomy as sexualized object regardless of their own desires (see Chapter 13 in this collection, Ringrose and Renold).

Girls might try to hide the size of their breasts under baggy clothes, yet in preparing to run Molly and Caitlin had to remove their school sweatshirts to avoid overheating. Thus their bodies became more exposed to the gaze of others. Breasts will not remain still as women run. The motion of running inevitably heightens the experience of breasts not as objects contained and bound within bras but as weighted, moving masses of flesh that swing in rhythm according to the length of the stride and the upward and downward bounce of the running body. We saw how Molly and Caitlin tried to support their breasts as they ran by holding their arms close to their torso, and this contributed to the jolting discontinuity of their movements.

We think it was because we shared the girls' self-consciousness that we decided to undertake some of the first runs. Each time we arrived at a new location within the Park someone had to run across the chosen terrain to allow the camera girl to practice the shoot and check the angle of the camera. As adults, relatively secure in our bodies, we were able to run unashamedly, not worrying which parts of our anatomy might be moving and deliberately not worrying about attracting unwanted attention. By modelling running we hoped to encourage the girls to lose their inhibitions. On reflection we recognize that the girls' self-consciousness is linked to the cultural significance attached to the breast as sexualized object. Young encourages us to pay attention to the specific materiality of breasts and the way this affects women's experience of their bodies. The breast in phallocentric, male Western culture is a fetishized object valued from the point of view of men, as a thing that is supposed to look pert and upright, as an object to be sized up, measured and commented upon (Young, 2005, p. 78). Young suggests that 'the chest is a center of a person's sense of being-in-the-world and identity' (2005, p. 76) and that girls and women have quite different experiences of being-in-the-world due to their anatomical differences. Those of us women who jog and who have sizeable breasts come to know that if we persist we can achieve a comfortable attunement with the anatomy of our moving bodies. Even so, it takes some time to acclimatize to the weightiness of the flesh being pulled inside the skin of the chest as feet pound up and down, and having the right clothing helps considerably. Throughout the day we watched as Caitlin and Molly gradually came to inhabit their bodies in more comfortable ways. While we expected the camera to increase the girls' self-consciousness, to our surprise it had the opposite effect, as will become apparent next.

The anonymous gaze

Each time we arrived at a new location, we enacted a ritual that involved setting up the tripod, attaching the camera to it and looking through the eyepiece to scan the land and scenery. We wanted to ascertain if the footage would be aesthetically interesting and would add something to the moving bodies of the runners. Then one of us, usually Gabrielle, ran across the chosen terrain to check that we had a long enough stretch of path to allow the runners to gather the speed that we felt suited the atmosphere of the place – slow near lilies, fast on the tarmac path beneath the open sky. The camera girl practised moving the camera on the tripod to ensure that she could follow the runner for the full length of the chosen section of the trail. Another girl observed the surrounding area to warn us of any possible approaching people or dogs that might interrupt the shoot. When all was ready we focused on capturing footage and an intense concentration took hold of us.

The first runner, Molly, got into position, crouched down and waited for the command 'Camera, rolling – ACTION'. The group watched intently and in silence as Molly set off, quickened her pace and accelerated to a slow, medium or fast jog. The camera girl pressed her eye to the eye of the camera and so fused, trained the apparatus on the moving body of the runner, swivelling the camera in a wide arc. Another girl extended an audio boom out into the air above the camera and, wearing headphones, listened for any sounds of the runner or from the environment; her breathing, the thud of her feet on tarmac, a bird squawking, twigs snapping underfoot or the squelch of mud. Once the runner was out of shot of the camera, one of the girls shouted 'STOP'.

Caitlin took up position exactly where Molly had previously started and again waited for the command 'Camera, rolling – ACTION'. Caitlin accelerated and we all watched intently as she too ran the stretch until she was out of camera sight. Again, the camera girl followed the runner's moving body. At the end of the first shots, we readjusted the angle of the camera and waited for everyone to take up position again. Our ritual was repeated as Molly and then Caitlin ran consecutively across the patch of ground a second time exactly as she had done the first time while the eye of the camera followed this time from the new perspective. Sometimes we took a third shot in the same location so that by the time we moved on there had been up to seven (one by Gabrielle and three each from Molly and Caitlin) similar running events. We worked smoothly as a team and under Pete's tuition, paying attention to every minute detail to make sure that each shot was as perfect as we could make it. During the course of the five hours we spent together in the Park we canned over 50 short shoots. Each take was initiated by one of the girls shouting loudly into the stillness/silence of the forest: 'Camera, rolling...ACTION', creating a sonic vibration that still echoes in our imaginaries.

As a material object, the camera features a nonhuman, artificial eye (Deleuze, 1985/1989), with lenses that can zoom in and out. Our camera also had the ability to tilt and, with the help of a human, to follow movement. The camera was usually placed on a tripod and Pete ensured that it was most often a girl who controlled the camera's movements. So it was girls with a camera that followed the runner's moving body as she ran quickly or slowly on tarmac, on mud, across the forest floor or through grass.

Deleuze saw the mode of film as an example of a form with the possibility to change our very perception and so alter the possibility for thinking and imagining (Colebrook, 2002, p. 29). Influenced by 'the French philosopher Henri Bergson, Deleuze uses cinema to theorise time, movement and life as a whole' (Colebrook, 2002, p. 29). He suggested that the first shock of cinema was to open up the visual field to give us as 'a direct expression of movement' and so to extend philosophy to allow us to think about the 'very mobility of life' (ibid.). 'Deleuze was interested in two broad concepts: the movement-image of early cinema and the time-image of modern cinema' (Colebrook, 2002, p. 29). The way the camera angle scans the visual field is the crucial issue here. Thus in the descriptions of our film-making we pay attention to camera angles and the way the girls used the camera with some facility. While we did not know and could not anticipate the specific shots that would be selected to compose the film 'Still Running', we were all cinematically literate enough to be in the present and at the same time anticipate the possibilities that would become scenes within the film in the future. Thus as we worked in the present we anticipated the future in terms of the film that would eventually be made. As we ran and shot film we created a temporal doubling as if we were already ahead of ourselves. Yet given that the Park had belonged to a wealthy male industrialist, we wonder if we felt another haunting, one that came from the past, hinting of patriarchy and the self-confident masculinity that might have owned this territory and occupied it as a place for riding, shooting and hunting.

Reading our cinematic-running-movement assemblages diffractively through the posthuman film critic Giuliano Bruno (2007), we are reminded of women's roles in film. All too often women are the stilled objects of the camera's gaze, subordinately positioned in relation to the active acting men. In our film-making, girls were in motion and it was us, as a group of women and girls, who orchestrated the composition of the shots. It was as if the ubiquitous sense 'of always being watched' by an imaginary predatory male was neutralized by the anonymous eye of the camera. The camera seemed to displace a threatening gaze with a specific, purposeful gaze of our choosing. In effect, the material, machinic, depersonalized eye of the camera released us all from the fears of the wild and instilled in us a new sense of freedom and belonging. Our dynamic terrain-camera-girl assemblages reterritorialized the Park, allowing us to traverse the landscape in new ways.

Reclaiming space and movement

As the day wore on the girls' movements took on a different quality. Each time Caitlin and Molly ran and reran the same stretch of trail, something changed. Gradually our attention to detail, the intense focus of the whole group and especially the eye of the camera honed on the moving body, seemed to lend legitimacy to the girls' movements and their actions gained in purposefulness and in confidence. As the day progressed they seemed to become more and more at ease with the process of moving and as they moved the jarred and fragmented parts of their bodies gradually became synchronized and the running started to flow. Their sprinting became bolder and faster, more determined and we could feel their energy increase as they warmed up. They seemed to come into their bodies, to inhabit them more fully over time. Their running seemed attuned to light and shade as sun glinted through trees and across the lily ponds. Their feet seemed to respond to different terrains of mud, grass or tarmac and their gait lengthened or shortened in respond to the various textures of the ground. In this way, assemblages of the girl-body-landscape emerged and fused.

It seemed that the repetition of running the same terrain again and again shifted movement from a series of discrete events into a flow (Manning, 2013). As Manning reminds us, the sense of movement, like any sensing, is a 'topological activity'. When we sense we experience

Figure 10.1 'Still Running'

and create folds in space-time (2013, p. 53). We sense on top of sense and one sense-experience is embedded in another, such that repetition can be imagined not as recreating the same but as a process of transformation. Through repetition the girls seemed able to overcome a struggle that Iris Marion Young (2005, p. 44) suggests forces girls to 'take a distance from and exist in discontinuity with her body'. The girls appeared enlivened, inhabiting their bodies more fully as if newly incorporated. They gradually lose the self-consciousness that had accompanied their initial hesitant running. The ease with which they came to move seemed testament to a further transformation, as if they lost the experience of their breasts as objects of a phallocentric gaze and their anatomy became integrated within the flow of movement. We suspect that this transformation was accomplished by repetition, yet a repetition framed within a specific configuration of 'containing' elements including the all-girl film crew, the sympathetic landscape and the nonhuman, non-judgemental eye of the camera (Figure 10.1).

We inhabited the Park and through our repeated actions claimed it for a period of time as *our* territory. Through movement and sense we became haunted by the landscapes of the Park and in turn these places called us into being in new ways (Bollas, 2006). As we developed a shared rhythm across the day we felt the affective charge intensify and we seemed to become more closely bonded. At times we seemed to fuse with the landscape as a kind of dreaming (Bollas, 2006), our concentration blended with the rhythmic moves of the runners and at times a collective hush befell us. The sweeping curve of the camera trained on the girls' bodies attuned us to the minutiae of sound: the snapping of twigs, the squawk of a bird, the bark of a distant dog or a runner's laboured breathing, and to the cadences of light: the shadowy stillness of the woods, the glinting sparkles across the water of the lily pond, the open sky above the hard coldness of a tarmac path. The landscapes of the Park became part of our intimate entanglement that invaded our inner worlds of experience.

The soothing monotony of repetition, the girls' moving bodies running across a landscape again and again, enacted a time-space warp as we and they repeated the same kind of motions; our heads following their moving bodies. These synchronized body movement patterns had the effect of stopping time even as it moved forward. The repeated movement of running the same trail again and again took on the intensity of a refrain (Manning, 2013), as if we were being constantly brought back to the place where we had started. As we came back again and again to the same place, through continuous movement, the act of running gained an increasing density.

Through the more-than-human assemblages of film equipment, our running and filming rituals and our focused, collective attention we created traces across the landscape that had once been the ironmaster's home. As we ran and reran we engraved the Park's pathways with our own intentions. The anonymous eye of the camera witnessed the girls' moving bodies; bodies that so often in this ex-mining place have been stilled and immobilized by the ubiquitous gaze of masculinity: the rule of the father. The camera, along with a now familiar yet relentless repetition, forged a new experience of moving; a moving freed of this gaze, bringing the girls back into their bodies, allowing them to becoming fully corporeal and fluid again. In this way we created a cartography that displaced the past purpose of the gardens and parks of Cyfarthfa Castle with our intense awareness and imagination. Next we diffract this cartography through a lens inspired by the feminist philosopher Luce Irigaray.

From stuckness to fluidity

For a Valleys girl, as Young suggests, to 'open her body in free, active, open extension' is to 'invite objectification' and this 'objectifying regard' is 'what keeps her in her place' (2005, p. 44). The objectifying male gaze is particularly intense in post-industrial valley communities where many men had a proud tradition of working in the physically demanding and dangerous steel and mining industries. Holding onto the values of hard manual labour, and the strong gender role divisions that support this, provides a way to manage the loss, pain and alienation of mass unemployment. Far from giving up their sense of male supremacy in post-industrial conditions this becomes a protective skin; a bulwark against despair (Walkerdine and Jimenez, 2012). So, girls experience high levels of sexual harassment and gender-based bullying in schools (Renold, 2013) and high levels of scrutiny, negative commentary and wolf whistling as they walk the streets of their localities. Boys and men have much to lose if they blur the boundaries between femininity and masculinity, so girls are continuously objectified and kept in their place. Thus the girls' initial hesitancy when running, mingled with the imaginary threat of capture and attack can be understood as assemblages which territorialized and stilled girls' movements (see Ivinson and Renold, 2013, 2014).

Reading fixity and movement diffractively, we recall that Irigaray provocatively suggested that men rely on the logic of solids to allow phenomena to become visible. As Mary Beth Mader (2002) points out, for Irigaray the status of the law of identity on which Western logic is based (a=a) acts to block becoming and deny flux and change. In opposition to masculinity Irigaray refers metaphorically to femininity as a mixture of amniotic fluid, blood, milk and even air. Female subjectivity escapes solid capture and representation and as such, women can be characterized by fluidity.

Irigaray repeatedly appeals to fluidity and fluids to articulate an identity that could break with the solid consistency of the *logos*. For her, fluidity always exceeds reason and rationality as they are expressed through the solid forms of textual representations. She accuses Lacan of a form of psychoanalytic monism (Irigaray, 1985, cited in Mader, 2002, p. 31) that views adult sexuality and systems of representation (language, law, the logos) as being organized around the ultimate signifier – the phallus. Sexual subjectivities are acquired or distributed in reference to this standard (Mader, 2002; Renold and Ringrose, 2015). According to Irigaray, women lack subjectivity because they lack a language of their own. She argues that women's perspectives and sense of being have not been fully elaborated in philosophy and so their self-defined expression has not been defined (Irigaray, 1985). She goes a step further to suggest that women's fluids are the materials that make the solid form of man possible. Fluidity is the background that allows solids to stand out:

> 'Philosophers forget that without fluid' their thought 'would have no possible unity, since the fluid always subsists *between* solid substances to join them, to re-unite them. Without the intervention of fluids no discourse would hold'.
> (Irigaray, 1985, cited in Mader, 2002, p. 32)

But this fluid, supportive condition does not itself stand out, and to draw attention to it is to risk revealing that a mobile, nonsolid necessity is actually the 'ground' for the 'solid' formations of *logos*.

Caitlin and Molly had embarked on the film-making process from a near silence. It had only been their offering of objects, namely their running certificates, that gave us an entry into their desires. Our film 'Still Running' denies the logic of solid, visible form on which 'the male language is based' (Mader, 2002, p. 31) and legitimizes the fluidity of women's movement. For a little while we glimpsed Caitlin and Molly as they fully committed to running, blossomed and became something more. The movement of repeated running seemed to herald a different way of becoming that embraced motion, breath and fluidity; perhaps, a yet to be constructed, specifically female expression, a yet to be imagined subjectivity if not quite yet a new language of expression?

Concluding comments: Ghostly assemblages and new becomings

We want to make a bold claim that through our collective and predominantly female entanglements with the camera, together with the girls' repeated running, a new kind of dynamic was set in train, one characterised by fluidity. The emerging girl-body-camera-landscape assemblages that we co-produced interrupted dominant flows that block girls from becoming mobile, energetic and in their bodies in the post-industrial places where they are growing up.

To make this claim we have worked diffractively. We have been thinking about the camera as a posthuman player in the film-making assemblage in relation to Barad's proposition that apparatus is always part of the phenomena produced and as she says, 'part of the on-going dynamism of becoming' (2007, p. 142). The becoming we have focused on here is how the film-making assemblage created a 'cut' in the flow of movement-time that Young (2005) refers to as a 'transcendent ambiguity', which interfered with strong historical legacies that pin girls into sedentary and fixed corporealities due to a heightened awareness of a patriarchal male gaze still prevalent in ex-mining communities.

We have been thinking about diffraction in relation to rhythm and repetition, emplacement and the specific configuration of girls-with-camera which literally 'called the shots'; and the wider film-making event without which this intra-acting assemblage (which revealed to the girls again their love of movement and the sense of freedom, enjoyment, accomplishment and autonomy epitomized by their running certificates) would not have happened.

We feel that the rhythm and repetition demanded by the film-making sequencing and the need to create multiple shots with each shoot discursively framed by the girls' refrain of 'Camera rolling...ACTION' drove the movement and scrambled the linearity of our common-sense ordering of time to reconfigure the schizoid body movement practices of girls who were running, yet who usually no longer run. This diffraction of time-space we felt was also enabled by running in the very same park where the girls used to run, a way of putting ourselves in the midst of things. Furthermore it was not *any* place, but a specific place that vibrated with the 'haunting fantasies' of earlier body movement practices. So, we suggest, the place literally called girls' bodies to run again, to become other.

Indeed, the posthuman assemblage of girls-with-camera brought the phenomenon of girls' moving bodies into view in new ways – so the 'gaze' is experienced through multiple media with different registers. The repetition, together with the uncritical, artificial eye of the anonymous camera, seemed to help the girls to transgress again and again the social conventions of feminine comportment – producing positive affects – affects that flowed as the girl-camera-crew assemblage invoked bodies to move in new, enlivened ways as the day wore on.

We have suggested that these ghosts (Barad, 2010) resonate throughout girls' talk, yet more importantly territorialize their corporeal beingness, training their bodies to become docile. We also suggest that this process creates a dis/continuity with the past that influences girls' movements today. Furthermore, in remembering and experiencing repeated movements that came from the necessity to film the same girls running in the same patch in order to provide footage taken with different camera angles and lenses, the imaginary end product – that which came to be the 'Still Running' film – set up some very peculiar time/space enfoldings. So, to conclude we recall Barad's provocation that

> What is needed is a posthumanist understanding of the role of the apparatus and of the human and the relationship between them.
> (2007, p. 145)

We have begun to explore how film-making assemblages 'cut' phenomena in ways that mattered differently and for a brief moment extended an agency of 'doing' and 'becoming' differently – as girls experienced their running bodies without hesitation, without perhaps 'leaving a little bit of themselves behind'.

Acknowledgement

This publication is based on research supported by the Wales Institute of Social and Economic Research, Data and Methods (WISERD) funded by the UK Economic and Social Research Council (Grant number: RES-576-25-0021) and the Higher Education Funding Council for Wales. The full research team included Gabrielle Ivinson, Emma Renold, Kate Moles and Mariann Martsin. We thank also Pete Moles of Talpini Media who enabling us to create six short films with young people.

References

Barad, K. (2007) *Meeting the Universe Halfway: Quantum Physics and the Entanglement of Matter and Meaning* (Durham and London: Duke University Press).
Barad, K. (2010) 'Quantum Entanglements and Hauntological Relations of Inheritance: Dis/continuities, Spacetime Enfoldings, and Justice to Come', *Derrida Today*, 3(2), 240–268.
Blackman, L. (2013) *Immaterial Bodies: Affect, Embodiment, Mediation* (Los Angeles, London, New Delhi, Singapore, Washington, DC: Sage).
Bollas, C. (2006/1993) *Becoming a Character: Psychoanalysis and Self Experience* (London and New York: Routledge Taylor & Francis Group).
Braidotti, R. (2013) *The Posthuman* (Cambridge: Polity Press).
Bruno, G. (2007) *Atlas of Emotion: Journeys in Art, Architecture and Film* (New York: Verso).
Colebrook, C. (2002) *Gilles Deleuze* (London and New York: Routledge Taylor & Francis Group).
Deleuze, G. (1985/1989) *Cinema 2: The Time Image* (H. Tomlinson and R. Galeta, Trans.) (Minneapolis: University of Minnesota Press).
Deleuze, G. and F. Guattari (1987) *A Thousand Plateaus: Capitalism and Schizophrenia* (B. Massumi, Trans.) (Minneapolis: University of Minnesota Press).

Haraway, D. (1992) 'The Promises of Monsters: A Regenerative Politics for Inappropriate/d Others', in L. Grossberg, C. Nelson and P. Treichler (eds.) *Cultural Studies* (New York: Routledge), pp. 295–337.

Irigaray, L. (1985/2002) *Speech Is Never Neutral* (New York: Routledge).

Ivinson, G. (2014) 'Skills in Motion: Boys' Motor Biking Activities as Transitions into Working Class Masculinity', *Sport, Education and Society*, 19(5), 605–620.

Ivinson, G. and E. Renold (2013a) 'Valleys' Girls: Re-theorising Bodies and Agency in a Semi-Rural, Post-industrial Locale', *Gender and Education*, 25(6) (Special issue: Feminist Materialisms and Education), pp. 704–721.

Ivinson, G. and E. Renold (2013b) 'Subjectivity, Affect and Place: Thinking with Deleuze and Guattari's Body without Organs to Explore a Young Teen Girl's Becomings in a Post-industrial Locale', *Subjectivity*, 6(4), 369–390.

Mader, K. (2002) 'The Forgetting of Feeling', in K. Oliver and S. Edwin (eds.) *Between the Psyche and the Social: Psychoanalytic Social Theory* (Lanham, MD: Rowman and Littlefield Pubs inc.), pp. 29–46.

Manning, E. (2013) *Always More than One: Individuation's Dance* (Durham and London: Duke University Press).

MacLure, M. (2013) Classification or Wonder? Coding as an Analytic Practice in Qualitative Research', in B. Coleman and J. Ringrose (eds.) *Deleuze and Research Methodologies* (Edinburgh, UK: Edinburgh University Press), pp. 164–183.

Renold, E. (2013) *Boys and Girls Speak Out: A Qualitative Study of Children's Gender and Sexual Cultures* (age 10–12) (Cardiff: Cardiff University).

Renold, E. and G. Ivinson (2013) 'Girls, Camera, (intra)Action: Applying a Diffractive Analysis to Teen Girls' Engagement with Visual Participatory Methodologies in Ethnographic Research on Gender, Subjectivity and Place', paper presented at *American Education Research Association* conference, San Francisco, 27 April –1 May.

Renold, E. and G. Ivinson (2014) Horse-girl Assemblages: Towards a Post-Human Cartography of Girls' Desires in an Ex-mining Valleys Community', *Discourse*, 35, 361–376.

Walkerdine, V. and J. Jimenez (2012) *Gender, Work and Community after de- Industrialization: A Psychosocial Approach to Affect* (Basingstoke: Palgrave Macmillan).

Young, M. I. (2005) *On Female Body Experience: 'Throwing Like a Girl' and Other Essays* (Oxford: Oxford University Press).

11
Decolonizing School Science: Pedagogically Enacting Agential Literacy and Ecologies of Relationships

Marc Higgins

Introduction

Within science education, 'the conventional goal' is one 'of thinking, behaving, and believing like a scientist' (Aikenhead and Elliot, 2010, p. 324). Through the two predominant methods of teaching and learning science, this entails: coming-to-know what scientists know (i.e., cognitivism, intra-personal learning, scientific knowledge as representation of nature) and/or enculturation into how scientists come-to-know (i.e., socio-constructivism, interpersonal learning, scientific knowledge as representation of culture). Both approaches construct and uphold the subject position 'Scientist' that is emblematic of the masculine, Eurocentric and anthropocentric subject of humanism that is presented through Western modern humanistic modes (e.g., representationalism, universalism, nature/culture divide). This (re)produces science as a human(ist) practice through which nature is knowable and representable (i.e., quantifiable, generalizable and predictable), and neither the culture of science nor the agency of nature can be accounted for or be held accountable. Accordingly, this type of scientific literacy and its entangled culture of 'school science' produce experiences of cultural *assimilation* and *acculturation* rather than *enculturation* for the vast majority of students (approximately 90 per cent of *all* students; Aikenhead and Elliot, 2010; McKinley, 2007). Rather than a harmonious interfacing of cultures (i.e., enculturation), this encounter is more often one where the potential for dialectical negation is either actualized (i.e., assimilation) or remains unactualized through students' complex and complicated curricular navigation (i.e., acculturation). Furthermore, for students whose daily lived experiences continue to be negatively impacted by Eurocentrism (re)produced with/in (and beyond) science, be they Indigenous, diasporic, or other postcolonial bodies, learning with/in the cultural practice of 'school science' largely continues to be a form of epistemic violence as the frequently cited experience is one of assimilation.

There is a growing body of work within science education that addresses humanism's Eurocentric legacies that is often referred to as decolonizing science education (e.g., Aikenhead and Elliot, 2010; Belczewski, 2009; Higgins, 2014a). Decolonizing education (Battiste, 2013) is a 'two-prong process' that entails: *deconstruction* of (neo-)colonial structures and strategies; and *reconstruction* that centres and takes seriously Indigenous, diasporic and other postcolonial ways-of-knowing and ways-of-being in reshaping the place-based processes and priorities of education and educational research. The work of decolonizing science education has primarily entailed addressing the ways in which Eurocentrism (re)produces science education as a space of cognitive and cultural imperialism in order to make space for learning that is epistemologically diverse and pedagogically pluralistic (McKinley, 2000, 2007; Sammel, 2009; see also Battiste, 2005, 2013).

However, 'given the pervasiveness of assimilationism in Western science education' (Sammel, 2009, p. 653), to only address the colonial episteme leaves the systemic strategies and structures that 'push for assimilation of students into Western science ontology' to continue functioning implicitly. While there might be some space for diverse ways-of-knowing through such a critique, Sammel (2009, p. 653) invites us to consider how science pedagogies and curriculums often 'include the mandate of improving scientific literacy and then proceed to define it, or refer to it by way of usual contemporary science education definition'. These position diverse ways-of-knowing-nature that are not Western modern science (WMS) but different, and often lesser, ways to attain the same goal of knowing nature with/in the ontology of Western modernity. The underlying and problematic message is that ontology is a singular affair. Cartesianism, the classical Western ontological process through which meaning and matter are individuated through separation from that which co-constitutes them (e.g., mind/body, nature/culture; Apffel-Marglin, 2011; Barad, 2007), becomes *the* (only) ontology onto which diverse ways-of-knowing differentially map. This not only re-centres WMS as the meter stick which is best suited to work with/in this ontology, but also complicates the entangled relationships held with/in 'school science' for bodies enacting other-than-Cartesian ways-of-being, such as Indigenous ways-of-knowing-in-being.

Herein, I use the expression ways-of-knowing-in-being to signal the following. First, learning is always already a relational process (i.e., coming-to-knowing, a verb) rather than an independent product (i.e., knowledge, a noun). Second, coming-to-knowing is inseparable from coming-to-being: they are ongoing and interconnected processes woven into the fabric of everyday life (Aikenhead and Michell, 2011; Cajete, 1994, 1999, 2000; Peat, 2002). Lastly, this plurality does not entail relativism (McKinley, 2007).

Battiste (2013, p. 107) argues that decolonizing approaches to education 'first and foremost must be framed within concepts of dialogue, respect for educational pluralities, multiplicities, and diversities'. However, science education dialectically subsumes, sublates and sutures over many of these 'pluralities, multiplicities, and diversities' through a centring of Cartesianism, while simultaneously working to erase other ontologies and its own workings by presenting itself as *the* (only) ontology. Accordingly, there is productive value in 'getting lost' (i.e., strategically straying off the beaten path) within science education, 'not as "losing *one's* way" but as losing *the* way – as losing any sense that just one "way" could ever be prefixed and privileged by the definite article' (Gough, 2006, p. 640).

To 'get lost' in science education, in this chapter I engage the question: *How might scientific literacy be enacted otherwise if it is configured with/in other-than-Cartesian ontologies while still privileging knowing nature (i.e., space, time and matter) through empirical observation?* This experimental wandering with/in science education plays out in three parts. The first section activates a decolonizing sensibility to explore two ways-of-knowing-nature that employ other-than-Cartesian ontologies in order to deconstruct/reconstruct science and science education. In particular, I think with Karen Barad's (2000, 2007) quantum philosophy-physics and Gregory Cajete's (1994, 1999, 2000) Indigenous science, while considering points of convergence and divergence between their ontologies. The second section employs these ontologies to explore one possibility for school-based decolonizing science pedagogies: relationally storying nature (i.e., space, time, matter). In the last section, I analyse two pedagogical productions that work against the ontological closure of Cartesianism to produce a different horizon of possibilities for decolonizing science education.

Towards ontological pluralism in science education

Within and against Cartesianism: Posthumanisms

As a Euro-settler trained within the physical sciences and education, I recognize the importance of not simply rejecting my tradition's epistemic, ontological and ethical commitments and enactments when they become problematic. I understand this move as a process of accounting for and being accountable to difference, as this tradition (re)produces me as researcher and educator (Higgins, 2014a). To attempt to move beyond without working within and against runs the risk of reproducing its structures, strategies, processes and practices elsewhere, albeit differently. This is of particular significance given the deep gravitational pull of Western modern humanism that makes it difficult to break from its epistemological and ontological orbits (Barad, 2007; Battiste, 2005; Braidotti, 2013).

Posthumanisms extend the driving push of antihumanism work within and against the epistemological limits of humanism by: decentring the human through considering other-than-human bodies, and troubling its Cartesian ontology. Cartesianism's relationship to decolonizing science education is twofold. First, it is an ontological medium through which power can, and does, operate (see Apffel-Marglin, 2011; Barad, 2000, 2007; Braidotti, 2013). The colonial apparatus requires the separation and separability of nature and culture to produce binary and hierarchal relationships between 'civilization' and its others (e.g., 'uncivilized' peoples and land). Second, Cartesianism continues to operate as *the* only ontology through forced colonial diffusionism (see Battiste, 2005; Blaut, 1993) while at the same time erasing its very presence. By presenting the world as something that exists a priori and always already separated in discrete units, the ontological enactment of cut-making is presupposed and rendered an absent presence. Cartesianism not only cuts across the multiple ways in which co-constitutive Indigenous and other postcolonial ways-of-knowing-in-being enact relationality, process and flux; but also cannot account for itself ethically, epistemologically, or ontologically (Aikenhead and Michell, 2011; Cajete, 1994, 1999; Peat, 2002).

Karen Barad: From scientific literacy to agential literacy

Drawing from quantum physics, Barad's (2007) theory of agential realism questions the humanist a priori status of nature before culture, as well as the antihumanist corollary statement of culture before nature. This work disrupts the notion that Cartesianism is *the* (only) ontology, not by negating it but rather by positioning it as one ontological configuration among many. These configurations are presented and produced as open-ended processes that are enacted rather than static. In particular, Barad's concept of intra-action enables us to gain insight into how relationality, flux and process are conceptualized and enacted:

> The neologism 'intra-action' signifies the mutual constitution of entangled agencies. That is, in contrast to the usual 'interaction', which assumes that there are separate individual agencies that precede their interaction, the notion of intra-action recognizes that distinct agencies do not precede, but rather emerge through, their intra-action.
>
> (Barad, 2007, p. 33)

In other words, intra-action accounts for and is accountable to the various ways in which bodies of meaning (e.g., social, cultural, political, historical) and bodies of matter (e.g., biology, ecology, physics, engineering, architecture) are co-constitutive. This acts as an invitation to consider the ways in which these bodies of meaning-matter are not only produced through Cartesian norms of bodily production (i.e., subjects and objects) but also through other-than-Cartesian entanglements that would comprise and cut across multiple Cartesian subjects and objects. This is not simply a way of redrawing the lines of bodily production (e.g., researcher + instrument interaction –> researcher-instrument intra-active entanglement), it is also a (re)consideration of how they come into being. As Barad (2007, p. 140) states, 'phenomena are constitutive of reality. Reality is composed not of things-in-themselves or things-behind phenomena but of things-in-phenomena.' Accordingly, the production of natural-cultural bodies and their bodily norms are enacted, in flux, process-based and performative rather than something that always already *is* (or *is not*).

The consequences of agential realism for scientific literacy are drastic. The task of epistemologically establishing a representational (i.e., humanist) relationship of equivalence with either nature (i.e., through cognitivism) or culture (i.e., through socio-constructivisim) breaks down because their separation was never a priori. Rather, Barad (2000, p. 237) invites us to consider how 'scientific literacy becomes a matter of agential literacy – of learning how to intra-act responsibly within the world' around the matters of science (i.e., space, time and matter). This is significant as agential literacy goes beyond scientific literacy's accounting for the diverse natural and cultural agents that constitute experimental phenomena studied and produced within the context of science education. First, it considers the ways in which agents are always already natural-cultural. Secondly, it accounts for the ways in which these agents not only constitute but are also constituted by phenomena. Third, agential literacy ethically re(con)figures accountability as a process of not only accounting for, but also being accountable to these agents and their intra-action in the world's ongoing becoming.

Gregory Cajete: Indigenous ways-of-knowing-in-being and science curriculum as 'all my relations'

Articulating relationality, flux and process differently and for different purposes, Indigenous science educator Cajete (1994, 1999, 2000) proposes that we consider ways-of-knowing-in-being – that is, the co-substantiation of epistemology and ontology – as ecologies of relationships. These ecologies of relationships that are enacted with/in these ways-of-knowing-in-being are often referred to as both external and internal to a human(ist) subject, while noting that some of the relations external to the subject do not require a subject at all. Externally, we often speak of relationships with other humans, relationships with other-than-human bodies (e.g., plants, rivers, mountains), as well as relationships with more-than-human bodies (i.e., spiritual beings) (see also Apffel-Marglin, 2011). Internally, the relationships between heart, mind, body and spirit are often called upon.

Furthermore, the boundary between exteriority and interiority is one that is porous, and it is this porosity that allows us to be with/in relation. This ontological porosity extends to space and time to make being in the world a question of process, flux and holistically being *of* the world. As Cajete (1994, p. 27) states, 'a constant building upon earlier realities is a basic characteristic of Indigenous processes... [in which] we engineer the new reality built upon earlier ones, while simultaneously addressing the needs, and acting in the sun, of our times'. The intentionality here signals that Cajete's ecology of relationships (sometimes referred to as 'sense of place') is not simply a way-of-knowing-in-being in which the world is enacted through the flux of relationships, but that there is also an ongoing accounting for and accountability to the ecology of relationships such that it is (re)generated and sustained. It is for this reason that Cajete (2000) reminds us that within many Indigenous languages there is an expression akin to 'all my relations' (e.g., *Mitakuye Oyasin* in Lakota). 'All my relations' is an epistemological, ontological and ethical accounting for and being accountable to the ecologies of relationships we find ourselves in and constituted by which extends beyond the immediate present to include generations past and those still yet-to-come. It is a metaphysical principle through and by which 'people understood that all entities of nature – plants, animals, stones, trees, mountains, rivers, lakes and a host of other living entities – embodied [and (will)] continue to embody] relationships that must be honoured' (Cajete, 2000, p. 178).

An Indigenous 'science education curriculum' of 'all my relations' has been in place since time immemorial in the form of land- or place-based education (Cajete, 1994, 1999, 2000). Despite disruption by ongoing (neo-)colonial practices, Cajete (2000) reminds us that Indigenous knowledge holders continue to engage these traditional yet ever evolving contemporary ways-of-knowing-in-being by 'seeking, making, sharing, and celebrating' (Cajete, 2000, p. 178) the ecological relationships they find themselves with/in. Accordingly, with/in Cajete's (1994, 1999, 2000) conception of Indigenous science education, scientific literacy would not simply be a task of knowing *about* nature but rather knowing-in-being *with* nature as an inseparable and co-constitutive part of the ecologies of relationships in order to learn 'the subtle, but all important, language of relationship' (Cajete, 2000, p. 178).

This teaching of knowing-in-being *with* is woven into and enacted through traditional Indigenous approaches to teaching and learning, such as storywork. As Barnhardt and Kawagley (2008) remind us, while Indigenous stories hold rich representations of nature (i.e., knowledge *about* nature when read with/in Cartesian representationalism), their potential lies in honouring a knowing-in-being *with* the plants, the animals and a wide range of other-than-human bodies that are teachers with/in the ecologies of relationships particular to a place. As a pedagogy through which Indigenous peoples 'came [and come] to perceive themselves as living in a sea of relationships' (Cajete, 2000, p. 178), it is a way to witness already existing relations and foster the possibility of new ones.

Points of convergence/points of divergence

While there are deep and productive points of resonance between quantum and Indigenous ontologies, there are still patterns of difference that matter. As Cajete (2000, p. 14) states,

> Native science is a product of a different creative journey and a different history than that of Western science. Native science is not quantum physics or environmental science, but it has come to similar understandings about the workings of the natural laws

through experimentation and participation with the natural world. The groundwork for a fruitful dialogue and exchange of knowledge is being created.

Thus, while quantum physics is a recent phenomenon in which Western modernity is irrevocably facing its ontological limits, Indigenous ways-of-knowing-in-being have been developed, practised and honoured since time immemorial with a built-in ethic of (re)generation and sustainability. Constitutive of these ways-of-knowing, and also another difference that matters, is the relationship to spirituality and more-than-human beings:

> Scientists study the tracks of subatomic particles that exist only a millionth of a second. They find the human observer influences the energy relationships and even the nature of existence of these subatomic particles. Humans do participate with everything else even at this level of natural reality. Indigenous people understood this relationship of human activity as concentric rings that extend into the spirit realm.
>
> (Cajete, 1994, p. 55)

Within Indigenous ways-of-knowing-in-being, spiritualties cannot be disentangled from co-constitutive epistemologies and ontologies: 'it is no accident that learning and teaching unfolded in the context of spirituality in practically every aspect of traditional American Indian [Indigenous] education' (Cajete, 1994, p. 41). Given Western modernity's ongoing and complex relationship with religion, spirituality often becomes a contested and complicated cultural interface that can result in the dialectic negation of Indigeneity (see Battiste, 2005; Blaut, 1993). While it is beyond the scope of this chapter, an ethic of dialogue might invite consideration of these patterns of difference that shape this interfacing (e.g., Western modernity's relationship to, and conflating of religion and spirituality; see Apffel-Marglin, 2011).

Designing and enacting a pedagogy with agential literacy and ecologies of relationships

Designing an intra-active pedagogy which stories ecologies of relationships

For Cajete (1994, p. 23), 'education is an art of process, participation, and making connection'. There are many ways to enact a pedagogy with agential literacy and/or ecologies of relationships, including learning through a curriculum of natural-cultural entanglements within Western modern scientific practices (Barad, 2000), posthuman(ist) science fictions (Gough, 2006), and land-based pedagogy (Barnhardt and Kawagley, 2005; Cajete, 1999). However, I took my cue from former students who reminded me that science is in everyday practices (Higgins, 2014a). Accordingly, I was interested in how students engage with, in and come-to-know everyday ecologies of relationships, namely their school space. This, as Lenz-Taguchi (2010, p. 11) states, entails designing an 'intra-active pedagogy' that

> shifts our attention from only giving attention to the intra-personal ...and inter-personal...to give explicit attention to the intra-active relationship between all living organisms and the material environment: things and artifacts, spaces and places that we occupy and use in our daily practices.

However, there is a certain degree of pedagogical side-stepping or 'wandering' required in order to imagine nature as other than separate, separable, static and passive as in a WMS-based traditional 'school science'. As Gough (2006, p. 640) says,

> to 'wander' away from the semiotic spaces of science education textbooks and scientific media reports, and to experiment with making passages to hitherto disconnected systems of signification, is neither 'haphazard' nor 'careless' but a deliberate effort to unsettle boundary distinctions and presuppositions.

In order to enact pedagogically the process of 'getting lost', two significant methodological moves were made.

First, I used participatory visual methods. In particular, I used photovoice as it is already being used within the context of science education to explore socio-scientific issues with a wide range of students (e.g., Cook and Buck, 2010) and it maintains science's centring of visuality as a means of engaging empirically with the world (Peat, 2002). Photovoice 'is a process by which people can identify, represent, and enhance their community through specific photographic technique' (Wang and Burris, 1997, p. 369). This is significant, as participatory visual methods lend themselves to working within and against science education with decolonizing goals in mind (Higgins, 2014a).

Second, I deconstructed/reconstructed photovoice. Like all methodologies, photovoice is open to re(con)figuration through a differential entanglement of theory, practice and ethics. Through deconstructive (mis)readings, the absent presence of critical humanist theories entangled with/in photovoice (i.e., standpoint theory and praxis) were misread as and substituted with differential conceptions of these same theories in order to reconceptualize photovoice (Higgins, 2014b). From this work two major openings were created: first, considering photovoice 'not only as individualistic and only possible through human agency, but also stemming from a place-based community that includes humans, other- than-humans, and more-than-humans' (Higgins, 2014, p. 215); and, second, an invitation to consider visual juxtaposition as a means of working 'against the epistemic violence that occurs and is made possible by reading practices that do not interrupt, and potentially make readers cognizant of the ways in which too simple readings are already sutured over by colonial imaginaries' (ibid., p. 216).

Using these openings, photovoice is reconfigured drawing inspiration from Indigenous storywork and comic book theory. Indigenous storywork is a pedagogical approach that is often already a rich site of knowledge about, and more importantly *with* nature (Cajete, 2000; Kawagley and Barnhardt, 2008). Furthermore, it is a relational and performative act in which the whole (i.e., the ecology of relationships) is enfolded with/in the part (i.e., the story). Comics are 'juxtaposed pictorial and other images in deliberate sequence, intended to convey information and/or to produce an aesthetic response to the viewer' (McCloud, 1993, p. 9). The characteristics of Indigenous storywork are complemented by the relational medium of comics. Producing and reading comics enacts a tacit relationship between author and reader in which meaning is an emergent process that occurs in between the elements of a comic book (e.g., panel-to-panel, image-to-text, panel-to-page, page-to-page) that are currently available to our field of vision (i.e., the two page spread). It is for this reason that McCloud (1993) states that the 'gutter', the space between the panels that frames reading, is where 'the magic' of comics happens.

Enacting an intra-active pedagogy which stories ecologies of relationships

Working with two middle-school classes in an urban Canadian school for a one-month period, this pedagogical project encouraged participants not to 'read' nature through scientific literacy but rather to narrate *with* nature as agential literacy. That is, to create the pedagogic conditions for pupils to tell the stories that 'nature' would tell (with) us were we able to listen anew through a different attunement. While differentially approaching science through other-than-Cartesian ontologies, this 'getting lost' worked within/against many of the nodes of science. For example, the content was still the 'stuff' of science (i.e., space, time and matter) and the process differentially privileged science's visual empiricism (Peat, 2002).

In the first half of the project, and leading up to the visual storying introduced above, a web of intra-active pedagogical activities engaged students in further developing a relational practice and language that works towards knowing *with* nature within the context of their schools. These activities were intentionally designed to produce literal and tactical wandering about and with/in school spaces. Students were encouraged to stop in places that were significant to take note of how this significance registered upon their bodies, in terms of the heart, mind and body (e.g., senses). This in turn encouraged students to think about how their own bodies are porous and how senses intra-act with/in an affective flow. Students were invited to document these affective encounters and bodily significances through written notes, and by photographically documenting their intra-actions and spatial mappings. This entailed accounting for and being accountable to the multiple relationships present, how they registered through sensory knowledge that exceeds representationalism, how spatial interiority/exteriority is produced through the agential cuts we call mapping, as well as how space becomes place. This was supported through engaging with/in Indigenous storywork, its teachings, its medium, and how it has been dialogically interfaced with comics (Yahgulanaas, 2009). Concurrently, hands-on skill building activities supported the creation of digital comic books, through the development of photography skills (e.g., composition), story-writing, -building and -boarding abilities, as well as learning about the aesthetics and technicalities of comic book creation, and the computer software used (i.e., *Comic life*; see http://plasq.com/).

In the second half of the project, the students engaged in iterative cycles of affective observation, photography and visual storying. Within the computer lab, students engaged in the *mise-en-page* of comics by juxtaposing multiple visual-textual elements of comic books (e.g., speech bubbles) in order to story their everyday ecologies of relationships within (and beyond) their school.

Narrating with everyday ecologies of relationships as agential literacy

In this section, two short narrative vignettes are presented and read with the other-than-Cartesian approaches that inform this work. A differential telling of students' visual-linguistic stories emerges through and between my reading of and *with* two students' comic books that are with/in and beyond their school as an everyday ecology of relationships. Also agentic within these entangled vignettes, albeit unevenly and unequally, are the following: student interviews, participant observations of pedagogical activities described, the school space, reflexive (researcher) photography and videography, interviews with the collaborating teacher and traditional Indigenous stories.

The diary of 'The Diary of a Wimpy Kid': Considering other-than-human bodies within schools

Within the school, a girl enters the library to take out a book. A cacophony of consternated cries of 'Pick me, pick me!' arises from various novels, encyclopedias and graphic novels (kids simply don't seem to read books as much as they used to). A big sigh of relief arises from The Diary of a Wimpy Kid *when this student reaches for her and takes her to the librarian to sign her out. Excitement wells up in* Diary *as she wonders what adventures are in store for her that day, 'Going outside [the library]! What a rush!' What might the diary of* The Diary of a Wimpy Kid *hold for that day? Being stuffed in a locker? Being lovingly read? Being left in the wet grass of the playground?*

While a library book is not the typical subject or object of study within the context of science education, there are still important lessons to be learned in considering this for, and as, decolonizing science education. Because books themselves are perceived as cultural repositories whose materiality is but a medium whose properties are taken for granted, it is important to consider the ways in which other-than-human bodies within schools are always already natural-cultural and participating agentially in entanglements in ways that come to matter. One of the first questions one might ask when considering the following is: Whose narrative voice emerges through the telling of this story? Within Cartesian frames, one has few options. As stories are forms of knowledge, they require a cultural body to enunciate them. Here, this leaves our student author Danielle (pseudonym) as *the* sole source of voice that is telling a story *about* a book through projecting anthropomorphic values onto it. However, Barad (2007) encourages anthropomorphism (i.e., attributing cultural values to bodies otherwise deemed acultural) if it can be put to the service of working against anthropocentrism (i.e., the centring of humans). However, what if the story is actually narrated by the book?

Thinking with Barad's agential realism and Cajete's ecologies of relationships, and the points of resonance between, encourages considering the ways in which bodies that are typically considered natural, rather than cultural, to have agency. Furthermore, these lines of thought invite us to think about the ways in which agency is distributed and enacted intra-actively. Barad (2007) refers to the 'doing' and 'undoing' of intra-action as posthumanist performativity. This extends the Butlerian notion that epistemology is always already performative. Performativity, a persistent theme through Butler's work, is the anti-ontological doing and undoing of epistemological categories, concepts and conditions such as identity (Butler, 1990), ethics (Butler, 2005) and framings (Butler, 2010). For Butler, there is no doer behind the deed or foundational essence behind epistemology, but rather, knowing and ways-of-knowing are always enactments within a citational chain. Barad (2007) extends Butler's notion of performativity by including materiality as performative and co-consititutive of discourse. In turn, this grants materiality a similar flux and undecidability, and in the process extends the range as to which bodies can and do engage in performativity, as well as the norms by which bodies come into being.

Accordingly, the voice that would arise would entail, at very least, Danielle narrating *with* the book. However, the body who is voicing is simultaneously neither and both the book nor/and Danielle as they are classically conceived within a Cartesian ontology, as neither pre-exist their enactive entanglement (i.e., no doer behind the deed). Rather, they emerge from a re(con)figured narrative body which would comprise and cut across multiple Cartesian entities through an iterative process that is always already happening. Thus, there was no essential 'Danielle' or a 'Diary of a Wimpy Kid' prior to this entanglement. Rather, they were always already enactments of their ongoing material-discursive historicity of ongoing entanglements past, present and to come. This means that (re)considering the voice as an intra-active entanglement would entail accounting for, and being accountable to, a plurality of natural-cultural bodies within the ecology of relationships which come to constitute the phenomena at hand. While it is impossible to fully account for all of the agencies which might enact this narrative, which includes both Danielle and *The Diary of a Wimpy Kid*, their respective and intertwined material-discursive historicities and futurities-to-come always already matter. Although, as Barad (2007) reminds us, while everything comes to matter, not everything comes to matter equally.

To begin to consider other-than-human beings as agentic is a productive step in the direction of taking seriously the Indigenous notion that the plurality of other-than-human bodies such as animals, plants, rocks and rivers constitute a sentient landscape which is always already teaching us, should we choose to and/or be able to listen *with* it (Battiste et al., 2005; Cajete, 1994, 1999, 2000). As Leroy Little Bear puts it 'trees talk to you, but you don't expect them to speak in English or Blackfoot' (in Peat, 2002, p. 288).

It is also interesting and worthwhile to consider the other-than-human bodies that co-constitute schools, such as books, as de/colonizing agents – bodies who are positioned with/in the indeterminate space between upholding and subverting coloniality (see Battiste et al., 2005). While books are often considered as enacting knowledge as a thing-unto-itself that is already made, it is worth noting that while Cartesianism is totalizing, it is never fully totalized. Entangled within the production of the comic, *The Diary of a Wimpy Kid* acted as a pedagogical pivot that facilitated and enhanced already existing relationships. As Barad (2007) reminds us, the ways in which we enact our intra-actions matter because 'each one reconfigures the world in its becoming – and yet they never leave us; they are sedimented into our becoming, they become us' (p. 394). In other words, the ways in which we enact our ecologies of relationships leave their marks upon the bodies connected with/in the entanglement. One of the ways in which the entanglement of *The Diary of a Wimpy Kid* and Danielle can be accounted for is through considering the multiple ways Danielle might have differentially taken up the book's ways-of-being-in-the-library.

One of such marks upon Danielle's body, or ways in which she registered the entanglement, was through developing a more active version of her already existing relationship with the school librarian and library (e.g., learning about the everyday engagements of books, such as being shelved or loaned, through discussions with the librarian). To extend this line of thinking further is to consider the ways in which, as Battiste et al. (2005) posit, the very materiality of schools as institutions upholds and enacts Eurocentric values: for example, books as intra-acting with/in neo-colonial knowledge commodification practices, re-centring the human of humanism. This has at least two important problematics and possibilities. First, it invites a double(d) deconstruction of schools' binary relationship between nature/culture and inside/outside (i.e., nature+outside/culture+inside) in order to (re)consider schools as not only cultural but also 'natural', or more specifically as natural-cultural places. To only consider the 'outside' of schools as natural spaces runs the risk of forgetting and neglecting the ways in which the inside of the school is always already enacting its very materiality. Secondly, while they are perceived as upholding (neo-)colonial values, it worth considering the ways in which schools and their ecologies of relationships are never fully totalized and are already enacting subversive possibilities.

Days of future past: Considering non-linear spacetime in science, technology, society and environment issues

Elsewhen in the school, Bill (pseudonym) is becoming a future self that may never come to be. Space and time as Bill knows it have momentarily unravelled, unwound as Bill quantum leaps into an unknown and (im)possible dystopian future. Arriving upon the very school grounds he would have been a student at, he finds the site in disrepair and deserted. All that remains of the forest that should be surrounding the school is but blackened earth. With no one around, he begins to explore the ruins. However, suddenly, he is pulled back into the timeline he is all too familiar with, as if awaking from a bad dream. What will Bill do with this knowledge of an uncertain but potentially possible and deeply problematic future?

A strong theme that permeates this story is the ever-present possibility of a future that is shaped by socio-politico-ecological disaster. Entangled with/in the story are conversations with the author, George and other students which suggest a partial and distributed understanding of how he and others are always already enacting (neo-)colonial systems. In other words, an understanding of the ways in which such systems privilege capital gain over growing social, political and ecological concerns that result from ongoing processes such as the entangled unregulated resource extraction and pollution, and highly uneven (re)distribution of wealth as well as basic human necessities such as food, water and space. As Smith (1999/2012, p. 58) reminds us about this entanglement, 'one of the concepts through which Western [modern] ideas about the individual and community, about time and space, knowledge and research, imperialism and colonialism can be drawn together is the concept of distance'. By means of separability, separation and distance through exclusionary individualism, the individual(istic) human(ist) subject can operate at a distance from culture, nature and ethics. Metaphysical individualism obscures an ongoing accounting for and accountability to the ways in which we are always already iteratively, epistemologically and ontologically co-constituted (Barad, 2007). Further, engagement in the ongoing and ever-needed possibility of ethics is foreclosed (see also Apffel-Marglin, 2011; Cajete,

1994, 1999, 2000; Peat, 2002). Here, part of the pedagogical possibility offered by this story towards subverting a singularizing (neo-)colonial settler futurity is not only directly addressing the many ways in which the humanist subject maintains and (re)produces power through distance and separation, but also how humanism separates, distances and organizes space, time and matter (i.e., nature).

Thinking with posthumanist performativity helps us think about the ways in which this story employs futurity and its subversive potentiality through ontological indeterminacy. Rather than using the language of predictability and certainty implied through a linear and causal relationship between past natural and cultural events towards an ever certain present, this story invites us to consider a natural-cultural future as a possible possibility that shapes the present with/in a non-linear causal relationship: *Does the past produce the present? Does the present shape the past? What about the relationships with the future?* On time, Barad (2007, p. 180) states:

> Time is not a succession of evenly spaced individual moments. It is not simply there as substance of measure, a background uniformly available to all beings as a reference or an ontological primitive against which change and stasis can be measured.

For Barad, time is performative and comes into dis/continuous being through its enactment. This dis/continuous being, or to vacillate between *being* and *not being*, is, in short, what it means to be ontologically indeterminate. If even the past is open to being re(con)figured (e.g., quantum tunnelling; see Barad, 2007) in the present, then what happens to the temporal linear causality that WMS relies upon to make knowledge claims? What if time were always already an entangled variable to account for and be accountable to rather than a control (or controllable substance)?

This resonates with Indigenous ways-of-knowing-in-being that recognize that the world itself is in flux and in process, such that it might be more appropriate to state that it is ontologically *becoming* rather than *being*. Such ontological indeterminacy has significant consequences for pedagogy. For Cajete (1994, p. 54), 'learning involves a transformation that unfolds through time and space' and that enfolds space and time. This is significant as it makes space for a plurality of ways-of-knowing-in-being to include other ways of enacting temporality such as Indigenous forms and flows of time such as non-Euclidian circularity (Cajete, 1994, 2000; Peat, 2002). Also, considerations of time as enfolded and time as always already more than an inert, immutable and linear backdrop upon which nature and culture play-out invite an ongoing consideration of the ways in which time makes itself intelligible through its entangled performativity with other agencies.

The ways in which multiple space-time-matterings make their presence known in singular instances in bi-directional causal ways (Barad, 2007; Cajete, 1994, 2000; Peat, 2002) invite us to consider not only how the past shapes the present and the futures-to-come, but also how the plurality of undeterminable futures shape the present, as well as the past. This non-linear causality invites us not only to consider how we are shaped by potential futures-to-come, but more importantly, how we are always already ethically bound to these potentialities that we can never fully come-to-know. 'Everything leaves a track, and in the track is the story: the state of being of each thing in its interaction with everything else' (Cajete, 1994, pp. 55–56). Potential futurities are always already with/in us. However, just as this story ends with the protagonist waking up from what seems to be a bad dream, there is always an ethical hope in the subversive potentiality of the future as it is always at once yet-to-come and not-yet-to-come.

Conclusion: De/colonizing science education

Decolonizing science is an ethical call to account for, and be accountable to, ways in which culture and nature intra-act with/in the learning journeys of all students, including Indigenous, diasporic and other postcolonial human bodies, as well as the other-than-human bodies with whom they interact. While there have been great strides in addressing the 'culture of science' and the 'Scientist' as subject (i.e., masculine, Eurocentric, anthropcentric), the human of humanism is reinstated by (re)defining practices of scientific literacy with/in the ontology of Western modern humanism (i.e., Cartesianism) and positioning this ontology as the only one, onto which all knowledge systems map.

If we consider decolonizing science education as a process or a journey that works against the normative and entangled set of onto-epistemological practices and enactments that constitute humanism's Eurocentric legacies, we must also recognize that it too is always on the move. As 'learning and teaching are occurring at all times, at all levels, and in a variety of situations' (Cajete, 1994, p. 40), education too is re(con)figured with/in relational ways-of-knowing-in-being that co-substantiate it, just as neo-coloniality is an incomplete yet never fully separate evolution of coloniality. Posthumanisms and Indigenous sciences provide important insights into the entanglement of knowing and being, as well as how we might imagine them otherwise. As this chapter has shown, with/in the points of convergence between Barad's *agential realism* and Cajete's *ecologies of relationships* lie ways-of-knowing-in-being that are shaped by ethics, accountability and responsibility to the (re)generation of that which we, as humans, co-constitute and are co-constituted by. This, of course, has great consequence for what scientific literacy *is, is not*, and most importantly *can be*.

As this chapter has shown, engaging in and through pedagogies that work within, against and beyond humanism's epistemology and ontology by bringing attention to other-than-Eurocentric and other-than-Cartesian possibilities to make space for plural ways-of-knowing-in-being can be(come) fruitful steps in knowing and being with space, time and matter otherwise. This moves away from *is* or *is not* towards a re(con)figuration of the possible possibilities in working towards enacting the world's ongoing becoming in a manner that (re)generates and sustains its ecologies of relationships. As Barad suggests, 'intra-actions iteratively reconfigure what is possible and what is impossible – possibilities do not sit still' (Barad, 2007, p. 234). There are always multiple possible possibilities with respect to pedagogies that account for and are accountable to the ecology of relationships one finds oneself in, enacts and is enacted by. However, this work is never over, nor is it individualistic in nature.

References

Aikenhead, G. and D. Elliot (2010) 'An Emerging Decolonizing Science Education in Canada', *Canadian Journal of Science, Mathematics and Technology Education*, 10(4), 321–338.

Aikenhead, G. and H. Michell (2011) *Bridging Cultures: Indigenous and Scientific Ways of Knowing Nature* (Toronto, ON: Pearson Canada Inc).

Apffel-Marglin, F. (2011) *Subversive Spiritualities: How Rituals Enact the World* (New York: Oxford University Press).

Barad, K. (2000) 'Reconceiving Scientific Literacy as Agential Literacy', in R. Reed and S. Traweek (eds.) *Doing Science+Culture* (New York: Routledge).

Barad, K. (2007) *Meeting the Universe Halfway: Quantum Physics and the Entanglement of Matter and Meaning* (Durham, NC: Duke University Press).

Barnhardt, R. and O. Kawagley (2005) 'Indigenous Knowledge Systems and Alaska Native Ways of Knowing', *Anthropology and Education Quarterly*, 36(1), 8–23.

Barnhardt, R. and O. Kawagley (2008) 'Indigenous Knowledge Systems and Education', *Yearbook of the National Society for the Study of Education*, 107(1), 223–241.

Battiste, M. (2005) 'You Can't Be the Global Doctor if You're the Colonial Disease', in P. Tripp and L. Muzzin (eds.) *Teaching as Activism* (Montreal, QC: McGill-Queens).

Battiste, M. (2013) *Decolonizing Education: Nourishing the Learning Spirit* (Saskatoon, SK: Purich Publishing).

Battiste, M., L. Bell, I. Findlay, L. Findlay and J. S. Henderson (2005) 'Thinking Place: Animating the Indigenous Humanities in Education', *The Australian Journal of Indigenous Education*, 34, 7–18.

Belczewski, A. (2009) 'Decolonizing Science Education and the Science Teacher: A White Teacher's Perspective', *Canadian Journal of Science, Mathematics and Technology Education*, 9(3), 191–202.

Blaut, J. (1993) *The Colonizer's Model of the World: Geographical Diffusionism and Eurocentric History* (New York: Guilford Press).

Braidotti, R. (2013) *The Posthuman* (Cambridge, UK: Polity).

Butler, J. (1990) *Gender Trouble* (London: Routledge).

Butler, J. (2005) *On Giving an Account of Oneself* (New York: Fordham University Press).

Butler, J. (2010) *Frames of War: When Is Life Grievable?* (London: Verso).

Cajete, G. (1994) *Look to the Mountain: An Ecology of Indigenous Education* (Durango, CO: Kikavi Press).

Cajete, G. (1999) *Igniting the Sparkle: An Indigenous Science Education Model* (Durango, CO: Kivaki Press).

Cajete, G. (2000) *Native Science: Natural Laws of Interdependence* (Santa Fe, NM: Clear Light Books).

Cook, K. and G. Buck (2010) 'Photovoice: A Community-based Socioscientific Pedagogical Tool', *Science Scope*, 33(7), 35–39.

Gough, N. (2006) 'Shaking the Tree, Making a Rhizome: Towards a Nomadic Geophilosophy of Science Education', *Educational Philosophy and Theory*, 38(5), 625–645.

Higgins, M. (2014a) 'De/colonizing Pedagogy and Pedagogue: Science Education through Participatory and Reflexive Videography', *Canadian Journal of Science, Mathematics and Technology Education*, 14(2), 154–171.

Higgins, M. (2014b) 'Rebraiding Photovoice: Putting to Work Indigenous Conceptions of Praxis and Standpoint Theory', *Australian Journal of Indigenous Education*, 43(2), 208–217.

Lenz Taguchi, H. (2010) *Going beyond the Theory/Practice Divide in Early Childhood Education: Introducing an Intra-active Pedagogy* (London: Routledge).

Mazzochi, F. (2006) 'Western Science and Traditional Knowledge', *EMBO Reports*, 7(5), 463–466.

McCloud, S. (1993) *Understanding Comics: The Invisible Art* (Northampton, MA: Kitchen Sink Press, Inc.).

McKinley, E. (2000) 'Cultural Diversity: Masking Power with Innocence', *Science Education*, 85(1), 74–76.

McKinley, E. (2007) 'Postcolonialism, Indigenous Students, and Science Education', in S. K. Abell and N. G. Lederman (eds.) *Handbook of Research on Science Education* (Mahwah, NJ: Lawrence Erlbaum).

Peat, D. (2002) *Blackfoot Physics: A New Journey into the Native American Universe* (Newbury Port, MA: Weiser Books).

Sammel, A. (2009) 'Turning the Focus from "Other" to Science Education: Exploring the Invisibility of Whiteness', *Cultural Studies of Science Education*, 4, 649–656.

Smith, L. T. (1999/2012) *Decolonizing Methodologies: Research and Indigenous Peoples* (2nd ed.), (New York: Zed books).

Yahgulanaas, M. N. (2009) *Red: A Haida Manga* (Vancouver, BC: Douglas & McIntyre).

12
Student Community Engagement through a Posthuman Lens: The Trans-corporeality of Student and Sea

Jocey Quinn

Understanding student community engagement

This chapter draws on my educational research on university student community engagement, but will explore the emerging data through the lens of posthumanism. Taylor says data invites us 'to follow it on nomadic theoretical journeyings, on to-and-fro zig zags and "backwards" readings as we work "on" it to make sense of it' (2013, p. 691). As we shall see, this journey sometimes takes us to some unfathomable deeps.

Community engagement has become part of the narrative of contemporary higher education. The belief that students should volunteer and engage with the communities in which they are located has become almost a truism in the UK and is even more emphasized internationally, in the USA and Australia for example. This promotion of student volunteering

> is premised on a number of key assumptions; that students benefit from volunteering through acquiring new skills and extending their employability profile; universities gain through improved relations with local communities and organisations, and the beneficiaries of volunteering activities are able to access additional or enhanced local services and amenities.
>
> (Holdsworth and Quinn, 2012, p. 386)

Thus, despite many dedicated individuals acting in good faith, rather than being a moral imperative and a sign of civic responsibility, student community engagement has become a marker of individualism and instrumentalism; another way that students can 'up' their profile. In a market-led system which prizes skills, employability and the production of demonstrable graduate attributes, being able to engage becomes another commodity. There is also a strong, related drive for academic staff to engage with their local communities, which is linked to the growing need to demonstrate the impact of research on practice, in order to gain research funding and to score highly in research ranking exercises. This too raises debates, with academics questioning how far community engagement is a radical act and absolute imperative for academics who care about social inequality, or whether it is rather a gesture of submission to an instrumental agenda which has very little to do with the generation of new knowledge (see, McKenzie, 2014; Taylor, 2014; Quinn et al., 2014). Whatever the position, universities and their students are expected to play some role in the regeneration of their localities and this is especially true when so many students are actually local students and already part of the communities in question. This is particularly the case for institutions which only gained university status after 1992 and are located in areas of industrial decline where they may be the main employer.

This chapter continues a line of research into student volunteering and community engagement (Holdsworth and Quinn, 2010, 2012) which questions neoliberal assumptions that such activities are neutral and win-win for both students and the various communities with which they engage. This research has produced new theoretical understandings. In Holdsworth and Quinn (2012) a critical and close analysis of biographical accounts of student volunteering activities among 20 students in one institution generated the concepts of 'reproductive' and 'deconstructive' volunteering:

> Reproductive volunteering characterises volunteering activities that do not challenge but rather reproduce and re-enforce existing power relations and inequalities. Deconstructive volunteering allows for volunteering activities that reveal power structures and inequalities and thus potentially create the conditions of their own critique, thus making their innocent performance impossible. (p. 293)

So, students whose engagement positioned themselves as 'helping' those whom they perceived to be in deficit simply reproduced their sense of natural superiority and reinforced their sense of what was normal (white and middle class) and what was deviant (poor and multicultural). On the other hand, those who engaged on equal terms with others to help develop community resources gained opportunities to deconstruct their own privilege and the structures that perpetuated it. The paper argued that deconstructive volunteering provided a positive learning experience that helped students to understand and also critique their fields of study. However, this was a two-way process and universities needed to prepare students for community engagement and provide them with the intellectual tools to make this leap of understanding possible. This is a curricular issue, rather than one that can be tackled by community engagement professionals. In the sample at least, there was little evidence that students had been given this grounding.

This current chapter takes data from some further research on student community engagement which sought to employ the concepts of reproductive and deconstructive volunteering. This project was a larger qualitative study employing a socio-cultural perspective and thematically coding the emerging data. Drawing particularly on the work of Stacey Alaimo (2012, 2011, 2010) and Jane Bennett (2013, 2010) and on related poetry and fiction, I make the move to reconsider this research through a posthuman lens. This lens has a destabilizing effect on both the issue of community engagement and the concepts of reproductive and deconstructive volunteering, enriching the research study and demonstrating the utility of posthumanism even in this rather unlikely area of educational research.

The research study

The most recent research project, as discussed in this chapter, aimed to use the concepts of reproductive and deconstructive volunteering in a wider case study. The aim of the project was to explore how far and in what ways students engaged with a range of learning outside their university studies: for example via volunteering and other forms of community engagement, via work, the outdoors, leisure and creative activity and via activism. It aimed to explore whether these activities enhanced their studies and whether they were acknowledged and built upon within the university curriculum. It also sought to analyse how far and in what ways these activities were actually contributing to the local community. The study began with eight focus groups involving a total of 80 students. These focus groups included students across disciplines and stages of their university career. They had randomly responded to an invitation to take part in the study circulated on the university website, by the volunteering centre, by academic colleagues, by the Students' Union and by student groups and organizations, with a small remuneration as an incentive. After analysis of this initial data, the project identified some issues of particular interest, then targeted relevant groups of students and ran four thematic focus groups with local, international, rural and mature students. We then specifically invited further students who were very active to take part in in-depth interviews and then analysed eighteen biographical accounts of active student community engagement. Finally, we interviewed the community partners linked to these activities in order to gather their perspectives on the contributions students made to the local community. The research generated a large amount of data and for the purposes of this chapter the focus will be on community engagement rather than other types of activity. All the participants have been given pseudonyms.

The place of engagement

The city in question is a fascinating mix of the maritime and the urban set on a border between two counties and surrounded by fields and coastline. It is large, sprawling and often ugly on the eye, cut across by busy roads and hasty post-war developments, following bombing in the Second World War. It also has a picturesque harbour area and a sweeping and spectacular seafront. Negotiating the city and familiarizing oneself with it is not easy. Storms have threatened the coastline, recently destroying the only railway line and for some months leaving the area stranded and at the mercy of TV crews and visiting politicians seeking to capitalize on the drama. The main university campus is centrally located and positioned on a hill overlooking and close to the main shopping centre. Despite these bare facts, the city, like all places, constantly shifts its meanings.

Space of course can be appropriated, rewritten and reimagined. For example, in *Heaven Is a Place* (Parker, 2014) LGBT dance and performance artists come together to bring out and claim the hidden beauty of the city for themselves:

> The film places bodies of the present in the places of the past... is set in the liminal, waterfront spaces of the city's border with the sea, the decommissioned military installations, the crumbling recreational structures, including the iconic place – which was once the (in) famous nude men's bathing area – and the brutal beauty of the 1950s-built bus station.
>
> (press release)

The university too re-imagines it as a place where the city tends to disappear. In publicizing the university and encouraging students to apply there the university particularly emphasizes the pleasures of nature, declaring: 'Walk the moors and feel the waves' (University website, 30 January 2015). It also makes great play of its international reputation in Marine Science, setting a scene that emphasizes maritime heritage and marine life.

The university makes efforts to create 'belonging' for home and international students. For example, its International Café is an initiative for overseas refugee and home community members to come together, share cooking and food. In walking around and observing the campus it is possible to see some interesting and heartening juxtapositions.:

> *In the canteen today saw a flock of Saudi Arabian women in burkas sitting next to a trans student in full make up and dress.*
>
> (JQ research diary)

Nevertheless the literature on 'diversity' in education calls their readability as marks of inclusion into question (see Taylor, 2014) and the university is both open and closed in multiple ways. In terms of the research project discussed here a close analysis of the focus groups shows the relationship between the university and the place where its students must engage to be complex and fractured, with unexpected connections and painful ruptures. Cutting the data further, and at a different angle, through the use of Alaimo (2010, 2011, 2012) and Bennett (2010), expands this connectivity to the very confluence of land and sea on which the university is (temporarily) lodged.

Off to the sea

During the initial eight focus groups, which took place in early 2013, the students were asked to discuss any activities they took part in outside their studies and a particular emphasis was laid on the issue of volunteering and community engagement generally. The responses to and accounts of community engagement varied widely. For many students time pressures and a desire to focus exclusively on their studies meant that they did not consider community engagement as a viable option. Others were disposed to become involved in the local community, but felt they lacked knowledge about what to do or the means to take part. Despite the predominance of non-engagement, there was widespread agreement that the university should do more to encourage these links, either within the curriculum or by promoting them in a more vigorous and targeted way. Engagement was seen as both moral and useful. A smaller number of students were very active, which had both opened up their fund of knowledge and contributed to their CVs in an instrumental way. Some were able to be critical and reflexive about this process, as these comments from the mature students' focus group from the second wave of focus groups (May, 2013) indicate:

> That's everything everyone goes on about, volunteering at this university: (telling us that) 'Volunteering, it looks good on your CV'. I just do it because I enjoy it, quite frankly, I wouldn't do it if I didn't enjoy it.
>
> (Laura)
>
> For me, if there's a volunteering opportunity for an hour every day, if it's related to my subject I'm ready to do it. Absolutely ready. But only, like I said, if it's related. It's not only that you enjoy it, but you also take the advantage of learning from it. I'm absolutely ready to do that.
>
> (Emma)

Those students who were active felt that, although volunteering was actively encouraged as a mark of enterprise and employability, their tutors did not acknowledge or reward community engagement, apart from vocationally oriented courses such as Social Work. As they saw it there was little integration of external and degree-based knowledge within their university studies. This was seen as a profound missed opportunity, as there were so many ways in which engagement added perspective to the subjects at hand and also enhanced the capacity of students to discuss and analyse them critically. Their concern was not restricted to seeking academic credit for volunteering, but rather that there should be a convergence of the different types of knowledge throughout the whole of the curriculum. In this sense the students seemed to validate the deconstructive potential of engagement, but feel that was neither acknowledged nor employed within their programme of study.

A tale of two cities

On exploring the focus group data a revealing picture of the local community emerged, one in which the people of the city were generally perceived as problematic and other. The university was seen as a city in itself, 'a little hub of people all in one place', and was enjoyed precisely because these others were not present:

> Everything's here. I very rarely go into town if I don't have to because I hate all the people, just too many people. Quite weird people sometimes! ... and it's nice to walk about and see only see young people and I feel like kind of this is my city.
>
> (Tom)

On venturing out and encountering these 'strange people' only bad things seemed to happen. 'With community things there – I had a lot of trouble with my neighbours last year. There was a house full of heroin addicts.' (Nick) Indeed the focus groups rarely talked about the people of the city except in relation to crime. This was not based on any actual evidence, rather hearsay and media speculation.

Of course many students were already people of the city and they were very conscious of this negative tendency among other students:

> I've had a lot of students that are always complaining about the locals here ... They're always going around saying 'oh bloody Janners'. And I just turn around and say I'm a Janner as well!!
>
> (Josh)

Actively being one of the *humans* who lived in the city was not the incentive or the focus for engagement for most students: 'I've come here to study not to directly engage in the community.' Rather the focus shifted to a very particular form of *nonhuman matter:* the sea. As a local student observed,

> They love it here in the sense that they love the beaches and the outdoors and they love the coast ... But they never really talk about the people as such. Only things like when someone may be had something stolen ... So I think it's more about actually like physical geography rather than the people and the culture.

By setting their horizons on the sea, the students leave the city and its problems behind. Culturally and historically this is a common move: 'many cultures have revered the sea and at the same time they have made it to bear and to wash away whatever was construed as dangerous, dirty, or morally contaminating' (Patton, 2006, p. xi). The move to the sea helpfully seemed to vitiate any responsibility for intervening on behalf of people. It seems that the university marketing is successful in selling it, not as a city with people in it, but as a gateway to nature:

> There are loads of students that have come down here from other areas and they love it down here because there are so many different types of wildlife, different habitats so close.
>
> (Matt)

Rural students who commuted complained of restricted opportunities for community engagement when living in a village where networks and minds could be closed. They compared this to the city, not in terms of a more open-minded community, but in terms of a more open engagement with wild spaces. 'And I think here in the city you've got everything haven't you. You've got the Moors not 20 minutes away and you've got the sea' (Jane). Students who were active did many different things such as working in schools and for charities and community organizations. However, a surprising number saw it as their role to reconnect humans with the sea: 'It's focused on getting community engagement, the natural environment that you're looking at, getting them to see what's actually there and close to them' (Simon). It was commonly suggested that somehow the coast creates different and valuable ways of being: 'I think you get a different outlook on a lot of things if you're in a coastal area... it's a lot more relaxed' (Jane). When asked to think of potential engagement activities that the university could foster, again attention turned to the sea: 'It's supposed to be the Green University, so doing stuff green within the city... maybe doing things like beach cleaning' (Holly). While it would be an exaggeration and a researcher's 'Hollywood story' to claim that the narrative of student community engagement here is simply and uniquely one of marine adventure, the part played by the sea seems worthy of reflection and discussion.

Using posthuman theory to explore the trans-corporeality of students and the sea

This polarized view of people and nature within the data might be seen as quite unremarkable and 'natural', given dominant discourses about seasides and the urban poor: the sea is nice and these people are not. It can also be seen as a common cultural construction where the sea represents escape and being among people represents confinement. This trope is everywhere: after all, my favourite tee-shirt says 'Free in the sea' on the front. Social class too obviously plays a part in this narrative, whereby the people of the city are positioned as an underclass and the students, although by no means predominantly middle class, create physical and symbolic distinction from them (Bourdieu, 1984). This may be a necessary move in their eyes. They will predominantly have come from the region, but not necessarily the city itself. Overall, the region is not an area of high employment. By doing a degree in the first place they are trying to manoeuvre some advantage and their privilege has to come at the expense of someone.

The sea can be seen as a mark of mobility and privilege: as the poet Baudelaire said, 'A free man loves the sea' (Man and Sea, in McClatchy, 2001). Travel across the city and access to beaches and sea was something that young working class people had highlighted as a problem at a recent Economic and Social Research Council (ESRC) Festival of Social Science event I organized (2011). The cost of public transport within the city itself was deemed prohibitive, still more travel down the coast. Yet students claimed freedom to 'go surfing up and down the coast' (Tom). This may be because of easier access to car loans and railcards, but it is also part of casting themselves as being mobile and having freedom and agency, all of which have high symbolic capital.

What then does a posthuman lens add to these more symbolic and structural interpretations? Posthuman theorists insist on the meanings of matter, and 'highlight what is typically cast in the shadow: the material agency or effectivity of nonhuman or not-quite-human things' (Bennett, 2010, p. ix). In this instance, by engaging with the matter of the sea posthumanism makes strange what may at first glance seem normal. Why do these students engage with water and not humans? Why is the matter of other humans, which is shared and familiar, experienced as weird, addicted and defective, so that engagement with it is inconceivable? Why is the sea, seemingly so alien in matter and so dangerous, seen as welcoming and relaxing? The posthuman work of Stacey Alaimo helps to explore but not necessarily explain this strange phenomenon. There is a physical link to the sea, a thread of human ancestry in amphibian life that Alaimo (2012, p. 482) unpicks: 'The sea surges through the bodies of all terrestrial animals, including humans- in our blood skeletons and cellular protoplasm.' This unspoken connection forges strong and evocative links. Images of this heritage seem to recur very often in human image-making. For example, Ben Marcus in his recent story 'Leaving the Sea' shows the desperate narrator (who is experiencing mental breakdown) looking back to a better, simpler body: 'where I would have gills, if I were something better that had never tried to leave the sea, something more beautiful that could glide underwater and breathe easily' (Marcus, 2014, p. 224). This form of posthuman thinking backwards actually disrupts a humanist narrative of progress whereby becoming 'fully human' is the apotheosis of life.

Jane Bennett (2013) traces 'onto-sympathy' between humans and plants, a mirroring of shapes and patterns that promotes empathy and recognition. She suggests that poetic imagery can 'amplify' these patterns across different domains and this idea has proven useful to my paper, helping to explore what can be sensed but not spoken in everyday human communication. So when in the poem 'Mana of the Sea' D.H. Lawrence claims: 'I am the sea, I am the sea' as the culmination of an extended metaphor of sea/body, tracing 'the tide in my arms', 'the flat recurrent breakers of my two feet', he enacts the fact that 'the environment is not located somewhere out there but is always the very substance of ourselves' (Alaimo, 2010, p. 4). Turning in/to the sea is both a compelling material and metaphysical act. In my writing I have always drawn on my reading of poetry and fiction (see Quinn, 2010) and so have a habit of thinking metaphorically. Posthumanism did not release this capacity, but rather poetry inclined me to posthumanism. Thinking poetically helps one to think materially and make the indivisibility of matter and mind comprehensible via an image, rather than through abstract explanation. This tends to be an intuitive process which is difficult to break down and subject to exegesis.

Across her work, which also draws on her knowledge as a professor of American literature, Alaimo (2010, p. 22) develops the notion of trans-corporeality that moves from 'the disembodied values and ideals of bounded individuals toward an attention to situated, evolving practices'. She pays particular attention to the sea and sea creatures. She invites thinkers to 'follow the submersible' as 'submersing ourselves, descending rather than transcending is essential [to recognizing] we dwell within and as part of a dynamic intra-active, emergent material world' (p. 283). 'Sea life hovers at the very limits of what humans can comprehend' (p. 477) and so to Alaimo is salutary in helping us to recognize our humanist presumptions and challenge our human exceptionalism. In this sense the students' engagement with the sea helps to broaden our conception of what engagement and contribution might be. The local community includes the sea; it is not merely bounded by it. By responding to the sea, the students, living in an age of posthumanism, are simply acting as posthumanists.

Implications for student community engagement: Changing the perspective

Discussion on community engagement has tended to be conducted in humanist terms, whether it be from neoliberal, critical or more poststructural positions. The existing focus is on human relationships and networks and on how they facilitate engagement. In contrast, this study goes beyond these networks across humans to consider human and nonhuman assemblages, looking closely at matter and its meaning. In this case what does the sea do and what does that mean? As Bennett (2010, p. 62) says, 'What would happen to our thinking about nature if we experienced materialities as actants, and how would the direction of public policy shift if it attended more carefully to their trajectories and powers?' Community engagement tends to be couched in terms of values and ethics; for Alaimo (2012) trans-corporeality engenders new forms of ethical responsibilities. Therefore the literature on community engagement needs to move beyond the ethos of 'doing good' to humans. This does not mean simply transferring attention to 'doing good to the sea', but understanding and taking account of the sea as an active part of community life. Posthumanism opens up the category of both what counts as harm and what entity might be harmed. It also tends to shift the time frame, making us think beyond the limits of our own lifetime, which is rather difficult for students who see themselves as passing through. Finally, it does not allow for divisions into good matter and bad matter. Thus the university cannot be engaged and also hold itself apart, and neither can students.

So it may be that this new form of engagement is deconstructive in a way that our original conception did not address. It deconstructs boundaries between human and nonhuman and deconstructs the human as a bounded non-porous subject. This is methodologically challenging to qualitative research which is still, despite its protestations, wedded to the notion of identity. In practice, analysis of qualitative data in educational research is informed by what I group together as 'the authentic self', 'the inescapable self' or 'the self-made self' (Quinn, 2010, pp. 16–17). Posthuman theory instead helps to operationalize what I have called 'the unself: subjectivity engaged in a perpetual process of flux' (p. 18) by moving with it in the sea. Perhaps it also helps deconstruct notions of agency as the students must give up control to the sea. However, there are some dangerous reproductions also going on: namely that some humans are un-fit, are somehow sub the category of human occupied by the young, healthy student. The city is bypassed for the sea and with it any sense of responsibility for it, or even that this is a common ground. Some matter has the capacity to help you transcend, some just drags you down. Being by and near the sea affords physical pleasure and traditionally a sense of being part of something bigger and restorative:

> O ye! Who have your eye-balls, vexed and tired,
> Feast them upon the wideness of the Sea
>
> ('On The Sea', John Keats)

Rather than a chance of deconstruction, engaging with the sea may offer a respite from thinking (and eyeball-vexing studying). It may especially provide an escape from the difficult thinking needed to address social inequality.

Conclusion

Student community engagement seems a rather bounded topic, limited by a number of positions, which may be critical, but also assume a humanist pedagogy and curricula. Using a posthuman lens reveals the student and the university are porous, subject to tidal rhythms and waves of transformation. All is unstable, all is connected, so pedagogy and curricula framed around the autonomous individual cannot hold. Collective engagement with the matter of the world must become the heart of higher education. However, how that world is conceptualized is still up for debate. The posthuman emphasis on the sharing of matter across human/nonhuman does not preclude the consideration of the socio-cultural, the economic etc. in shaping how that matter exists and is understood. However, in practice there are dangerous moments of slippage where, in enthusiasm for matter, both the structural and the ineffable become obscured. This is something I have emphasized in my previous writing on posthumanism (Quinn, 2013a and 2013b). I want to sail out to sea on a tide of enthusiasm for posthumanism, but the city as a socio-cultural phenomenon and lived-in place also calls me back. The sea in my case study is used as a pragmatic tool as well as being 'vibrant matter' (Bennett, 2010). It is tied to the economic life of the town, as a maritime centre with related industries, as a site of leisure events bringing in customers, and as a potential for tourism. The university has invested in marine research and teaching in the anticipation this will bring kudos and financial reward and this too seems to pay dividends. In the symbolic realm, countless research and cultural activities based in the city tie themselves to the sea as a mark of distinction. This chapter is simply the next in line. There are numerous 'signposts' leading students to the water. All these meanings intertwine with the vital play of matter that occurs when students 'engage' with the sea. These meanings do not supersede the significance of trans-corporeality but neither are they obliterated by it. It is in adding to and revisioning the socio-cultural (rather than eliding it) that posthuman theory has most to offer the study of education.

References

Alaimo, S. (2012) 'States of Suspension: Trans-corporeality at Sea', *Interdisciplinary Studies in Literature and Environment*, 19(3), 476–493.
Alaimo, S. (2011) 'New Materialisms, Old Humanisms, or Following the Submersible', *Nordic Journal of Feminist and Gender Research*, 19(4), 280–284.
Alaimo, S. (2010) *Bodily Natures: Science, Environment and the Material Self* (Bloomington and Indianapolis: Indiana University Press).
Bennett, J. (2013) *Vegetal Life and Onto-Sympathy*, Visiting Lecture (Birkbeck: University of London), 4 October 2013.
Bennett, J. (2010) *Vibrant Matter* (London: Duke University Press).
Bourdieu, P. (1984) *Distinction* (London: Routledge and Kegan Paul).
ESRC Festival of Social Science (2011) *Creating Our Place*, November.
Holdsworth, C. and J. Quinn (2012) *Antipode*, 44(22), 386–405.
Holdsworth, C. and J. Quinn (2010) 'Student Volunteering in English Higher Education', *Studies in Higher Education*, 35(1), 113–127.
Marcus, B. (2014) *Leaving the Sea Stories* (London: Granta).
McClatchy, J. D. (2001) *Poems of the Sea* (London: Everyman's Library).
McKenzie, L. (2014) 'Being a Link between the Academic World and Local Communities', *The Sociological Imagination* website, posted 6 March, Sociologicalimagination.com, accessed 15 February 2015.
Patton, K. C. (2006) *The Sea Can Wash Away All Evils* (New York: Columbia University Press).
Parker, K. (2014) *Heaven Is a Place* (Press Release (for a Film): Sundog Media).
Quinn, J., K. Allen, S. Hollingworth, U. Maylor, J. Osgood and A. Rose (2014) 'Dialogue or Duel?: A Critical Reflection on the (Gendered) Politics of Engaging and Impacting', in Y. Taylor (ed.) *The Entrepreneurial University: Engaging Publics, Intersecting Impacts* (Basingstoke: Palgrave Macmillan), 202–223.
Quinn, J. (2013a) 'Theorising Learning and Nature: Post-human Possibilities and Problems', *Gender and Education*, 25(6), 738–754.
Quinn, J. (2013b) 'New Learning Worlds; The Significance of Nature in the Lives of Marginalised Young People', *Discourse: Studies in the Cultural Politics of Education*, 34(5), 716–730.
Quinn, J. (2010) *Learning Communities and Imagined Social Capital* (London: Continuum).

Taylor, C. (2013) 'Objects, Bodies and Space: Gender and Embodied Practices of Mattering in the Classroom', *Gender and Education*, 25(6), 688–704.
Taylor, Y. (ed.) (2014) *The Entrepreneurial University: Engaging Publics, Intersecting Impacts* (London: Palgrave Macmillan).
Taylor, Y. (ed.) (2012) *Educational Diversity: The Subject of Difference and Different Subjects* (London: Palgrave MacMillan).

13
Cows, Cabins and Tweets: Posthuman Intra-active Affect and Feminist Fire in Secondary School

Jessica Ringrose and Emma Renold

Introduction: Towards a posthuman feminism

> I think one of the main turning points for me and my interests in this (feminist) group was when we got loads of the year nine girls (age 13–14) in and we were talking about the normalized cat-calling and the skirt being lifted up and you kind of think 'that happened to me too'. And they're these thirteen year old little girls and it's really sad and it's so common that you just kind of blank it out. But when you see these young girls quite petrified and upset by things, it really sets off a little fire in you and it shouldn't be tolerated.
>
> (Stella, Parkland School, Focus Group)

> I think that girls have this taught thing to be kind of quiet and if we are upset... if something's happened to us that we are not happy about we can't really talk about it we just carry on and I think you kind of realize that when girls are given a platform or even a class room where they can talk about things and they are safe then how much people feel they can say, and that's important.
>
> (Anna, year 11, Parkland School, Focus Group)

Feminism has always been incendiary and fiery, spreading and catching through group affects and generating fierce reactions. The key orienting slogan of second-wave feminisms was 'The personal is the political', which challenged the privatization and pathologization of emotion and the subordinate status of the 'feminine' (Boler, 1999). The pivotal mechanism for addressing the personal was often through 'consciousness raising' or the sharing of experiences in groups. Feeling 'safe' in the sharing of experience has always been a central debate within feminist groupings. However, a false commonality of collective experience, with erasures of race, class and other forms of difference was issued by what Braidotti calls antihumanist feminists who challenged universal human identity categories of manhood and womanhood (Braidotti, 2013, p. 27).

Indeed as noted in Chapter 1 of this collection, in Braidotti's influential book *The Posthuman* (2013 p. 80) she lays out her vision of posthuman feminism as that which 'rebels' against identity politics and dominant categories of identity. Posthuman feminism goes beyond antihumanist critique (*potestas*) to act and move (*potentia*) (ibid., p. 26). Posthuman feminism incubates and injects lethal viruses to shake 'the political economy of phallogocentrism and of anthropocentric humanism'. Braidotti specifically advocates that 'posthuman feminists look for subversion not in counter-identity formations, but rather in pure dislocations of identities via the perversion of standardized patterns of sexualized, racialized and naturalized interaction' (Braidotti, 2013, p. 99). Evoking the famous Deleuzo-Guattarian phrase about bodily capacities, Braidotti (ibid.) calls upon us to experiment with resistance and intensity in order to find out what 'posthuman bodies can do'.

Despite our longstanding love affair with Braidotti (see Renold and Ringrose, 2011 and forthcoming) we find her call for 'pure dislocations of identity' utopic and problematic. Challenging simplistic identity politics around universal womanhood or girlhood has never meant throwing out or simply blowing up identity categories. Critically engaging with strategic essentialism in the context of everyday political activisms has proven more useful (Spivak, 1990). Not satisfied with abstract treatises on what posthuman feminism should be, we want to use the important conceptual tools of posthumanism to think methodologically about the processes involved in feminist 'becomings' through our empirical research on feminist groupings and politics in secondary schools.

In this chapter we consider how feminist practices (e.g., identities, belongings and activisms) are reconfigured through posthumanism, which works within and against the binary of essentalized and universalizing categories of girl and boy (among other categories of identity). We explore what lethal injections, subversions and ruptures to phallogecentricsm *look like* in feminist practice and how they may well be performed through the embodied location of girl-feminist-body. We explore qualitative research generated through what we conceptualize as posthuman feminist intra-activist research assemblages (Renold and Ivinson, 2014). Thus our research was 'injected' with *posthuman feminism* from the outset, infecting every empirical encounter and the production of our 'data' and 'findings'. We demonstrate how posthuman feminist research processes allow us to explore the potentialities of the posthuman (but still gendered) body, enacting theories of assemblages, discursive-material intra-action, space-time-matterings and spatial affect.

Assemblages: Posthuman performativity, agential intra-action, space-time-matterings

Educational scholars have increasingly used assemblage theory to explain the workings of power relations in the social, cultural and material world. The concept of assemblage resonates with Foucault's theories of discourse and dispotifs/apparatus – sets of discursive relations of power that materialize through embodied relations in space and time (Legg, 2011). More generally, assemblage theory has formed an important frame for theorizing connections between phenomena to describe 'agencement' (Puar, 2011) or the agentic force relations between various agents. Assemblage theory is derived from Deleuze and Guattari's treatises *in Anti-Oedipus* and *1,000 Plateaus*, where they use assemblage (sometimes machinic assemblage) to articulate the flat, connective, affective relations in play (see also Fox and Alldred, 2014). Homing in on bodily relations, Deleuze and Guattari draw upon Spinoza, suggesting we find out the capacity of bodies or things to affect one another – the relative life force that is affected through assembled relations is what is of concern (Hickey-Moody, 2013).

We place assemblage theory in dialogue with Karen Barad's theories of posthuman performativity and her concept of intra-action. Although Barad does not explicitly use the Deleuzian notion of assemblage, the concept is compatible with her approach, which explores the human and nonhuman agencies at work within relational research encounters (be they in the science lab or the qualitative focus group). As noted throughout this collection (see chapters by Higgins, Gannon and Taylor, for example), Barad's posthuman performativity suggests discourses and material phenomena do not stand in a relationship of externality to one another; rather the material and the discursive are mutually implicated in the dynamics of intra-activity (Barad, 2007, p. 149). Barad draws our attention to the performative 'intra-action' between objects, bodies, discourses and other nonhuman things. Thus rather than exploring inter-action in which modalities can be separated out, she explores their intra-action, the blending or diffracting of elements or agents working together. Barad argues that 'discursive practices are ongoing agential intra-actions of the world' (ibid.) and it is in their coming-togetherness that creates what she terms differential 'matterings', which can never be known in advance, and are always in flow. Barad also talks about space-time-matterings of posthuman performativity – the lively intra-action of discourse and materiality to illuminate their iterative and dynamic qualities:

> Iterative intra-actions are the dynamics through which temporality and spatiality are produced and iteratively reconfigured in the materialisation of phenomena and the (re)making of material-discursive boundaries.
> (Barad, 2007, p. 179)

Barad thus advocates accounting for spatiality and temporality through the intra-actions that form matterings. This approach rethinks agency as happening in the spaces of the intra-actions rather than in the humanist sociological account of institutional structure vs human agency:

> Agency is a matter of intra-acting; it is an enactment, not something that someone or something has... Agency is the enactment of iterative changes to particular practices through the dynamics of intra-activity... particular possibilities for acting exist at every moment and these changing possibilities entail a responsibility to intervene in the world's becoming, to contest and rework what matters and what is excluded from mattering.
> (Barad, 2007, p. 144)

Thus agency shifts from an individual human property to a complex relational terrain of power relations that traverse the human and more-than-human. This is a de-centring of human consciousness which helps us to rethink the unit of analysis in agential intra-actions as more-than-human. For education scholars, it enables us to consider the intra-acting material forces in, for instance, a school eco-system and the surrounding environs, shaping the spatial and temporal potentialities of gendered subjectivities in school (Juelskjaer, 2013; Ivinson and Taylor, 2013).

Intra-activating feminist research assemblages

The research project we explore in this chapter was called 'Feminism in Schools: Mapping Impact in Practice'. We conceptualize this research process as part of a larger, feminist intra-activist research assemblage. Funded by Cardiff University, the project documented an engagement project between Jessica, Emma and *Elle* magazine. The *Elle* editorial team had approached us to help them develop and support (we thought!) a feminist resource pack for UK Secondary Schools. While ultimately the relationship between the fashion magazine and the researchers was unsustainable due to *Elle*'s desire to market their product to teen girls, under the guise of 'feminism' (Keller and Ringrose, 2015), it did spur an interesting experimental research assemblage where five[1] academics activated relationships with teachers across England and Wales to facilitate and/or run feminist lunch clubs and feminist after-school clubs in schools. Seven highly diverse secondary schools across England and Wales, including mixed, single-sex and fee-paying institutions and from a range of religious, ethnic and socio-economic backgrounds participated for at least six weeks, with some still ongoing one year later. We generated qualitative data with 75 young people, five academics and five teachers, using a combination of semi-structured group and individual interviews. Creative methodologies also formed part of the research design; including the visual documentation of a range of material intra-activisms (e.g., poems, writings, sculptures, and online posts from sites like Facebook, Tumblr and Twitter).

We put intra-action together with activism to gesture towards how our entanglement as feminist-driven researchers entangles in research encounters generated through this assemblage. This approach departs from practitioner action research or co-productive methodologies because our practice is situated in posthuman feminism, and an understanding of change and transformation as occurring in dynamic and shifting affect-laden assemblages which cannot be predicted in advance. It also conceives of human and nonhuman actors and actants not as separate inter-acting entities but intra-acting forces that create agency and change.

Posthuman spatio-affects

However, in Barad's conceptual moves to de-centre the humanist individual agent and re-privilege the materialities of nonhuman agents and matter, she has been critiqued as evacuating a concern with consciousness, the psychical and subjective (Clough, 2009). We wish to hold the subjective in play throughout our analysis, but via a posthuman lens. We think that affect is a useful concept, derived from assemblage theory and Spinoza's thinking about bodily affects (as above). For us affect is like conceptual glue that helps us to bridge the psycho-social divide in relational thinking (Bright et al., 2012). Gregg and Siegworth (2010 p. 6), outlining major theoretical frameworks for understanding affect, discuss a 'certain inside-out-outside-in difference in directionality: affect as the prime "interest" motivator that comes to put the drive in bodily drives (Tomkins); affect as an entire, vital and modulating field of myriad becomings across human and nonhuman (Deleuze)'. These authors suggest these two 'vectors' of affect theory are often separated and some seem keen to choose between non-subjective or subjective perspectives on affect.

In suggesting a posthuman approach to affect, we wish to hold various registers in play: affect is transpersonal in that it circulates among and between subjects (Massumi, 2002) as well as being embodied, situated and operating psychologically in and through discursive positioning but exceeding these boundaries (Wetherell, 2012). Affect can be useful as a concept to think about 'interfaces' or 'scaffolding' of relations (Khanna, 2012, p. 220); in that sense it works well with Barad's notion of intra-action within, between and beyond the human body. Affect is a way of thinking about how subjective experience leaks between one person and another; it has psychical, felt, experiential effects inside the human but it is also more-than-human with spatial, atmospheric and other effects (Bright et al., 2012).

Indeed, consider Sara Ahmed's (2004) theories of an affective, political economy where affects (happiness, disgust, etc.) travel, stick and circulate through space, instantiating norms around gender, sexual and racial privileges, for instance. Research on the 'spatio-affective' (Iedema and Carroll, 2015, p. 68) in geography and area studies is also very useful in attending to sensory embodied affects and 'spatial spheres' that 'arise from resonances that move people to act together'. Palipane (2011, p. 5) advocates thinking about 'spatial practice' as a way to explore the relationship between social thought and action where actors can 'appropriate official discourse and secrete their own social spaces'. Ben Anderson (2009, p. 71) writes about affective atmo-spheres as spatial zones of contact as operating 'across human and nonhuman materialities and in-between subject/object distinctions'.

Below, we explore these ideas further using our posthuman research lens to consider the space-time-matterings, intra-actions and spatio-affective dynamics of 'affecting feminism' (Pedwell and Whitehead, 2012) or what we theorize in this chapter as 'feminist becomings'. These include but are not limited to the naming and claiming of a feminist identity – rather our focus is on those feelings and attachments that are created within and flow inside and out from the school-based feminist group. Here we consider the experiences of participating in one of the feminist groups at Parkland Secondary School (a pseudonym). Situated in North West London in a fairly wealthy borough, Parkland had the largest operating feminist group of over 40 girls, which had been established the year prior by (at that time) a year 10 student, Stella. We learned about this feminist group through its growing reputation, which had reached one of our other research schools in the neighbouring borough. In order to interview all the year 9 and 10 members of the Parkland group, we assembled the three members of the voluntary research team and the paid researcher[2] to simultaneously conduct four focus group interviews during one of the lunchtime meetings. Then two team members conducted another focus group with the year 11 students later that week. In total we interviewed 30 participants at Parkland.

Cows: Girls herded as sexual meat in school corridors

The girls who participated in focus group interviews from the feminist club in Parkland School described the process of beginning their group to challenge the daily sexism they were experiencing as catalysed by a particular event. During a non-uniform day the previous year they told us 'two or three girls were sent home for inappropriate clothing... with no attention paid to the boys and we objected and the group was born'. It was serendipitous that the day that we visited the school for the year 9 and 10 focus group interviews was (coincidentally) another non-uniform day exactly one year after the uniform day that had sparked such controversy, outrage and action from the girls, as explained by one group:

Daphne: for men... they'd never think if I wear this will I get raped. It's non-uniform day today and it's so bad because everyone wearing shorts got stopped at the gate and it was all girls and I had to look in my mirror and change three times

	today because I was worried my outfit was too provocative for school... I shouldn't have to think twice before I go out the door, I'll wear what I need to wear in July, girls will wear shorts and crop tops and it's not a big deal anymore it's just legs, basic human anatomy.
Andrea:	and we have all these male teachers looking at us while they waste time we could be in lessons.
Lori:	and they lined us up and the head teacher decided if we could go in, like looking at how short our shorts were, and I was just thinking I don't feel comfortable with you staring at my legs, determining what I should wear and objectifying me.
Caroline:	and it's sexualizing legs.
Lori:	I don't come to school thinking I want to wear short shorts to attract the boys I came to school thinking I want to wear shorts because it's hot today and there's no breeze... they're sexualizing me, I'm not sexualizing myself.
Andrea:	they made it so shameful lining us up in a group, all girls, and both male middle aged teachers and they lead us in a group like cows through the main playground so everyone stared at you on the way to the hall.
Daphne:	its cos we will distract the boys.
Andrea:	and we were like half an hour later for our third lesson and that impacts our education based on what shorts we are wearing.
Caroline:	the boys are bad as well, I've already had my bum slapped twice today.

(Year 9 and 10 girls, Focus Group)

Feminist scholarship has long associated women's sexual regulation with masculine objectification (Bordo, 1993); and man's desire to conquer the natural and animal world has been linked extensively to control over women's bodies as sexualized commodities to be consumed metaphorically as meat. Take, for example, how the pick-up bar is referred to as 'meat market' (Adams, 2000) and the becoming-meat of women's bodies in fashion eco-feminism (e.g., Lady Gaga's raw beef meat dress worn at the 2010 MTV awards) and corporate eco-environmentalist campaigns (like 'Love Fish' where celebrities, mostly women, pose naked with sea-life draped over their bodies to raise awareness of overfishing). It thus came as no surprise to hear the girls connect their experience of being 'sexualized' and 'sexualizing' with being '[led] like cows' in ways that resonates powerfully with Carol Adams' (2000) provocative treatise on the 'pornography of meat'.

The girls talk about being surveilled ('looking at us', 'stared at'), 'lined up' and herded 'like cows' through the space of the main playground and hall way, as well as being 'slapped' by boys. They powerfully articulate how their bodies are felt as a sartorial and physical 'distraction' from the male teachers and boy pupils – an affective process that demands a posthuman analysis, as their own body parts are dissected and dismembered in the looking, staring and 'objectification' of legs and/in shorts. Indeed, the girls seem intensely aware of how they are 'becoming sexual-legs', when they contrast the anatomical leg ('just legs', that should be unremarkable, purely functional, there to enable you to move around) with the ways their legs are sexualized and subject to public shame and ritual humiliation. We see a gendered Cartesian split between the (female)brain/(female)body in their becoming-shorts and/or becoming sexual-legs when they juxtapose how the sartorial and somatic intra-act to sexually objectify in ways that interrupt their 'education' – the intellectual milk that feeds them, but which is interrupted to protect and serve the boys/male brain ('they think we will distract the boys' – where the 'we' is no longer mind and body, but solely 'body').

A posthuman feminist lens enables us grasp the affective and multi-sensory intensities of girls' embodied experience of 'sexualization' as the felt force of phallogocentric logic where regulatory gender/sexual norms invade and 'touch' (see Renold and Ringrose, 2015 for more on the 'phallic touch'). It enables us to explore these affective intensities (i.e., the girls' shame, discomfort and objectification) of feeling 'like cows', not as metaphor or simile, but through a discursive-material-physical sexuality assemblage (Fox and Alldred, 2014) of legs-cows-shorts-looks-slaps and in ways that connect to a wider enduring historical and contemporary assemblage of becoming-meat.

Indeed, the girls' outrage as they shared their collective experience with us and the group is what ignited the 'little fire' among some of the older girls in particular, as narrated by Stella in the opening sections of this chapter motivating the creation of the feminist group. As we illustrate throughout the chapter and have conceptualized elsewhere, it is in these moments in our research encounters that our data 'glows' (MacLure, in Ringrose and Renold, 2014) with the affective matterings and energetic life forces of a 'becoming-feminism' which are incubating lethal injections into phallocentric time-space.

The Portacabin: Safe space and feminist atmo-spheres

Enraged (fired up), Stella contacted the activist group UK Feminista, via their website. UK Feminista is an organization which helps set up feminist groups and campaigns, including school outreach. A UK Feminista representative visited the school with information about starting a group and campaign. With the support of a sympathetic teacher, Mr Hanson, who held the meetings in his classroom, the group was 'born':

Chloe: we had a big talk, learnt what it was about then everybody just shared their experiences of everyday sexism and everyone felt really at home and everyone seemed to have encountered something.
Theresa: it felt really nice, it was good to get it off your chest and you felt really included in the thing that you thought would make a difference, like everyone cares. If we talked about this stuff outside a meeting everyone would say there's so much worse going on in the world like other countries have it much worse.
Joanna: it gave you like a place to go with your problems, like before if someone shouted at you in the street you would have been like there's nothing I can do but now there's a place to go and talk about it and suggest things to stop it...
Chloe: it makes you more angry like before I'd be scared but now I'm like why am I scared?

(Year 9 and 10 girls, Focus Group)

Spatially the feminist group became situated in Mr Hanson's Portacabin. Mr Hanson is a sociology teacher and during the research visits to the school a wide range of students would come and go from the Portacabin – a dedicated place and space physically away from the main school. Some would go there to seek support on a wide range of safeguarding issues, such as 'bullying'. Others would simply visit and hang out, talking about the cabin as a safe space 'to go' that 'feels like home'. The Portacabin thus seemed to operate as a nurturing and safe haven for expressing troubling affects.

Human geographer Ben Anderson writes about the simultaneously indeterminate and determinate nature of 'collective affects' that make up what he terms 'affective atmo-spheres'. Affective atmo-spheres traverse 'human and nonhuman materialities and in-between subject/object distinctions' (2009, pp. 78–79) and provide a tangible way forward in conceptualizing the temporal and spatial contours of affective intensities and flows as they travel in and across bodies, place, objects and time. Anderson also develops Marx's concept of the 'revolutionary atmosphere' which 'exerts force on those that are surrounded by it and like the air we breathe it provides the very condition of possibility for life' (ibid.). This description is evocative for us insofar as it connects to the visceral political atmosphere that can be generated through collective engagements with feminism and the possibility for feminist becomings. Anna (below) talks about the Portacabin as a 'safe environment' for the sharing of 'collective affects' around everyday sexisms, such as 'touching' and 'cat-calling':

Anna: I feel like, especially through year 8 I always felt like I was isolated in holding feminist views so in the class room I'd say something and people would say like here she goes, and I think that made me think Stella's the only one who's a feminist but now I think not really as there's a whole classroom of people who are interested in feminism and it's nice to not feel so alone in your views.

Jos: yeah cos when we were 13 we didn't have any of that and I think what's nice about the group now is that there's something here now where girls can talk about their experiences and be in a safe environment to talk about it and share their views, and I think especially when we were in year 8 and things were happening like sexism, touching and cat-calling we were like 12 or 13.

(Year 11 Girls, Focus Group).

These feelings of safety were repeated many times over across the girls' interviews. The Portacabin and the affective matterings that were released inside its four walls began to emerge as an affective container for the sharing of often isolating and exclusionary experiences. Individual experiences intra-acted to form what Hemmings (2012) calls 'affective solidarity':

Daphne: it's like you feel like it's not just happening to you.
Andrea: it's quite a relieving.
Daphne: it's a bit depressing almost though because there's so much of it and you don't really realize how common it so it's a bit shocking, not depressing...
Andrea: it's almost like anger, you can feel these people being treated horribly, and all like the media and everything.

Zoe: you hear all these stories of girls being harassed and having these terrible experiences and you feel exactly the same and we're all kids and it's creepy.

Riley: but being in the group has made me more self-aware and confident and I can stand up to people when I know what they're doing is wrong and it's given me more insight, because when stuff happens to you every day sometimes you don't even notice but now I pick up on it a lot more ...

(Year 9 and 10 girls, Focus Group)

These comments highlight the affective intensities of being part of a group collective, and how 'affective solidarities' emerged over time, enabling feminist becomings and the sensations of everyday sexisms to surface with alacrity and frequency ('I pick up on it a lot more'). The discursive materialites of (sexual) 'harassment' and affect (feeling relieved, depressed, shocked, angry, creepy, confident) intra-act to produce an enhanced awareness ('insight') in ways that appear to ignite a shift in the constitution of abusive power relations as the group 'secretes' a new social space inside the safety of the cabin – a safe space for the creation of revolutionary feminist atmos-pheres,

Indeed, one of the key features of the girls' new-found 'affective solidarity' was in their capacity to 'notice' together. We witnessed this collective noticing during an earlier visit where the girls discussed the feeling of being photographed in public through mobile phones without their consent. In that instance a feeling of hopeless victimization travelled around like a contagion (Brennan, 2004) in the room as girls confirmed the experience had happened to them and very rapidly we were wrapped in a swirl of 'collective affects' that gripped us, in paralysis. Collective feminist experiences like these can topple and sink us into melancholic states about the feminist complaint or wound (Berlant, 2008). But they also can spark potential – they can enable feminist becomings of affirmative thinking and/or acting differently (Braidotti, 2013) as a result of the shared experiences of anger and confrontation that lead to 'confidence' from being with the group. Again, agency, or feminist becomings, are not the property of individual girls/bodies. They emerge in dynamic assemblages where girls' intra-act with each other, in specific times and spaces. The Portacabin was one such space (as we have defined above). However, feminist becomings were difficult to sustain inside the school (a sexist 'kitchen comment'), or in public space (from 'older' or 'physically stronger men'), and without the embodied collectivity and affective solidarities of the group ('never be able to get equality by myself'), where feminist becomings are blocked and transformed into 'negative' affects only fit for 'drama queens':

Interviewer: so through the group are you guys able to stand up for one another if there's an incident?
Zoe: I think it varies depending on the situation, like if someone at school makes a kitchen comment the group will come at them but if it's a situation where it's an older man or the person is physically stronger than you then you do feel like you can't come back at it quite as much ...
Eva: it's like our older peers are like don't be too much of a feminist and we don't want to argue but most of us do cos we have the energy and the drive to do it and then they say ah you're such a drama queen.
Zoe: oversensitive, not assertive they always make it negative.
Aubrey: I think the feminist club should be more active and start a blog or something cos I always come out feeling so inspired and within an hour I feel like I'll never be able to get equality by myself.

(Year 9 and 10 girls, Focus Group)

The affective solidarities expressed by the girls above in their talk of how 'drives', 'energies' and 'inspiration' can spark revolutionary feminist atmospheres, to 'get equality', were not only difficult to sustain outside the group, but were always precarious, operating in a liminal space that could at any moment be punctured, most notably by the boys, who, in the words of one participant said they 'reacted quite badly not being invited'. After discussing the many ways in which they experience sexism and sexual harassment, Lauren describes the negative reactions of the boys to the feminist lunch club:

Lauren: they're upset by it but it's what happens to us every single day and we feel a lot more powerful about it and they don't like it, it threatens them when we come up all fired up.

(Year 9 and 10 girls, Focus Group)

Being 'fired up' in the nurturing cocoon of the Portacabin provided fuel for the girls' feminist becomings to thrive. In the regulatory school space, their feminist fire becomes incendiary and threatening as it intra-acts with other historical fiery narratives of 'bra-burning feminists' (boy pupils and teachers). Attempts to extinguish the girls' flames also include their return to the animal world of the previous section, where they intra-act with verbal attacks of being furry 'bitches' who 'don't shave'.

It is in this context and these territorializing assemblages that the founder of the group, Stella (year 11), talks further about her ambivalence about wanting and not wanting to embrace the boys by inviting them into the Portacabin:

Stella: I often get a bit scared, when there's a group like this. I fear the introduction of boys could mean you lose the core of what it really for in the first place. I want every girl to feel comfortable in the group and I think it's so important or boys to come along as well as girls as it impacts their lives as well but... I fear that the girls who gained confidence through this group would suddenly lose all their new confidence again and get scared... you do need to introduce boys but it needs organizing well so the boys don't take over cos that defeats the purpose. This was to make a space for girls and all these issues include boys but what we don't want to do is introduce the boys to please them because this what it's all about, everyday boys are pleased and we are not pleased and they are and we can't live our whole lives censored to please the boys although.

The girls very quickly became aware that they had created a space which enabled assemblages to be formed free from 'fear', 'insecurity' and 'censorship' – a space where girls could shake off the shackles of 'femininity', where girls are not required to please boys or satisfy the phallic bound desire that Braidotti urges us to rupture. Stella's struggle to find ways of enabling boys to feel their pain, while maintaining a safe space that sustains the flow of the girls' new-found/shared feminist becomings is palpable. Indeed, the more the girls released their feminist becomings into the school space (and beyond), the more they found themselves intra-acting with and defending against attacks on their swelling feminine-other-non-pleasing body/mind, and the Portacabin emerged and intra-acted in and as a unique material-spatial assemblage for the safe expression and circulation of affective solidarities and feminist becomings for girl bodies only.

234 Cows, Cabins and Tweets

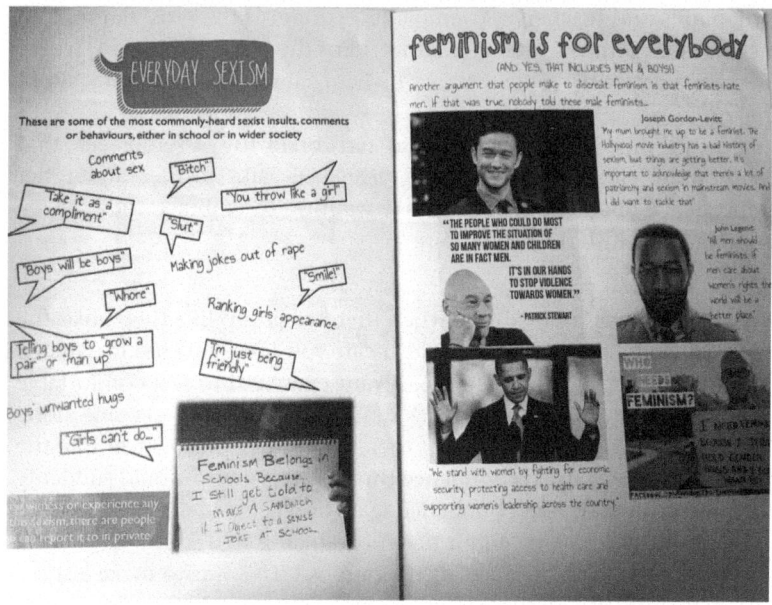

Figure 13.1 Feminism is for everybody

Intra-active material change agents: Leaflets, memes and tweets

In previous sections we have explored how the affective solidarities of feminist becomings emerge and/or are blocked through foregrounding the ways body parts, animals, talk, space and place intra-act in dynamic more-than-human assemblages and how embodied feminist-talk/practices in mainstream school space were experienced as precarious and risky. In this final section, we explore the affective intensities of material artefacts and their potentialities, as nonhuman actants, to keep the girls' feminist fires burning (see also Renold, forthcoming). The first artefact we want to explore is the 'Feminism is Cool' leaflet produced by the group to distribute at school:

Stella: I think when we had the first meeting...we just said okay this is...what feminism is and talked about the ideology but also how it can be utilized. So we made a leaflet and broke it down...There was one boy who was in my science class that

I'd always have these discussions with, he'd be like feminism is pathetic, feminism is stupid and then like coming to this group, there was a leaflet that Sir (Mr Hanson) gave out that explained what a feminist is and the importance of it and the statistics about experiences girls had had, and I gave him the leaflet and he took it home and came in the next day and he was like do you know what Stella, I've got something to tell you that's quite important and he was like I would now declare myself a feminist.

(Stella, year 11, Focus Group)

Here, using the information provided on campaigning from UK Feminista, the group puts feminist 'ideology' into intra-action with the school through a material agent in the form of a leaflet. 'Broken down' into facts and statistics, the leaflet operates as a nonhuman agent – a means of communicating about what feminism means and why the girls' feminist becomings matter. Stella describes how one of the boys takes the leaflet home and arrives at school the next day boldly revoking his identification against feminism and declaring himself 'a feminist'. It is perhaps through the leaflet which traverses time-space by travelling with the boy from school to home (where he can perhaps digest in his own time, in his own space) that the girls' feminist affective solidarities attach and flow in ways that enable Stella's hopes that boys need to 'feel' what they 'feel everyday' to materialize.

Another important way the girls talked about promoting feminist 'ideologies' was via a range of social media, where they intra-acted with members of the school and a wider audience through various forms of digital learning and sharing. There has been plenty written on cyber-feminism and the posthuman extension of the body through digital cybernetics. What we want to emphasize here is how the posthuman dimension of the girls' virtual engagements and transmission of their feminist views are still connected to and intra-acting with the school-based assemblage of the feminist group:

Theresa: we've looked at hashtags on twitter, Everyday Sexism, 'yes all women', there was not an 'all men' and loads of people started tweeting not all men to do this not all men do that.

Violet: we had adverts all over the table too and they were sexist and we had to pick which ones were the worst, and we've probably seem them a thousand times in magazines but when you look at them close up you see so much sexism.

Joanna: we have TVs around school which show announcements and assemblies and stuff and one day it said 'I need feminism because' and it was all these girls saying why they need feminism... we made our own ones and took pictures and posted them on Twitter and Facebook and stuff.

(Year 9 and 10 girls, Focus Group)

Social media enables rapid fire creative engagements and affective transmogrifications (Papacharissi, 2015). The girls describe modifying the 'yes all women' hashtag and tweeting with the hashtag 'not all men', to offer examples of men who are not sexist. They also talk about remaking the Tumblr meme 'I need feminism because' to create their own posters documenting 'this is what a feminist looks like'; they then took photos of the group holding their posters.

They also produced a series of 17 photos of the girls holding up the photos with a 'Who needs feminism' Tumblr meme branded PowerPoint:

Figure 13.2 I need feminism because...

Figure 13.3 Who needs feminism?

which they showed in an assembly and displayed the images on the school TV system to be broadcast at regular intervals throughout the day, a form of knowledge circulation which, like the leaflet, seemed to operate affectively to interrupt the official school space and communicate their feminist matterings in the in-between spaces when students move from class to class. They also extended their reach beyond the school, by posting some examples on Facebook and Twitter:

Jos: it felt good putting it on Facebook and declaring like I'm a feminist I'm fighting for this, and like when people favourite your tweets and stuff you feel like part of a community... I'll tweet about feminism and it's not always appreciated by everyone, like I've had a lot more people saying I find your twitter really annoying, and I've had people say I respect you for your views, but a lot more say that's stupid or 'Oh god here she goes'. I think the places for feminists or young feminists to go have become a lot more publicized so we now know this is a good place to go to.

Anna: ...social media has definitely had like a huge impact for like spreading the word... and the reason why it's got so much bigger through social media is having this access to it, posting stuff on Facebook and sharing of information has allowed a lot of young

> feminists, as they use social media in particular to understand and view these everyday sexism and other projects online like change.org. For the first time ever we can take up any persona we want on the internet so anyone with feminist views and fears being scrutinized for those views can go okay well now I'm Anna something and I'm going to be tweeting and blogging about my feminist views, you can do your bit without being put it in the line of fire.
>
> (year 11, Focus Group)

Intra-acting with a larger feminist group or community through Facebook and Twitter has become a 'good place to go' for the girls, with cyberspace operating as an alternative safe haven in ways similar to the Portacabin. These spaces are particularly important since, when girls meet resistance to their feminist becomings at school, or in the street ('that's stupid' 'that's annoying' 'there she goes again'), they have others online supporting them. Anna specially relates how their digital feminist selves can be activated without 'being in the line of fire', since the intensity of engagements at school is sometimes too much to bear, so the digital community sustains them without being caught up 'in the line of fire'.

Indeed, as Jo's experience testifies, while Twitter and Facebook can operate a form of digital feminist resistance (Berridge and Portwood-Stacer, 2015) our posthuman complexity lens highlights that this is more than virtual; it is a digital-material-sensory-affective-spatial assemblage. The digital dimension cannot be dislocated from the everyday experiences of the walking girl body in school or in public on the street (see also Retallack et al., 2016). These experiences are part of the whole affective sensorium (Anderson, 2009) of dealing with sexism across variously assembled spheres of intra-action.

Conclusion: Iterative feminist becomings

Puar (2011) argues that contemporary feminist politics needs both intersectional identitarian politics (organized resistance around major structural power formations such as race, class and gender through which hierarchical differences are maintained) *and* posthuman assemblage theory to explore the relationships between signification/identity positions and bodily capacities/affective tendencies. We very much agree with this hybrid approach. Engaging with intersectionality and class and race privilege has never been more important, given resurgences in popular feminism and what have been termed neoliberal, celebrity and commodity forms of feminism (Rottenberg, 2013) which fail to address the complexities of power and therefore largely offer life-support rather than lethal challenges to phallogecentrism.

Parklands Secondary is a privileged school in a wealthy borough of the large urban context of London. The girls had discursive-material access to organized feminist activist groups who provided outreach (UK Feminista), and a supportive teacher who enabled a protected space (the Portacabin room of their own) to experiment with feminist becomings including cultivating online social media skills. Critically, not all of the schools in the research assemblage shared in the discursive-material resources of Parkland. Other schools had different intra-active *potesta*, or restrictive, regulatory challenges to be worked through. For instance, several of our research schools were in economically deprived areas with high levels of racialized marginalization. When the London-based girls came together for a Feminist Saturday workshop bringing together four schools, familiar tensions arose around what feminism was and who spoke for whom.

Returning to posthuman assemblage theory and Barad, these are the very contextual iterative differential and relational matterings that count. Particular conditions – space-time-matterings – make dislocations and disruptions to phallogecentricsm possible. Focusing on Parkland, our posthuman lens enabled us to surface key spatialities and material actants such as the Portacabin; mainstream classroom space; virtual space and networks; leaflets; and the liminal visual medium of school TV. Posthumanism helped us to dwell upon the spatio-affective nuances of feeling safe or threatened. We explored the flow of affects, including the incendiary effects of the girls' feminist fire spreading and generating a range of reactions from insult to upset to acceptance. Indeed, taking heart with the boy declaring himself a feminist, we cannot second guess where and how feminist becomings might spring up. These will take different forms in every eco-system, in this case the discursive-material-affective terrain of schools.

Notes

1. The academic team included Jessalynn Keller (Middlesex University), Andy Phippen (Plymouth University), Emma Renold (Cardiff University), Jessica

Ringrose (UCL, IOE) and Victoria Showunmi (UCL, IOE), with research assistance from Victoria Edwards (Cardiff University), Gianna Tomassi (Cardiff University) and Hanna Retallack (UCL IOE).
2. The interviewers were Jessalynn Keller, Hanna Retallack, Jessica Ringrose and Gianna Tomassi.

References

Adams, C. (1990/2000) *The Sexual Politics of Meat: A Feminist-Vegetarian Critical Theory* (London: Continuum).
Ahmed, S. (2004) *The Cultural Politics of Emotion* (Edinburgh: Edinburgh University Press).
Anderson, B. (2009) 'Affective Atmospheres', *Emotion, Space and Society*, 2, 77–81.
Barad, K. (2007) *Meeting the Universe Halfway: Quantum Physics and the Entanglement of Matter and Meaning* (Durham and London: Duke University Press).
Berlant, L. (2008) *The Female Complaint: The Unfinished Business of Sentimentality in American Culture* (Durham and London: Duke University Press).
Berridge, S. and L. Portwood-Stacer (2015) 'Introduction: Feminism, Hashtags and Violence against Women and Girls', *Feminist Media Studies*, 15(2), 341–344.
Boler, M. (1999) *Feeling Power: Emotions and Education* (London: Routledge).
Bordo, S. (1993) *Unbearable Weight Feminism, Western Culture, and the Body* (Berkeley: University of California Press).
Braidotti, R. (2013) *The Posthuman* (London: Polity Press).
Brennan, T. (2004) *The Transmission of Affect* (Ithica: Cornell University Press).
Bright, G., H. Manchester and S. Allendyke (2012) 'Space, Place, and Social Justice in Education: Growing a Bigger Entanglement: Editors' Introduction', *Qualitative Inquiry*, 19(10), 747–755.
Clough, P. T. (2009) 'The New Empiricism: Affect and Sociological Method', *European Journal of Social Theory*, 12(1), 43–61.
Fox, N, J. and P. Alldred (2014) 'New Materialist Social Inquiry: Designs, Methods and the Research Assemblage', *International Journal of Social Research Methodology*, 18(4), 399–414.
Gregg, M. and G. Siegworth (eds.) (2010) *The Affect Theory Reader* (Durham: Duke University Press).
Hemmings, C. (2012) 'Affective Solidarity: Feminist Reflexivity and Political Transformation', *Feminist Theory*, 13(2), 147–161.
Hickey-Moody, A. (2013) 'Affect as Method: Feelings, Aesthetics and Affective Pedagogy', in R. Coleman and J. Ringrose (eds.) *Deleuze and Research Methodologies* (Edinburgh: Edinburgh University Press).
Iedema, R. and K. Carroll (2015) 'Research as Affect-Sphere: Towards Spherogenics', *Emotion Review*, 7(1), 67–72.
Juelskjaer, M. (2013) 'Gendered Subjectivities of Spacetimematter', *Gender and Education*, 25(6), 754–768.
Keller, J. and J. Ringrose (2015) ' "But then Feminism Goes Out the Window!": Exploring Teenage Girls' Critical Response to Celebrity Feminism', *Celebrity Studies*, DOI:10.1080/19392397.2015.1005402.

Khanna, R. (2012) 'Touching, Unbelonging, and the Absence of Affect', *Feminist Theory*, 13(2), 213–232.
Legg, S. (2011) 'Assemblage/Apparatus: Using Deleuze and Foucault', *Area*, 43(2) (June), 128–133.
Massumi, B. (2002) *Parables for the Virtual: Movement, Affect, Sensation* (Durham: Duke University Press).
Palipane, K. (2011) 'The Struggle to Belong: Dealing with Diversity in 21st Century Urban Settings', http://www.rc21.org/conferences/amsterdam2011/edocs/Session%201/RT1-1-Palipane.pdf, accessed 22 July 2015.
Papacharissi, Z. (2015) *Affective Publics: Sentiment, Technology, and Politics* (Oxford: Oxford University Press).
Pedwell, C. and A. Whitehead (2012) 'Affecting Feminism: Questions of Feeling in Feminist Theory', *Feminist Theory*, 13(2), 115–129.
Puar, J. (2011) 'I Would Rather Be a Cyborg than a Goddess: Intersectionality, Assemblage and Affective Politics, EIPCP', http://eipcp.net/transversal/0811/puar/en, accessed 22 July 2015.
Renold, E. (forthcoming) ' "Feel What I Feel": An Onto-cartography of Teen Girls, Sexual Violence and Creative Activism', *Journal of Gender Studies*.
Renold, E. and G. Ivinson, (2014) 'Horse-Girl Assemblages: Towards a Post-human Cartography of Girls' Desire in an Ex-mining Valleys Community', *Discourse Studies in the Cultural Politics of Education*, 35(3), 361–376.
Renold, E. and J. Ringrose (2011) 'Schizoid Subjectivities?: Re-theorising Teengirls' Sexual Cultures in an Era of "Sexualisation" ', *Journal of Sociology*: Special Issue: Youth Transitions, 47(4): 389–409.
Retallack, H., J. Ringrose and E. Lawrence (2016) ' "Fuck Your Body Image": Teen Girls' Twitter and Instagram Feminism in and around School', in J. Coffey Shelley Budgeon and Helen Cahill (eds.) *Learning Bodies: The Body in Youth and Childhood Studies* (London: Springer).
Ringrose, J. and E. Renold (2014) ' "F**k Rape!": Mapping Affective Intensities in a Feminist Research Assemblage', *Qualitative Inquiry*, doi:10.1177/1077800414530261.
Rottenberg, C. (2013) 'The Rise of Neoliberal Feminism', *Cultural Studies*, 28(3), 418–437.
Spivak, G. C. (1990) *The Post-Colonial Critic: Interviews, Strategies, Dialogues* (London: Routledge)
Wetherell, M. (2012) *Affect and Emotion: A New Social Science Understanding* (London: Sage)

14
Theorizing *as* Practice: Engaging the Posthuman as Method of Inquiry and Pedagogic Practice within Contemporary Higher Education

Ken Gale

Creating a research context?

The ongoing nature of the research that this chapter emerges from involves an inquiry into different forms of academic and professional writing within the context of teaching and learning practices in higher education in recent years. Specifically, by inquiring into and opening up engagements between discursive representations of practices and the substance of their material reality, this chapter offers a basis for creating new cartographies for research, teaching and learning. Such an approach is partly premised upon the view that attentiveness to research, teaching and learning engagements can no longer simply be about the social interactions of individual teachers and learners filling space and time with behaviour and practice. The approach will also be used to disrupt and displace writing as a location that is coded by humanist and phenomenological discourses where the individual will of the author is agentic in the production of a metaphysics of being.

The theoretical and practice based milieu within which these nascent rhizomatic practices are oriented can be described as a 'minor literature' (Deleuze and Guattari, 1986) and for the purposes of this research, as 'pedagogic and/or inquiry based assemblages'. Such assemblages will be recognizable through cartographies of (apparently) diverse elements, molecular fluxes and transmutational energies that might be present and brought together for different purposes in education settings such as lessons in classrooms, meetings in staffrooms and chance encounters between colleagues in corridors where various forms of communication take place. The following quotation from Deleuze in conversation with Claire Parnet offers a telling means of making sense of such complexity:

> Whether we are individuals or groups, we are made up of lines and these lines are very varied in nature. The first kind of line which forms us is segmentary – of rigid segmentarity... all kinds of clearly defined segments, in all kinds of directions, which cut us up in all senses, packets of segmentarized lines. At the same time, we have lines of segmentarity which are much more supple, as it were molecular. It's not that they are more intimate or personal – they run through societies and groups as much as individuals. They trace out little modifications, they make detours, they sketch out rises and falls: but they are no less precise for all this, they even direct irreversible processes. But rather than molar lines with segments, they are molecular fluxes with thresholds or quanta. *A threshold is crossed, which does not necessarily coincide with a segment of more visible lines.* Many things happen on this second kind of line – becomings, micro-becomings, which don't even have the same rhythm as our 'history'.
>
> (Deleuze and Parnet, 2002, p. 124)

This chapter employs this focus on molar lines with segments and on molecular fluxes with thresholds or quanta to provide the basis of a contention that within the orthodoxies of education research in higher education generally there has been a sustained focus upon lines of the former kind, those described by Deleuze as being of rigid segmentarity, to do perhaps with divisions of class, gender, ethnicity, ability and so on, to the neglect of those that might be seen to address becomings of a more molecular or particular kind that are more concerned with events and encounters, perhaps of a less tangible and more passing kind.

> (W)hat precisely is an encounter ...? Is it an encounter with someone, or with animals who come to populate you, or with the ideas that take you over, the movements which move you, the sounds which run through you... sounds hammered out, of decisive gestures, of ideas all made of tinder and fire, of deep attention and sudden closure, of laughter and smiles which one feels to be 'dangerous' at the very moment when one feels tenderness.
>
> (Deleuze and Parnet, 2002, p. 11)

Further, there is a sense in which it could be claimed that this attention to rigid segmentarity has been highly influential in creating a 'major literature' in conjunction with the paucity of 'minor literatures' that have been used to promulgate the presence of the second kind of line described above. In their reading of *Kafka* (1986) Deleuze and Guattari present 'minor literatures' as acting in political, experimental and performative ways to de-centre and deterritorialize the structural dominance, traditional idioms and forms and hylomorphic tendencies of 'major literatures'. The ongoing nature of the present research involves, in part, a redressing of this apparent imbalance and in so doing wishes to highlight the play between the molar and the molecular qualities of these lines that network, entangle and criss-cross in multiple, highly complex ways in higher education at the present time: as Deleuze says, these 'lines are immanent, caught up in one another' (Deleuze and Parnet, 2002, p. 125).

Therefore, in addressing the play between these 'literatures', the temporal and spatial orientation of this ongoing research project is substantively influenced by the employment of Richardson's (2000) practice of using 'writing as a method of inquiry' as a highly generative practice which has been agentic in terms of research practice and data creation. Given that writing, conceptualization, theorizing and so on are modes of practice which animate and *activate* in both pedagogical and research-based terms, in the early stages of this inquiry there was a temptation to signify the research as *action* research *qua* action. As has been suggested elsewhere,

> (I)t is also becoming clear that our responsibility for organisation and facilitation as writers and researchers is also being reconfigured, reconceptualised and so energetically questioned within the always becoming of our singular selves in a continual process of emergence. Within this process we are becoming aware of both participating in and creating an 'action research assemblage' (Gale, 2013) that requires us to begin to look at research process and practice in radically different ways.
>
> (Gale, Turner and McKenzie, 2013, pp. 13–14)

So, in the play and emergence of the methodological positioning of this chapter, the view is offered that enunciations and utterances exist in relational space and, as Deleuze and Guattari (1988, p. 80) claim, 'the social character of enunciation is intrinsically founded if only one succeeds in demonstrating how enunciation in itself implies collective assemblages'. The research therefore involves the participants, who all hold different academic positions within the institution, in engaging in a variety of narrative-based writing activities (Gale and Beaumont, 2015; Gale, 2013; Gale et al., 2013). By always working with the presence and activity of these writings as a 'simultaneity of stories so far' (Massey, 2005) the research methodology acknowledges, emphasizes and troubles the intended open-endedness, rhizomatic and processual nature of the research project itself. Arguments have been offered against describing research methodology of this kind as 'autoethnographic' (Wyatt and Gale, 2013a, 2013b) in relation to the phenomenological and humanist inclinations that are to be found in most conceptualizations of the term and the practices that this implies. However, the descriptive claim to be 'action research' can be sustained when action research is conceptualized as research which 'acknowledges and works with "assemblages" in all their complexity, operating within and working to promote an always differentiating seriality of fluid, transmutating and rhizomatically connected forms and possibilities' (Gale, 2013, p. 13).

Therefore, the origination of the current chapter is located within preceding praxis-based writing inquiries in which questions about subjectivity and relationality were seen to emerge within the entanglements of language and materiality. Here language is considered in an essentially Foucauldian, discursive form and materiality or, as Spinoza might express it, in terms of all things being animate in varying degrees: what Bennett refers to as 'thing-power' (2010, p. xiii). The complexity offered in examining entanglements in these ways has the potential to add richness to the continuous play between the latent and manifest possibilities of the not-yet-known which form an important part of these inquiries. This has promulgated a challenge to anthropocentric constructions of the phenomenological and humanist notion of the unitary, agentic self acting upon the passive materiality of the external world.

The current research, therefore, takes on an emergent posthuman identity as it is tentatively characterized here in this 'minor literature'. In working with a sense of the irreducibility of things into a 'culture of objects' the chapter describes a methodological engagement with Bennett's contention that agency is always being re-distributed with the becoming of Deleuze and Guattari's theorizing and use of 'assemblages' (1988) and a consideration of how the writing being investigated here can be contextualized within what Bennett refers to as 'agentic assemblages' (2010, p. 21).

Assemblage as methodology?

Such an approach troubles and displaces those 'major literatures' that proffer phenomenological and sociological constructions of the 'individual' and the 'group' and, in so doing, work to open up inquiries based upon notions of singularity within 'pedagogic and/or inquiry based assemblages'. For Deleuze singularities can be conceptualized as events which are 'essentially pre-individual, non-personal, and a-conceptual'. In belonging to a dimension other than the purely representational, singularities can be 'turning points and points of inflection: bottlenecks, knots, foyers, and centres; points of fusion, condensation and boiling; points of tears and joy, sickness and health, hope and anxiety, "sensitive" points' (Deleuze, 2004, p. 63). According to Bennett (2010), 'agentic assemblages' can be seen as collections of singularities, heterogeneous elements that engage with the play, movements and flows of contingency, structure, organization and change that might be recognizable in any milieu at any given time.

However, Deleuze and Guattari's conceptualization of 'assemblage' is itself not fixed and takes different forms in the dynamic vitality of their work. The various translations of 'assemblage' are animated in their work in a variety of different ways: their repetitions always produce difference. So that 'assemblage' in its original form of 'agencement' (Massumi, 1993), while being suggestive of an intentional form of agency, actually has more to do with posthuman energy and force. It is less about the psychological sense of individual agency that with intent fights against structure and more about the continuous processual distribution and reconstitution of collective multiplicities that creates new vectors of becoming into the not-yet-known. In contrast, the more recently translated 'arrangement' (Dosse, 2010), while possibly suggesting organization and, perhaps, some kind of systemic sociological ordering of selves with function in mind, actually talks to the relative spatial and temporal impermanence of experience. So that as soon as relational ontologies are aligned in particular ways, something shifts; the 'pedagogic and/or inquiry based assemblage' disassembles and in so doing, follows a new and different line of flight, is part of new forms of affective relationality, striating space differently and always becoming. Of these dynamisms and vitalities Deleuze says:

> Creative functions are completely different, nonconformist usages of the rhizome and not the tree type, which proceed by intersections, crossings of lines, points of encounter in the middle: there

is no subject, but instead collective assemblages of enunciation; there are no specificities but instead populations, music-writing-sciences-audio-visual, with their relays, their echoes, their working interactions.

(Deleuze and Parnet, 2002, pp. 27–28)

So, for example, by encouraging students to work collaboratively in writing workshops through the use of what Deleuze has described as 'zigzagging' (http://www.langlab.wayne.edu/CStivale/D-G/ABC3.html) it becomes possible to generate a means of working that is not simply about individuals or groups of students and that is more to do with 'aggregates of singularities' and with bringing spatial and temporal potentialities and relational energies into play.

Theorizing *as* practice?

So, 'pedagogic and/or inquiry based assemblage' is a term that is used to describe, within this 'minor literature', cartographies of multiple, diverse, contingent and heterogeneous singularities that are coalescent and constitutive, that have no central locus of control and that in terms of movements and moments offer a complex relational engagement with space and time. The research is further animated by ongoing consideration of what these 'assemblages' do in different education settings: how might they be seen to work and to animate the particularities of practice? Bennett argues that '(t)he effects generated by assemblages are, rather, emergent properties, emergent in that their ability to make something happen...is distinct from the sum of the vital force of each materiality considered alone' (2010, p. 24) Crucially, such an approach can be seen to provide a further basis and justification for the methodological mapping, central to the becoming of this chapter, of theorizing *as* practice. Expressing the contiguity of theorizing *as* practice with the emergence and affective nature of assemblages is partly to address the tyranny of the theory/practice dualisms that are present in education research and pedagogy and partly to trouble and disrupt the data collection and analysis binary that works to construct research practice within the constraining limits of (post) positivist thinking and practice. By animating Deleuze and Guattari's contention that 'there is no heaven for concepts' (1994, p. 5), concepts must be created; they exist as events and the process of creating concepts, conceptualization, is an active process; theory comes to life in doing, as a verb.

As a means of further methodologically conceptualizing this emergent research process, the project advances St. Pierre's (1997) notion of 'transgressive data' to promote further particular iterative responses and to place the signifier 'data' under erasure in a sustained troubling of the 'major literature' of conventional research practice. In this early paper St. Pierre identified 'sense', 'dream', 'response' and 'emotional' as forms of data and characterized them as 'transgressive'. While the rhetoric of her paper is more forcefully explicated in her more recent conceptualization of and argument for post-qualitative research as practice (St. Pierre, 2014), the practice of theorizing data as 'transgressive' directs attention towards empirical practices that are positioned outside of the concerns of the orthodoxies of (post) positivist research.

In many respects Deleuze and Guattari's integrated applications of 'concept, affect and percept' (1994, p. 163) and Foucault's arguments for a 'getting free of one self' (1992) serve to further intensify St. Pierre's claims. Further, her assertion that data, in its traditional, coded and representational form, needs to be articulated in relation to the 'transgressive' serves to promulgate the view that theorizing as practice is active in the processes and praxis of using forms of writing to disrupt a metaphysics of being and in the promotion of the flows and transmutations of becoming-researcher. Theorizing as practice has the potential to bring to life within its process active consideration of and engagement with the 'entanglements' (Barad, 2007) of the discursive and the material as a means of inquiring further into notions of subjectivity, practice and space. This approach also offers a means of providing insights into the way in which Barad's conceptualization of 'intra-action' (ibid.) can be used to advance, refine and animate an emergent engagement with the relationalities that exist between discursive representation and material reality.

Such an approach can be contextualized within Braidotti's (2013) recent advocacy of forms of posthuman theorizing and practice that work to point our thinking, our very 'becoming' (Deleuze and Guattari, 1988) in the direction of a life, not exclusive from but beyond the self. In taking such an approach Braidotti offers an incisive challenge to the unitary subject of the Humanities and points us towards pedagogic and research-based practices whose concerns are to do with 'a more complex and relational subject framed by embodiment, sexuality, affectivity, empathy and desire as core qualities' (ibid., p. 26). There is clearly a resonance here between her claims and the continuing potential emergence of a 'minor literature' dealing with the kinds of supple and molecular lines identified and presented earlier.

Non-individuated transformative practice?

The rhetorical, theoretical and practice-based initiatives that this research continues to open up are clearly transformative and suggestive of a newly imaginative and sustainable approach to teaching, learning and inquiry. While recognizing and in part acknowledging that transformative learning can be conceptualized as 'a deep, structural shift in basic premises of thought, feelings, and actions' (Transformative Learning Centre, 2004), this chapter is designed to argue for transformation and transformative practices that extend beyond the human and that can be spatially and temporally animated as what Deleuze and Guattari might describe as 'nonpersonal individuation' or 'haecceity' (1988, p. 261). Using forms of writing practices that encourage theorizing as practice through opening up spaces that are not yet known offers a research practice that both recognizes and immerses itself in complexity and multiplicity and in so doing asserts that the spatiotemporal relations of the classroom, the studio and the workshop are as much a part of teaching and learning as the 'becoming' of the teachers and the learners who exist in such relationality. So these classroom, studio and workshop assemblages will be involved in the production of widely differentiated teaching and learning practices that are wholly and intensively imbricated within a multiplicity of visible and indistinct vectoral and material forces. As De Freitas points out, such complexity can be seen as being

> composed of humans, writing implements, writing surfaces, texts, desks, doors, as well as disciplinary forces whose power and agency are elicited through various routines (singing the anthem) and references ('In algebra, we always do this...').
>
> (2012, p. 562)

So, for example, by using Barad's notion of 'diffraction' as an encouragement to write outside of and beyond humanist constructions of the self, the research is active in beginning to disrupt and challenge the colonizing phenomenological tendencies of reflective and reflexive practices that have dominated academic and professional writing practices for a considerable time. Writing diffractively engages interference and works to trouble and distort those images of self that the 'mirror on reality' of reflective writing is often encouraged to produce.

As non-individuated transformative practices this proliferation of human and posthuman energies and forces that exist in always changing spatial and temporal states can be articulated in a number of ways. Again, Bennett's conceptualization of 'agentic assemblage', and 'thing-power' alerts us to the vibrancy of these intra-acting human and posthuman energies. Further, the productive desire operating within these diffractive writing practices and cartographic strategies generates multiple and diverse associative capacities and can be responsible for enabling a new and vibrant form of empiricism to emerge. Drawing upon Haraway's fascination with 'the molecular architecture that plants and animals share' (2000, p. 132) the imagery of the 'vignette' as being something that is written on a vine leaf can possibly be used to suggest a new, different and anti-positivist empirical approach:

> It makes more sense to me to think of *vignetting*, of actively and performatively bringing the world into becoming through drawing attention, through blurring the peripheral for a moment to sharpen and clarify the central, through interfering with false binaries to represent in the play of making temporally and spatially hesitant the real. It is momentary; it lives in the wink of an eye: aeon.
>
> (Gale, 2014, p. 1,000)

In relation to the emergence of these inquiry-based activities there is also a sense in which classroom practitioners will need to pay attention to the following observation offered by Bennett when she says: 'Spinoza's conative, encounter-prone body arises in the context of an ontological vision according to which all things are 'modes' of a common 'substance' (ibid., p. 21). Time and space is to do with encounter; it is no longer simply something to be filled: associative and metonymic writing practices can be used to transform inquiry in non-individuated and highly networked ways.

In referencing and building upon Deleuze's conceptualization of the virtuality of selves as 'molecular girls', Lenz Taguchi (2013) offers such a posthumanist way of thinking that serves to decentre selves from dominant anthropocentric positioning. Her approach offers a helpfully incisive challenge to approaches to teaching and learning that might allow the discursively constructed proclivities of such materialities to flourish. She posits selves as constituting 'a collective researching-body-assemblage, a collective body of thinking' suggesting with Deleuze and Guattari (1994) that this operates as 'a tool for thinking'. For her,

> The researching 'subject' cannot... be understood as a singular, independent or autonomous agent. As a researching-collective-body,

being used by thought, you are in a state of inter-connectedness, and companionship with other beings, matter and discourse.
(Lenz Taguchi, 2013, p. 1,109)

'Molecular girls' comes to represent a challenge to what she sees as the masculinized norms and the molar politics of positivist and postpositivist research practices. She offers a process that acts towards and in terms of transformation and change. Within the networks and complexities of these potentially transformative material and discursively inflected spaces concepts are events and the 'becoming' that her thinking refers to inseparably exists within and, at the same time, creates them. Lenz Taguchi uses the becoming of 'molecular girls' to animate transformations in research selves and practices by offering differentiation, challenge and resistance to the concept of 'man' as representative of the fixed category of being of dominant and dominating research and pedagogic practice. And when she asserts that as a 'researching-collective-body' you are in 'a state of inter-connectedness, and companionship with other beings, matter and discourse' she echoes Deleuze and Guattari's suggestion that 'Climate, wind, season, hour are not of another nature than the things, animals, or people that populate them, follow them, sleep and awaken with them' (ibid., p. 263). Indeed, and in relation to these potentially transformative practices Bennett's notion of 'distributive agency' employs the associative and affective qualities of Spinoza's conative bodies as a way of showing 'the power of a body to affect other bodies (which) includes a "corresponding and inseparable" capacity to be affected' (2010, p. 21).

Writing with a logic of sense?

Offering this form of posthuman theorizing as practice in relation to the strategies and practices of teaching and learning also, and perhaps paradoxically, pays at least referential attention to Merleau-Ponty's (2005) humanist concerns with the pre-linguistic and his setting up of a method of inquiry into the creative potential of forms of perception that do not find meaning pre-existent in the world but rather call meanings into existence through collective experience of the world. In his later work Merleau-Ponty (1968) put forward a philosophical approach that offered substantive challenge to the essentially humanist qualities that characterized his earlier phenomenological studies. In this he presented arguments promoting a consideration of a conflation of the senses which encourages a working with the world, not as disengaged observers objectively examining and offering determinations of the world from the outside but, rather, where senses of self and of the world are emergent phenomena in the kinds of 'becoming' described in the previous paragraph. In proposing what can be characterized as a synthesis of the senses, Merleau-Ponty put forward an approach to language and meaning suggesting that bodies function among, in, with and between aspects of materiality and discourse without being explicitly or obviously aware of doing so. He used the term 'intercorporeity' to describe 'a new kind of being, a being of porosity, pregnancy, or generality, and he before whom the horizon opens is caught up, included within it' (1968, p. 149). By offering a seemingly posthuman, to appropriate Deleuze's (2014) phrase, 'logic of sense', such an approach adds weight to Lenz Taguchi's critique of those dominating anthropocentric tendencies that traditionally work to centrally position selves in terms of their relationality to thinking, knowing and practice.

In a similar vein, while engaging with the vibrancy of matter, Bennett (2010, p. 5) animates what Virginia Woolf (1985) described as a 'moment of being' in which, when out walking one day, she glimpses an apparently random collection or arrangement of items which, for her, exist as 'a culture of things irreducible to the culture of objects'. Here we have an example of what Deleuze and Guattari (1988, p. 261) describe as 'haecceity' that 'consist[s] entirely of relations of movement and rest between molecules or particles, capacities to affect and be affected'. In sensing this moment of movement we can see haecceity as bringing to life a redistribution of agency in which objects are no longer seen in terms of passive materiality but rather as engaging the possibilities of producing affects. For Bennett there seems to be an onto-politics in this moment where a shift of power, a form of Deleuzo-Guattarian 're-territorialisation', takes place. She says:

> This window onto an eccentric out-side was made possible by the fortuity of that particular assemblage, but also by a certain anticipatory readiness on my in-side, by a perceptual style open to the appearance of thing-power.
>
> (Op. cit.)

Bennett promotes a sensitivity to the vibrancy and vitality of matter and also alerts us to acknowledge a redistribution of agency in terms similar to Barad's 'intra-action' between and with materiality and the discourses that tend to construct it in particular ways. Likewise this chapter takes its transformative and sustainable energy from a becoming awareness of and a working with the potentialities of a redistribution of agency that can be generated through diffractive writing practices and a theorizing of practice that such writing has the potential to promote.

Consequently, it no longer feels possible to think of teaching and learning outside of 'pedagogic and/or inquiry based assemblages', where rhizomatic relational tendencies can be seen to exist and that offer ways of conceptualizing teaching and learning practices in non-linear, multiple and highly complex vibrational ways. Such an approach to 'pedagogic and/or inquiry based assemblages' is therefore designed to provide a tangible point of both reference and departure and signifies a directional strategy that is designed to pay attention, not to the body *qua* unique unitary human form, but rather to its vital and transmutational relationality with and within material circumstance or what Deleuze and Guattari (1988) describe as its 'milieu'. So when Haraway, now almost apocryphally, asserts that our bodies do not end with our skin, the concerns of this chapter come alive in relation to the engagements, the 'entanglements', the 'intra-actions' (Barad, 2007) that the materiality of bodies have, not only with other bodies, but with the discourses that signify, represent and construct these bodies in particular ways.

Therefore, in advancing the later theoretical stance of Merleau-Ponty and in working with a Deleuzian (2004) 'logic of sense', which promotes the use of sense over reason and invokes a philosophy of the event that problematizes forms of rationality which are bound up in the search for totalizing of truth, this research is also designed to offer a challenge to those rationalist epistemologies that act to concentrate higher education practices as emergent from and exclusively concomitant with activities of the mind and that involve themselves in advancing and consolidating a metaphysics of Being. In terms of activating particular transformative writing practices through the employment of diffraction and a 'logic of sense', this chapter argues for teaching and learning practices that also involve what Thrift (2006) has referred to as a 'processual sensualism', where space is in constant motion and where sense is employed in a continual engagement with encounters and events. In an approach of this kind attention moves from and with the body in relation to subtle and nuanced energetic spatiotemporal forces and dimensions that might be seen to participate in its molecular and particular presence in the world and that troubles and, at the same time, pays attention to the problematic ascendancy of its molar and universalistic specifications and discursive positionings. As part of the research participants were encouraged to write short, diffractive pieces to do with their sensing of classroom noise, the use of visual modalities in learning encounters and so on, and to share these with colleagues. This was carried out as a means of challenging the use of reflective writing that is often involved in 'mirroring' reality and in moving towards the truth of the matter.

Problematizing the performative?

In many respects this chapter is more to do with educational practices than outcomes. This is not to say that outcomes are not significant or intended, rather that methodological procedures exist within substantive, dynamic and highly theorized situated and contextualized practices. Such an approach is designed, therefore, to divert attention from outcomes in themselves and to re-direct and focus upon ontologies of practice. By paying attention to Deleuze and Guattari's practice advocacy of 'plugging in' conceptualizations this chapter invokes the use of a 'logic of sense' through writing as a means of focusing upon and animating the processes by which teaching and learning and research-based outcomes are produced. In relation to this, one of the writing activities involved participants in, first of all, writing down a brief conceptualization of a particular practice mode and style in relation to the multiple spatial dimensions of pedagogic practice: these included such things as inquiry-based learning, peer evaluation, reflective writing and so on. Once this was done the participants were given a situation or a setting in which they were encouraged to write down a 'plugging in' or contextualization of their conceptualization that paid attention to these spatial multiplicities.

When Deleuze and Guattari (1994, p. 5) claim that 'concepts are not waiting for us ready-made, like heavenly bodies...they must be invented, fabricated, or rather created...(and)...would be nothing without their creator's signature' they instantiate the methodological intent of this chapter that theory, or more accurately its verbal form, theorizing, *is* practice. So the chapter itself can be located within and operate as an 'ethico-onto-epistem-ological' methodological approach which Barad (2007, p. 185) describes as

> an appreciation of the intertwining of ethics, knowing, and being-since each intra-action matters, since the possibilities for what the world may become call out in the pause that precedes each breath before a moment comes into being and the world is remade again, because the becoming of the world is a deeply ethical matter.

The becomings and non-individuating transformative aspirations and predictions that are embodied in Barad's account and the writing practices and methodological approaches that can be inferred from it allude to the possible emergence in education of fundamental and potentially challenging teaching, learning and research-based strategies. There has been present and growing for a number of years (Ball, 2003) a research-based and theoretically informed recognition of the substantial and substantive influence of performative processes and practices in many aspects of institutional educational life. Ball and others have forcefully argued and demonstrated that performativity is a new mode of state regulation that, through the implementation of numerous policy initiatives, makes it possible to govern in increasingly neoliberal ways. As Ball points out, the individualistic pressures on academics and practitioners to align themselves in response to external targets, standards and classifications of 'good practice' have become highly pervasive; 'performativity produces opacity rather than transparency as individuals and organizations take ever greater care in the construction and maintenance of fabrications' (2003, p. 215). While the performative inclinations of such reforms and policies have a tendency to reduce to and then offer understandings and interpretations of teaching and learning in quantifiable terms, I have argued in this chapter that pedagogical practices in higher education are better understood in terms of complexity, contextually situated events and posthuman relationalities that challenge attempts at classification and the convenience of crude systems of measurement.

In their critique of what they refer to as 'hylomorphism' Deleuze and Guattari (1988, p. 408), influenced by the work of Simondon, offer a challenge to the structural ordering and control of systems that are projected in advance by external agencies as a means of organizing these systems in particular ways. While 'hylomorphism' is a doctrine and an approach that might claim to address passivity and/or chaos, Deleuze and Guattari point to the political aspects of hylomorphic tendencies that become manifest through practices of 'territorialisation' (ibid., p. 314). Such 'territorialisations' become manifest as they are informed by a simplistic and rather bland view of education that posits linear input/output parameters for teaching and learning which are offered credibility and validity through the privileging and funding of positivistic and quasi post-positivist research practices.

Concluding in the middle?

This chapter advocates the use of diffractive writing, a logic of sense and a theorizing as practice that function within spatiotemporal relationality and which operate to 'smooth' space and to activate 'territorialisations' that both resist and offer radical alternatives to the confines of existing 'striations', delineations and practices of codification. In following these directions and by taking a methodological approach which promotes inquiry into the not-yet-known, through the use of writing practices which themselves are a form of inquiry, this chapter suggests possible engagements in higher education that are designed to promote potentially transformative teaching, learning and inquiry-based practices. In attempting to encourage methods of inquiry that are not mimetic, that discourage tracing or a lifting of texts or images from one medium to another, a practice described by Deleuze and Guattari (1988, p. 12) as 'decalcomania', the emergent nature of the research described is designed with cartographic tendencies in mind, whereby practices of representation and discursively influenced construction are problematized and challenged. Instead, through the use of diffractive (writing) practices, connections can be made with intensive and material processe,s working with creative concept making, in affect and with ethical sensitivity. With the micro-political challenge to the discursively constructed performative nature of orthodox education research practices in mind it is, perhaps, apposite to conclude with a final quotation from St. Pierre, who says: 'Not only do people produce theory, but theory produces people' (2001, p. 142). Based on this view, I suggest that transformation in higher education teaching and learning is not only possible but fundamentally necessary.

References

Ball, S. (2003) 'The Teacher's Soul and the Terrors of Performativity', *Journal of Education Policy*, 18(2), 215–228.

Barad, K. (2007) *Meeting the Universe Halfway: Quantum Physics and the Entanglement of Matter and Meaning* (London: Duke University Press).

Bennett, J. (2010) *Vibrant Matter: A Political Ecology of Things* (London: Duke University Press).

Braidotti, R. (2013) *The Posthuman* (Cambridge: Polity Press).

De Freitas, E. (2012). 'Classroom as Rhizome: New Strategies for Diagramming Knotted Interactions', *Qualitative Inquiry*, 18(7), 557–570.

Deleuze, G. (2004) *The Logic of Sense* (M. Lester,Trans.) (London: Continuum).

Deleuze, G. and F. Guattari, (1986) *Kafka: Towards a Minor Literature* (D. Polan, Trans.) (Minneapolis, MN: University of Minnesota Press).

Deleuze, G. and F. Guattari (1988) *A Thousand Plateaus: Capitalism and Schizophrenia* (B. Massumi, Trans.) (London: Athlone).

Deleuze, G. and F. Guattari, (1994) *What Is Philosophy?* (G. Burchell and H. Tomlinson, Trans.) (London: Verso).

Deleuze, G. and C. Parnet (2002) *Dialogues II* (H. Tomlinson and B. Habberjam, Trans.) (London: Continuum).

Dosse, F. (2010) *Gilles Deleuze and Felix Guattari: Intersecting Lives* (New York: Columbia University Press).
Foucault, M. (1992) *The History of Sexuality: The Use of Pleasure* (vol. 2) (R. Hurley, Trans.) (London: Penguin)
Gale, K. (2013) 'Action Research and the Assemblage: Engaging Deleuzian Pedagogy and Inquiry beyond the Constraints of the Individual and the Group in Education Settings', *International Journal of Qualitative Studies in Education*, 1–15, doi: 10.1080/09518398.2013.805447.
Gale, K. (2014) 'Moods, Tones, Flavours: Living with Intensities as Inquiry', *Qualitative Inquiry*, 20(8), 998–1005.
Gale, K. and E. Beaumont (2015) 'Teacher and Student Experiences of Collaborative Writing at Masters Level', in P. E. Kneale (ed.) *Masters Level, Teaching, Learning and Assessment* (Palgrave: London).
Gale, K., R. Turner, and L. McKenzie (2013) 'Action Research, Becoming and the Assemblage: A Deleuzian Reconceptualisation of Professional Practice', *Educational Action Research*, 21(4), 549–564.
Haraway, D. (2000) *How Like a Leaf* (London, England: Routledge).
Lenz Taguchi, H. (2013) ' "Becoming Molecular Girl": Transforming Subjectivities in Collaborative Doctoral Research Studies as Micro-politics in the Academy', *International Journal of Qualitative Studies in Education*, 26(9), 1101–1116.
Massey, D. (2005) *For Space* (London: Sage).
Massumi, B. (1993) *A User's Guide to Capitalism and Schizophrenia: Deviations from Deleuze and Guattari* (Cambridge, MA: MIT Press).
Merleau-Ponty, M. (1968) *The Visible and the Invisible* (A. Lingis, Trans.) (Evanston: Northwestern University Press).
Merleau-Ponty, M. (2005) *Phenomenology of Perception* (London: Routledge).
Richardson, L. (2000) 'Writing: A Method of Inquiry', in N. K. Denzin, and Y. S. Lincoln (eds.) *Handbook of Qualitative Research* (2nd ed.) (Thousand Oaks, CA: Sage), pp. 923–948.
St. Pierre, E. (1997) 'Methodology in the Fold and the Irruption of Transgressive Data', *International Journal of Qualitative Studies in Education*, 10(2), 175–189.
St. Pierre, E. A. (2001) 'Coming to Theory: Finding Foucault and Deleuze', in K. Weiler, (ed.) *Feminist Engagements. Reading, Resisting, and Revisioning Male Theorists in Education and Cultural Studies* (New York, NY: Routledge), pp. 141–161.
St. Pierre, E. A. (2014) 'Post-qualitative Research', *International Journal of Qualitative Studies in Education*, 26(6), 629–633.
Thrift, N. (2006) 'Space', *Theory, Culture & Society*, 23(2–3), 139–155.
Transformative Learning Centre (2004) from Transformative Learning Centre, http://tlc.oise.utoronto.ca/index.htm.
Woolf, V. (1985) *Moments of Being* (ed. J. Schulkind, 2nd ed.) (London: Harcourt Brace).
Wyatt, J. and K. Gale (2013a) 'Assemblage/Ethnography: Troubling Constructions of the Self in the Play of Materiality and Representation', in P. Short, L. Turner and A. Grant (eds.) *Contemporary British Autoethnography* (Rotterdam: Sense), pp. 139–157.
Wyatt, J. and K. Gale (2013b) 'Getting Out of Selves: An Assemblage/ Ethnography?' in T. Adams, C. Ellis and S. Holman-Jones (eds.) *The Autoethnography Handbook* (Thousand Oaks, CA: Sage), pp. 300–313.

15
A Femifesta for Posthuman Art Education: Visions and Becomings

Anna Hickey-Moody

This chapter revisits my concept of 'affective pedagogy' (Hickey-Moody, 2009, 2012) as a posthuman model of art education. In so doing, I mobilize the manifesto/manifesta/femifesta as a genre of feminist scholarship (Colman, 2008, 2014; Haraway, 1991; Lusty, 2008; Palmer, 2015). The manifesta, or femifesta (Palmer, 2015), has provided a model for advancing a call to action in scholarship, but also in popular culture. From Donna Haraway's *Cyborg Manifesto* to Riot Grrrl and the famous revisioning of gender advanced through the Jigsaw Manifesto (Piepmeier, 2009; Lusty, 2015), the manifesto has been mobilized in various forms and contexts as a feminist modality. I modulate Deleuze's (1998, 1990, 2003) Spinozist notion of *affectus* through a feminist lens as the material equation of an interaction as a means through which to map the posthuman material exchange undertaken through art. *Affectus* is a margin of change and the capacity to change; to be affected. This is distinct from the affection, which is the emotion and sensation felt. Working with *affectus* as a margin of actual and virtual change, I consider Deleuze (1990, 2003) and Deleuze and Guattari's (1987, 1996) writings on the politics of aesthetics. Affective pedagogy is a framework for thinking through the pedagogical shift in perception effected by the aesthetics of an artwork.

Aesthetic affect can be deployed to reconceptualize, or further develop, contemporary theories of posthumanism, in a manner congruent with imperatives to conceive educational practices outside identity. The affective pedagogy of aesthetics is posthuman education. The affect of art extends beyond the products of human labour. A dance piece, or a painting, is created by humans, but its impact on culture, the pedagogical work it undertakes in inviting new ways of seeing and relating, in effecting economies of exchange, cannot be confined to the labour of one artist or the perspective of one beholder. This affective pedagogy of aesthetics is a spatial, temporal assemblage in which historicized practices of art production, ways of seeing, spaces and places of viewing are plugged into one another and augmented. Subjective change is part of a broader assemblage of social change, activated by the production of new aesthetic milieus.

Affective relations

Affect is the concept of taking something on, of changing in relation to an experience or encounter. Deleuze employs this term in differing ways. I am interested in the notion of *affectus*, a kind of movement that encompasses subjective modulation. In *Spinoza, Practical Philosophy* Deleuze (1998) describes *affectus* as an increase or decrease of the power of acting, for the body and the mind alike. He expands this definition through arguing that *affectus* is different from emotion. *Affectus* is the virtuality and materiality of the increase or decrease effected in a body's power of acting. He states:

> The *affection* refers to a state of the affected body and implies the presence of the affecting body, whereas the *affectus* refers to the passage [or movement] from one state to another, taking into account the correlative variation of the affecting bodies. Hence there is a difference in nature between the *image affections* or *ideas* and the *feeling affect*.
>
> (Deleuze, 1998, p. 49)

Affectus is the materiality of change: 'the passage from one state to another' which occurs in relation to 'affecting bodies'. The image, affections, or ideas to which Deleuze refers are generated by a specific kind of movement. It is the movement of increasing or decreasing one's capacity to act: the virtual and material change that prompts the affection or 'feeling of affect' in the consciousness of the body in question. As a model for theorizing pedagogy, *affectus* differs from existing theorizations of subjective change as a kind of cultural pedagogy, such as those put forward by Giroux (1999a, 1999b; 2004a, 2004b), Lusted (1986) and McWilliam (1996), in the respect that *affectus* is a posthuman pedagogy. Posthuman because it is grounded in interpersonal relations, it is people responding to the *materiality* of art. *Affectus* is, in part, a rhythmic trace of the world incorporated into a body-becoming, an expression of an encounter between a corporeal form and forces that are not necessarily 'human'. Literature, sound, dance, are media that prompt affective responses and generate *affectus*: a synergy, a machinic-assemblage that is bigger than the sum of its parts. In creating subjective change or a 'modulation[1]' in the form of *affectus*, such media can be considered posthuman pedagogies: art as a material force of change.

Affect as pedagogy

Albrecht-Crane and Slack (2007), Ellsworth (2005), Kofoed and Ringrose (2012) and Watkins (2005) are theoreticians of education or pedagogy who work with the idea of affect. Albrecht-Crane and Slack (2007, p. 191) argue: '[t]he importance of affect... is inadequately considered in scholarship on pedagogy' and, while the work of theorists cited above moves to address this gap in research, this concept has the potential to reconfigure theories of pedagogy and indeed education in significant ways. One of these ways is through rendering the teaching object as a non human body. For example, art is a mode of producing subjectivity. Thus, it is pedagogical. Deleuze and Guattari (1996) argue that works of art can be thought as consisting of compounded collections of percepts and affects. A percept is a physical fragment of the world imagined in and through the artwork. An affect is the sense or feeling that is enmeshed with the materiality of the artwork. Combined in art, percepts and affects constitute a 'bloc of sensations' (1996, p. 176). Blocs of sensations are the language with which art, as a culture, speaks:

> Art is the language of sensations. Art does not have opinions. Art undoes the triple organisation of perceptions, affections and opinions in order to substitute a monument composed of percepts, affects and blocs of sensations that take the place of language... A monument does not commemorate or celebrate something that happened but confides to the ear of the future the persistent sensations that embody the event: the constantly renewed suffering of men and women, their re-created protestations, their constantly resumed struggle.
> (Deleuze and Guattari, 1996, pp. 176–177)

Art works are monuments, entities that propel the political agendas of those for whom they speak. Art works create a new sensory landscape for their beholder. These simultaneous acts of propelling a political agenda and creating a sensory landscape occur *through* an artwork's affective potential. This is the way a work of art can make its observer feel; the connection(s) a work prompts its observer to make. The materiality of the artwork, the blocs of sensation of which it is composed, embody the affect specific to the work. Each bloc of sensation has its own affective force or quality. In suggesting a bloc of sensations has an affective capacity, I am arguing that art has the aptitude to re-work a body's limits. Art can re-adjust what a person is or is not able to understand, produce and connect to. This is not to say that a work of art necessarily will change its viewers in prescribed ways, rather, that art works *can* create new associations and habits of clustering emotion around new images. In terms of the Spinozist idea of affects clustering around images, art has the capacity to construct new organized patterns of affect. This is, then, primarily a corporeal reconfiguration and, secondly, an emergent cultural geography of human feelings.

Deleuze and Guattari argue that percepts and affects exist within a work of art because they have been created as part of a work of art, upon terms established by the work, terms that are specific to the *way* the work of art has been constructed. Yet they also develop an inherently masculinist perspective on art and affect which articulates through language and through the milieu of work with which they engage. Here, an affect is a new milieu of sense, or series of personal associations, that are created in relation to percepts: '*Affects are precisely these nonhuman becomings of man*' [sic] (Deleuze and Guattari, 1996, p. 169). Such minor transformations are nonhuman because although an affect is an embodied change, a readjustment of personal 'limit' or capacity, affect is not produced in relation to another person (i.e., a writer, a dancer, a painter) but rather, in relation to the material product, the work. A dancer performing a tightly choreographed ensemble piece is a de facto condition of the production of affect. The art piece would not work without the dancer, yet the piece is far more than the variable of a single body. A work of art develops a miniature universe that can perform a pedagogic function through crafting and imbuing previously non-existent elements of difference upon its spectator.

The term 'percept' is a way of describing aspects of the physicality of the artwork in its completed form. In describing the way a percept works, Deleuze and Guattari (1996, p. 166) suggest:

> A percept is material crafted into a sensation...it is difficult to say where in fact the material ends and sensation begins; preparation of the canvas, the track of the brush's hair, and many other things besides are obviously part of the sensation.

The affects produced by percepts are not affinities of lived experience. They can only be developed 'internally' to a work of art, and on terms specific to the work in question. However, new lived sensibilities, or personal vocabularies, are often the *products* of artistic affects. On a work of art, blocs of sensation are offered up to the world. In describing this potential for the creation of newness and transformation, Deleuze and Guattari (1996, p. 166) argue:

> 'Blocs' of percepts and affects are innovative by *nature;* they are not about preserving previous events or works of art, but are the creation of a new solidarity... Even if the material only lasts for a few seconds it will give sensation the power to exist and be preserved in itself in the eternity that exists for that short duration.

The implications of translating this sentiment into subjective or 'human' terms, Deleuze and Guattari (1996, p. 166) suggest, are that the person who experiences the force produced by an affect can retain this force, and can also be changed as a result of their experience. However, the way an affect is experienced, and the way(s) in which an affect works, will always be specific to the body in question. Indeed, whether or not a work of art is perceived as having affect at all, is always specific to the body in question. As Deleuze and Guattari (1996, p. 164) contend, '[a work of art] is no less independent of the viewer or hearer, who only experience it after, if they have the strength for it'. The power of percepts and affects must be seen as context-specific and highly subjective. The forces produced by works of art exist in relation to those who experience them, those who 'have the strength for it' (1996, p. 164). Having established the subject-specific, yet materially powerful, nature of art, I now turn to the differences between a bloc of sensations (a work of art) and a terrain, or cultural habitat.

Interspecies junction points

In Deleuze and Guattari's terms, the production of art is contingent on its opening up to chaos; a line of deterritorialization that opens up a territorial refrain and connects it to other spaces (rhizome) and other cultural melodies. This connection, facilitated by opening up to chaos, forms a chorus:

> Every territory, every habitat, joins up not only its spatiotemporal but its qualitative planes or sections: a posture and a song for example, a song and a colour, percepts and affects. And every territory encompasses or cuts across the territories of other species, or intercepts

the trajectory of animals without territories, forming interspecies junction points.

(Deleuze and Guattari, 1996, p. 185)

These 'interspecies junction points', rhizomes, are created through artistic methods, specific, technical material workings, practices that craft compounds of sensations. A compound of sensations is quite distinct from a general collection of bodies, an unstructured dance, or the singular bodies and choreographies that are worked together until they pass into a sensation. Deleuze and Guattari are adamant that it must be an artistic method that serves to extract material, blocs of sensation, percepts and affects, from a territory. In explicating the role of artistic method in constructing the force of a work of art, Deleuze and Guattari (1996, p. 167) argue that

> By means of the material, the aim of art is to wrest the percept from perceptions of objects and the states of a perceiving subject, to wrest the affect from affections as the transition of one state to another: *to extract a bloc of sensations, a pure being of sensations. A method is needed, and this varies with every artist and forms part of the work.*

(emphasis added)

Art encounters difference through creating and presenting differences yet unknown. The act of constructing new ways of feeling is at once a contextualized, local event and a vehicle of timeless creation. This is because art work occurs within, and writes over, a specific cultural territory and thus possesses a political significance relative to the cultural geography it reinscribes or reconfigures. However, the sensations produced in this act of reconfiguration are not bound to the cultural terrain they are written upon. Sensations can abide, potentially infinitely, in cultural memory, embodied memory and artistic vocabularies. Deleuze and Guattari (1996, p. 163) explicate this pedagogical process through suggesting: 'If art preserves it does not do so like industry, by adding substance to make the thing last. The thing became independent of its "model" from the start.' Art as an affective entity must be considered a culturally active agent. Art (objects, events, or a relation between people, spaces and places) has the capacity to change people. It can teach us to be different.

A piece of art is evidence of the technical work of an artist, a substantiation of the methodological labour of the artist. In this respect, art mediates an interchange between artist and viewer, but the process of material mediation is the pedagogical exchange.

> The artist's greatest difficulty is to make it [an artwork] *stand up on its own*. Sometimes this requires what is, from the viewpoint of an implicit model, from the viewpoint of lived perceptions and affections, great geometrical improbability, physical imperfection and organic abnormality.
> (Deleuze and Guattari, 1996, p. 164, original emphasis)

The labour of the artist remains implicit in the analysis quoted above. Deleuze and Guattari's analytic tools of beings of sensation and aesthetic figures theorize the ways artworks, as entities, hold power, or force. A *bloc* of sensation is a compound of percepts and affects, a combination of shards of an imagined reality and the sensible forces that the materiality of this micro-cosmos produces. Building on, or consolidating blocs of sensation, a *being* of sensation is the sensibility of a work of art. A being of sensation can also be thought as the inhabitant of an artwork, as living on the work and consisting of its affective potential. Operating in a similar realm, yet in relation to the cultural context of an artwork, aesthetic figures offer us a way of thinking through the cultural politics of art. Deleuze and Guattari (1996, p. 177) describe aesthetic figures by suggesting:

> Aesthetic figures, and the style that creates them, have nothing to do with rhetoric. They are sensations, percepts and affects, landscapes and faces, visions and becomings. But is not the philosophical concept defined by becoming, and almost on the same terms? Still aesthetic figures are not the same as conceptual personae. It may be that they pass into one another, in either direction... insofar as there are sensations of concepts and concepts of sensations.

By inviting us to think outside the boundaries of 'majoritarian' thought, aesthetic figures push sensory becomings into the realm of the conceptual by creating experiences in which one is challenged to partake in 'the action by which the common event itself eludes what it is' (Deleuze and Guattari, 1996, p. 177). Beings of sensation are created within artworks and these beings 'think for' (Deleuze and Guattari, 1996, pp. 63–68) the observer, in the respect that they translate materiality into a particular sensation. The concept of 'affective pedagogy', of being changed by art and seeing this change as a kind of learning, mobilizes the idea of a being of sensation as teacher, in order to interrogate the nature of affective forces produced by art works and the social, machinic assemblages they are produced within and which, in turn, they effect. As a femifesta for paying attention to the impact held by the materiality of art and feminist scholarship, this chapter constitutes a folding together of multiple pasts and opens up many little futures in which we can think about artistic affect as a materialist, posthuman pedagogy. Art teaches in ways we are only beginning to see.

Note

1. I employ the term 'modulation' because it avoids teleological overheads that accompany the idea of 'transformation', which is another word used to articulate the materiality of change from on state to another.

References

Albrecht-Crane, C. and J. Daryl Slack (2007) 'Toward a Pedagogy of Affect', in A. Hickey-Moody and P. Malins (eds.) *Deleuzian Encounters: Studies in Contemporary Social Issues* (Houndmills, Basingstoke, Hampshire and New York: Palgrave), pp. 99–110.
Colman, F. (2008) 'Notes on the Feminist Manifesto: The Strategic Use of Hope', *Journal for Cultural Research*, 14(10), 375–392.
Colman, F. (2014) 'The Practice-As Research Manifesto', *Tate Working Papers*, http://www.tate.org.uk/research/research-centres/learning-research/working-papers/practice-as-research-manifesto, accessed 24 January 2015.
Deleuze, G. (1990) *The Logic of Sense* (New York: Colombia University Press).
Deleuze, G. (1998) *Spinoza: Practical Philosophy* (Minneapolis: City Light Books).
Deleuze, G. (2003) *Francis Bacon: The Logic of Sensation* (Minneapolis: University of Minnesota Press).
Deleuze, G. and F. Guattari (1987) *A Thousand Plateaus: Capitalism and Schizophrenia* (Minneapolis: University of Minnesota Press).
Deleuze, G. and F. Guattari (1996) *What Is Philosophy?* (London: Verso Publishers).
Ellsworth, E. (2005) *Places of Learning: Media, Architecture, Pedagogy* (New York: Routledge).
Giroux, H. (1999a) 'Cultural Studies as Public Pedagogy: Making the Pedagogical More Political', *Encyclopaedia of Philosophy of Education*, www.vusst.hr/ENCYCLOPAEDIA/main.htm, accessed 15 February 2005.
Giroux, H. (1999b) Cultural Studies as Public Pedagogy: Making the Pedagogical More Political, *Encyclopaedia of Philosophy of Education*, www.vusst.hr/ENCYCLOPAEDIA/main.htm, accessed 15 February 2005.
Giroux, H. A. (2004a) 'Cultural Studies and the Politics of Public Pedagogy: Making the Political More Pedagogical', *Parallax*, 10, 73–89.
Giroux, H. A. (2004b) 'Education after Abu Ghraib: Revisiting Adorno's Politics of Education', *Cultural Studies*, 18, 779–815.

Haraway, D. (1991) 'A Cyborg Manifesto: Science, Technology, and Socialist-Feminism in the Late 20th Century', *Simians, Cyborgs and Women: The Reinvention of Nature* (New York: Routledge), pp. 149–181.

Hickey-Moody, A. C. (2012) *Youth, Arts and Education* (London: Routledge).

Hickey-Moody, A. C. (2009) 'Little War Machines: Posthuman Pedagogy and Its Media', *Journal of Literary and Cultural Disability Studies*, 3(2), 273–280.

Kofoed, J. and J. Ringrose (2012) 'Travelling and Sticky Affects: Exploring Teens and Sexualized Cyberbullying through a Butlerian-Deleuzian- Guattarian Lens', *Discourse: Studies in the Cultural Politics of Education*, 33(1), 5–20.

Lusted, D. (1986) 'Why Pedagogy?' *Screen*, 27(5), 2–15.

Lusty, N. (2008) 'Sexing the Manifesto: Mina Loy, Feminism and Futurism', *Women: A Cultural Review*, 19(3), 245–260.

Lusty, N. (2015) 'Beyond Repair: Feminist Manifestos and the Idiom of Rupture', *Centre for Feminist Research* Goldsmiths, Wednesday 3 June.

McWilliam, E. (1996) 'Pedagogies, Technologies, Bodies', in E. McWilliam and P. G. Taylor (eds.) *Pedagogy, Technology and the Body* (New York: Peter Lang), pp. 1–22.

Palmer, H. (2015) 'BE-CONTRA-: A 21th Century Prefix Femista', *Centre for Feminist Research* Goldsmiths, Wednesday 3 June.

Piepmeier, A. (2009) *Girl Zines: Making Media, Doing Feminism* (New York: NYU Press).

Watkins, M. (2005) 'No Body, Never Mind: Interest, Affect and Classroom Practice', *M/C Journal*, 8(6), http://journal.media-culture.org.au/0512/06-watkins.php, accessed 12 May 2015.

Index

accountable, 186, 189, 190, 191, 198, 200, 203
accountability, 5, 15, 16
actant, 83, 88, 89, 90, 98, 99, 102–6, 216, 224, 234, 239
action research, 244–5
action research assemblage, 244
activism, 20, 95, 208, 221, 224
actor network theory, 6, 26, 68
aesthetic figures, 264
affect, 15, 19–21, 71, 95–6, 98–100, 103, 105, 116–17, 128–9, 136, 139, 142–4, 157–8, 161, 168–9, 180, 183, 196, 222, 225, 228, 239, 247, 251–2
affective atmos-phere, 229–30
affective neuroscience, 49–51
affective pedagogy, 3, 258, 260–5
affective solidarity, 231–5
affect theory, 6, 25
affectus, 258–60
affirmative politics, 13, 16, 20, 231
agency, 3, 63, 66, 82, 89, 112, 184, 223, 231, 246
  agency of matter, 113
  congregational agency, 13, 134
  distributive agency, 96, 98, 103, 198, 245, 251–2
  posthuman agency, 21, 94–5, 152, 164, 195, 214
agential literacy, 186–203
agential realism, 13–14, 18, 48, 190, 198, 203
agentic assemblage, 99–102, 104–5, 106, 250
Alaimo, Stacey, 40, 83, 208, 210, 214–16
animals, 8, 11, 13–14, 32, 66, 119–23, 138–9, 143, 150–62, 192, 199, 214, 227, 233, 243, 250, 251

animal studies, 6
anthropocentric, 2, 5, 8, 12–14, 61–7, 95, 103, 111–14, 119–20, 133, 150–1, 186, 221, 245, 250
antihumanism, 189
archives, 68, 71, 75
art education, 258
artistic method, 51, 98, 262–3
assemblage, 1, 2, 6, 10, 16, 21, 27, 31, 42, 82–3, 94, 128–34, 140, 168, 171, 182, 222, 231, 245
  assemblage theory (deLanda), 26
  machinic assemblage, 42, 100, 222, 260, 265
  pedagogic assemblages, 142, 242, 253
  posthuman assemblages, 172–3, 180, 183, 216, 234, 239
  research assemblage, 144–6, 224, 246
  see also agentic assemblage
atmo-sphere, 225, 229
atmosphere, 12, 14, 20, 174, 176, 230, 232
  revolutionary atmosphere, 231–2
author, 82, 195, 197, 200, 242
awkward relations, 108

Barad, Karen, 1, 13, 15, 18, 21, 48, 81–3, 95, 114–16, 134, 168, 171, 183, 189, 198, 202–3, 222–3, 239, 248, 253
  see also agential realism, phenomena
Battiste, Marie, 187–9, 193, 199
becoming, 10–11, 31, 61, 72, 82, 99, 115, 121, 124, 133, 151, 171, 181–3, 199, 201, 215, 223, 246, 248, 254, 259, 261
  feminist becoming, 221, 226, 228, 230–5, 239

Bennett, Jane, 1, 13, 16, 19, 62–3, 81, 84–6, 94–106, 133, 208, 214–17, 245, 250, 252
  see also *Vibrant Matter*
binaries/binary, 5, 7, 10, 12, 38, 46, 61, 70, 82, 96, 133, 159, 189, 199, 221, 247, 250
Bogost, Ian, 19, 66–8, 73
Braidotti, Rosi, 1, 8, 12–13, 16, 20, 22, 27, 41, 59, 61, 112–13, 115–16, 121, 189, 221, 231, 248
Brassier, Ray, 59, 60, 66
building materials, 58, 61, 72
built environment, 59, 60, 69
Butler, Judith, 27, 198

Cajete, Gregory, 189, 191–5, 198–203
Carry that Weight, 93–104
cartography, 38–40, 42, 46, 53, 116, 180, 242, 247, 256
causality, 3, 14, 96, 101–3, 201–2
chatter, 41–3, 46, 49, 51, 121
circle of convergence, 43, 44, 46–52
civilize/civilization, 8, 60, 189
cogito, 10, 25, 27, 29, 34
Colebrook, Claire, 40, 42, 52, 78, 117, 177
colonialism, 3, 8, 9, 67, 163–4, 200
comics, 195–7, 199
common worlding, 150–1, 164
community engagement, 206–9, 211–13, 217
concrete, 58, 64, 69–71
correlationism, 59, 65
critique, 2, 5, 8, 16, 25–7, 39, 53, 78, 221
  critical practice, 9, 20, 39, 45, 81, 195, 221
curriculum, 20–1, 27, 129, 142–3, 187, 191–2, 208, 210–211
cyborg, 11, 258

dance, 116, 154, 157, 209, 258, 260–1
data, 1, 17–19, 27, 33, 75, 77, 82, 86, 105, 114–, 115, 119, 122, 129, 130–2, 135–9, 145–6, 206, 216, 222, 228, 244, 247–8
Davies, Bronwyn, 28, 129, 134, 139
decolonial thinking, 6

deep time, 64–5
Deleuze, Gilles, 30–4, 40, 108, 111, 113, 120, 122, 171, 177, 258
Deleuze and Guattari, 1, 9, 10, 18, 27, 29, 46, 52, 99–100, 103, 117, 133, 168, 222, 242–5, 249–56, 261
Descartes, Rene/Cartesianism, 2, 10, 15, 25, 26, 46, 118, 187–90, 196, 199, 228
deterritorialzation, 40, 43, 45, 50–1, 143, 244, 262
difference, 30, 41, 42, 129, 134, 143, 164, 189, 192
diffraction, 3, 134, 171, 183, 249, 253
  diffractive analysis/methodology, 19, 134, 171, 178, 181–2
  diffractive writing, 249, 250, 252–6
disanthropy, 60
doing, 14, 18, 26
  knowing and doing, 21
  new ways of doing, 6, 19, 77, 164, 171, 198

early childhood education, 44, 47, 112–13, 128, 150, 153, 158
ecology, 1, 20, 40, 49, 97, 163, 190
  ecologies of encounter, 13
  ecologies of relation, 191, 193–203
Edensor, Tim, 71, 73
edu-craft/ing, 5, 19–22
embodied/embodiment, 13, 19, 20, 37, 46, 69, 72, 79, 116, 157, 160, 171, 192
emergence/emergent, 14, 15, 18, 30, 95, 96, 104–5, 110, 128, 134, 144, 168, 172, 195, 215, 244, 247, 253
empiricism, 27, 64, 250
  transcendental empiricism, 29–34
  see also new empiricism
encounters, 13, 15, 20, 38, 40, 71, 80–1, 157, 164, 196, 224, 243, 250
  awkward encounters, 134, 152, 158–62
  pedagogical encounter, 128, 129, 142

Enlightenment, 10, 12, 59, 61, 78, 112, 114
  Western Enlightenment, 8, 10, 25
entanglement/entangled, 14, 18, 48, 69–70, 82, 104, 115, 134, 138, 151, 153, 182, 190, 194, 198, 224, 245, 248
epistemic violence, 187, 195
epistemology, 1, 6, 14, 26–8, 33, 72, 171, 191, 198, 203
ethics, 5, 8, 22, 63, 96, 138, 191, 202
  ethico-onto-epistomology, 18, 20, 254
  ethic of worlding, 13, 15, 22
  posthuman ethics, 12, 15–16, 53, 105–6, 160
eurocentric, 21, 186, 199, 202
event, the, 20, 32–3, 118, 243, 246, 253, 260
experiment (researching differently), 10, 18, 20, 21, 39, 51, 77–8, 83, 94, 104, 121, 129, 151, 194, 224, 244

Facebook, 224, 236–8
femifesta, 258, 265
feminism, 6, 7, 28, 112, 224, 230, 235–9
  affecting feminism, 226
  feminist materialism, 133
  new material feminism, 13
  posthuman feminism, 12, 220–2
findings, 150, 165, 222
focus groups, 130, 208–12, 226
Foucault, Michel, 7, 27, 113, 170, 222, 248
friction, 163– 4

Guattari, Felix, 110

Haraway, Donna, 4, 8, 11, 13, 16, 53, 69, 120, 151, 154, 162, 250, 253, 258
Harman, Graham, 19, 65, 66, 73
Heidegger, Martin, 65
higher education, 17, 21, 22, 131, 145, 206, 217, 242, 244, 256

human exceptionalism, 2, 105, 114, 138, 149, 150, 215
humanism, 2, 5, 6, 7–9, 15, 61, 112, 149, 187, 189, 199, 201–2
humble/humility, 16

immanent, 6, 10, 18, 30, 32, 34, 82, 86, 110, 244
indigenous, 3, 6
indigenous-settler, 75, 77–89, 187–202
individualism, 200, 207
Ingold, Tim, 17, 70–2, 79
intensity, 10, 30, 42, 60, 83, 105, 110, 128, 168–72, 230
interbeing, 13
intermezzo, 7
interpretivist, 75, 77, 85
interspecies, 7, 13, 16, 152, 262–3
interviews, 18, 28, 71, 98, 102, 130, 132, 138, 170, 172, 197, 209, 224, 226
in the middle, 17, 32, 49, 112–13, 246, 255
intra-action, 18, 82, 83, 134, 171, 190, 198–9, 203, 222–4, 238, 253
invent (method), 6, 18, 33–4, 53, 82, 115, 133

Kant, Immanuel, 29, 30, 32
knowledge practices, 2, 4, 18, 21, 33, 34, 52, 105, 145, 192, 199
  knowing-in-being, 16, 18, 189, 191–2
  politics of knowledge, 6
  situated knowledge, 53, 69, 117, 215

land deed, 75, 77, 80, 83, 86–7
Latour, Bruno, 68, 73, 85, 106, 150, 158, 165
learning, 21, 40, 48, 50, 52, 69, 72, 144, 149, 156–8, 161, 189, 193, 202
  learning assemblage, 250, 253
  transformative learning, 201, 249, 251
literature, major literature, 244, 246, 248

literature, minor literature, 244, 247, 248
Lyotard, Francois, 25

Manning, Erin, 13, 110, 116, 123, 178, 180
Manning, Erin and Massumi, Brian, 19, 20, 108, 110, 111, 114, 117
mapping, 39, 40–3, 45, 46, 53, 116
Massumi, Brian, 82, 116, 225, 246
materiality, 15, 60, 66, 70, 81, 95–101, 104, 131, 141, 171, 175, 198, 223, 245, 247, 260
material realism, 6
material-semiotic, 128
mattering, practices of, 14, 15, 145, 223, 228, 230, 239
meaning-making, 72, 77, 95, 152, 156, 214
Meillassoux, Quentin, 7, 59, 60, 66
Merleau-Ponty, Maurice, 251–3
methodology, 6, 7, 10, 26, 29, 34, 39, 41, 66, 245
  materialist methodology, 86
  spatial methodology, 94–6
  see also posthumanist methodology
molar lines, 43, 45, 47, 53, 243–4, 251
molecular lines, 12, 45, 244, 248
more-than-human, 3, 6, 11, 28, 52, 120, 122, 128, 135, 149, 152, 157, 165, 168, 180, 191, 223
Morton, Timothy, 14, 68
movement of thought, 110
multiplicity, 6, 10–11, 18, 31, 41, 46, 82, 170, 249
multisensory encounter, 156
multispecies ethnography, 149–54, 160, 164, 165

nature-culture, 3, 79, 82
  natural-cultural, 190, 194, 198
neoliberal, 22, 51, 113, 143, 207, 239, 255
neuro-ontologies, 37, 39–40, 42, 46, 47
neuroscience, 37–53
new empiricism, 1, 6, 26, 28, 133
new materialism, 26, 28, 83, 133
Nietzsche, Friedrich, 27, 33, 60

nihilism, 59, 66
nomad/nomadic, 32, 111, 115–20, 120, 206
nonhuman, 8, 13, 15, 18, 20, 26, 58, 66, 80, 86, 96–100, 112, 133, 152, 156, 177, 212, 225, 229, 261
non individuating transformations, 254
non-linear, 11, 200, 201–2, 253
non-sentient objects, 58, 66
notice, 63, 67, 69, 97, 99, 105, 118, 135, 158, 165, 231
noticing, 136, 162, 231

objective, 10, 77, 251
object-oriented ontology, 6, 13, 62, 65–6, 68
onto-epistemology, 13, 25, 63, 66, 71
ontology/ontological, 4, 5, 6, 10, 77, 97–9, 104, 115, 121, 189, 202, 246, 250
  flat ontology, 16, 62–3, 65, 133
  maori ontology, 78–81
  ontological turn, 25–8, 34, 135
organic monism, 46, 53
out-of-field, 122

participatory research, 171, 194
pedagogy, 21, 22, 72, 128, 192, 217, 247
  intra-active pedagogy, 48, 193, 194, 195
  land-based pedagogy, 194
  see also affective pedagogy, posthuman pedagogy
percept, 248, 260–4
performative, 13, 134, 190, 201, 223, 244, 250, 254–6
phallocentric, 174–5, 179, 228
phallogocentrism, 228
phenomena (Barad), 14, 18, 134, 182, 190, 198, 223
phenomenology, 65, 67, 242, 245, 246, 249, 251
  alien phenomenology, 6, 19, 66
philosophy of difference, 30
photovoice, 194–5
plane of consistency, 30–2
plasticity, 40, 47, 48

Index 271

poetry, 65, 208, 215
postcolonial, 10, 187, 189
post-disciplinary, 7, 19, 20
post-hoc analytical strategy, 135
posthumanism, 1, 5–9, 18–22, 59–65, 70, 105, 113–15, 129, 132, 143, 189, 202, 214–17, 221, 239, 258
posthuman methodology, 2, 6, 34, 39, 52, 66, 86, 94–6, 103–4, 134, 147
posthuman pedagogy, 58, 142–4
posthuman turn, 26, 28, 34, 112
post-qualitative, 1, 17, 27, 132, 146, 248
post-structural, 6, 8, 9, 10, 27, 39, 112, 114
potentia, 19, 20–2, 221
power, 4, 16, 42, 46, 58, 88, 104, 115, 134, 156, 201, 207, 222–3, 239, 252, 264
praxis, 16, 149, 195, 245, 248
'proper' child, 112, 120–4

qualitative methodology/enquiry, 2, 17, 26–8, 94, 104, 134
queer, 40, 41, 53, 155
queer theory, 6, 40

rational/rationality, 8, 10, 26, 102, 112, 113, 128, 157, 181, 253
relational, 6, 12–14, 20, 22, 80, 86, 110–112, 117, 143
relationality/relational ethics, 143, 155, 171, 189, 196, 239, 246, 249
research design, 18, 130, 131, 135, 224, 253, 256
responsibility/ethical responsibility, 15–16, 18, 53, 105, 138, 203, 223, 244
rhizome, 10–11, 18, 32, 121, 246, 262–3
    rhizomatics, 7, 39, 43–6, 52, 242, 245, 253
rupture, 11, 32, 135, 210, 233
    asignifying rupture, 45, 50, 51, 53

school, 17, 49, 51, 104, 128–31, 139, 145, 168, 175, 194, 197, 200, 221
    feminism in schools, 224, 229, 232, 235, 238

science education, 189
    decolonizing science education, 189, 197, 202
    indigenous science, 191, 192
    native science, 192–3
    western modern science, 187, 194
    scientific literacy, 187, 189–90, 195, 202
sea, 206, 209, 210, 212–17
senses, 11, 29, 67, 72, 108–9, 111, 144, 155, 156
shadow, 110–112, 116–21
signature, 78, 83–4, 87–8
singularities, 30, 32, 43, 46, 117, 246–7
Snaza, Nathan and Weaver, John, 6, 8, 16, 143
space-time-mattering, 145, 202, 222, 226, 239
speciesism, 8, 13
speculation, 19, 65, 117
speculative realism, 60, 66
Spinoza, Baruch, 15–16, 222, 225, 245, 250–1, 259
spirituality, 89, 191, 193
Stengers, Isabelle, 39, 48, 53, 78, 152, 164
storywork, 192, 195–6
student, 17, 20–1, 28, 50–1, 93–4, 130–2, 144, 186, 194, 196, 197, 206–18, 237
subjectivity, 9, 14, 59, 67, 77, 118, 181–2, 216

techniques, 19, 66
tendencies-to-form, 119
theorising as practice, 242, 244, 247–8
thing-power, 1, 13, 16, 82–8, 95–101, 133, 136, 245, 250, 252
thinking collectively, 162, 164
trans-corporeality, 206, 213, 215–16, 218
transdisciplinary, 7, 37–8
transgress, 40, 110, 183, 248
transhumanism, 59
truth, 3, 10, 25, 46, 53, 78, 112, 152, 160, 253

Tsing, Anna, 151, 152, 154, 162, 163, 165
Tumblr, 224, 236–7

university, 27, 93–5, 98, 100, 104, 145, 153, 206, 208–11, 213, 217
unself, 3, 216
use-value, 110, 111, 122

Vibrant Matter, 81, 82, 84, 95
vibrant matter, 95–9, 103, 105, 217

visual methods, 19, 170, 171, 194, 224, 247
vital materiality, 1, 95, 97–100, 104, 247, 254
voice, 17, 27, 41, 42, 135
volunteering, 206–11

wandering, 189, 196
world without us, 60–4, 66, 70, 72
writing, 19, 21, 111, 115, 116–18, 242, 245, 249, 251
writing as a method of inquiry, 244